5757453

D1544950

XINRAN is a British-Chinese author, journalist and activist. Before moving to London in 1997, she was host of 'Words on the Night Breeze', a groundbreaking radio show in China which invited women from across the country to discuss their issues live on air. Her first book, *The Good Women of China*, recounted some of these stories. Published in 2002, it became an international bestseller and has been translated into more than thirty languages. She has written one novel, *Miss Chopsticks*, and four further non-fiction books: *Sky Burial*, *China Witness*, *Message from an Unknown Chinese Mother* and *Buy Me the Sky*. A collection of Xinran's 2003–5 *Guardian* columns, *What the Chinese Don't Eat*, was published in 2006 and covers a vast range of topics as varied as food, sex education, the experiences of British mothers who have adopted Chinese daughters and whether Chinese people do Christmas shopping or have swimming pools. *The Promise* is her eighth book.

Xinran lectures and gives speeches on writing, and on Chinese women and history. In 2004, she set up the Mothers' Bridge of Love charity to foster understanding between China and the West. Xinran lives in London, but visits China regularly.

Praise for Xinran

'One would have to have a heart of stone not to be moved.'

Economist on *Message from an Unknown Chinese Mother*

'Groundbreaking... This intimate record reads like an act of defiance, and the unvarnished prose allows each story to stand as testimony.'

The New Yorker on *The Good Women of China*

'An absorbing, often startling, always persuasive exploration of contemporary China.'

Hilary Spurling, *Spectator*, on *Buy Me the Sky*

'Right here we see the red lines that many Chinese still draw for themselves in public discourse, or even privately, the boundaries they dare not cross even today. No other style of storytelling could have exhibited them with more clarity or greater rawness.'

Oliver August, *The Times*, on *China Witness*

'This story of an extraordinary woman written by an extraordinary woman will stay with you long after closing the book.'

Christina Lamb, *Sunday Times*, on *Sky Burial*

'Xinran writes with a fine balance of economy, compassion and wisdom, and manages to be at once proud, critical, forward-looking, nostalgic, sad, angry and hopeful.'

New Statesman on *What the Chinese Don't Eat*

'Xinran evokes the multiple, layered cultures and customs of modern China with bright, memorable detail and empathy for her characters.'

Guardian on *Miss Chopsticks*

The Promise

Love and Loss in Modern China

XINRAN

*Translated from the Chinese
by William Spence*

LONDON · NEW YORK

Published in 2019 by
I.B.Tauris & Co. Ltd
London · New York
www.ibtauris.com

References to websites were correct at the time of writing.

ISBN: 978 1 78831 362 9
eISBN: 978 1 78672 534 9
ePDF: 978 1 78673 534 8

A full CIP record for this book is available from the British Library
A full CIP record is available from the Library of Congress

Library of Congress Catalog Card Number: available

Typeset by Tetragon, London
Printed and bound by CPI Group (UK) Ltd, Croydon, CR0 4YY

FOR MY BELOVED HUSBAND,
TOBY EADY
28 February 1941–24 December 2017

In the twenty years we knew each other, we came to understand what it truly means to be in love. My darling Toby, without you, so many Chinese authors like me would still be buried seeds, never to sprout in Western literary soil. Without you, I would still feel like an orphan suffering in loneliness, never to become the person I am today — your beloved wife and a woman who can feel and understand love.

Thank you, my Toby. You are my soulmate, a man of letters, and your promise of love has led me to this book.

As the poem we both loved goes:

天不老, 情难绝,   *Heaven will never grow old, nor will my love for you.*
心似双丝网,   *Our hearts are like fishing nets,*
中有千千结。   *tied together by a thousand threads.*

Contents

Promises and 'Talking Love'

My Inspirations for This Book

Early one morning in February 2012, my husband Toby Eady and I went out for a stroll around Kensington Gardens. The gentle breeze hinted at the approach of spring. The first rays of morning sun danced in the trees, bathing buds still in hibernation. A patch of green on the ground failed to hide its growing presence. The parakeets larked around, greeting their neighbours the crows and the visiting seagulls. The whole scene gave off a most palpable sense of being alive. Toby and I walked in silence, hand in hand, along the narrow path, unable to speak for fear of interrupting the birds' peace.

I've always liked birds. As a child, I would wonder wide-eyed at the various types that visited the fruit trees in the courtyard of my grandmother's house. Some even made their nests up on the high branches. But then the birds disappeared, perhaps because they couldn't bear the human chaos playing out below. It wasn't until the 1980s, when I was working as a journalist in the countryside, that birds once again caught my attention. However, this time they were in peasants' cooking pots. ('There aren't enough food rations. We can only survive by eating whatever we can catch,' I was told.)

It is true. You could only find birds in China in cooking ingredients, fairy tales, and those beautiful old paintings.

There is a pond directly in front of Kensington Palace which I like to think of as my own 'Swan Lake'. There, the swans have mingled with the grandsons and -daughters of Queen Victoria for generations, carrying on their respective lines. At night, the royal household holds candlelight feasts for honoured guests from across the world; at dawn, the lake ripples as it welcomes back the swans and other migratory birds. The Chinese say that a person's character is inextricably linked to their local environment. Well, I say a bird's is too.

I am ashamed to say that I recognise very few types of birds. Except for swans, mandarin ducks and seagulls, I only know pigeons – those birds who seem to be ever-present, and ever looking for love.

That day, we walked along the side of the pond watching the birds stop by for breakfast and a morning shower. Three pigeons caught my attention. One 'young lady' was foraging for food on the bank, followed by two restless 'young men'. She didn't have a moment's peace.

'They're not like us, are they? With pigeons, it always seems to be the men who are nagging,' I said to Toby.

'They're talking about love,' said Toby, kissing me on the forehead.

'"Talking love"? You have this saying in English?'

'In English, we say "dating" or "making love", not "talking love". But there are no laws to language – only what we express and what we understand. What's so special about "talking love" in Chinese?'

That last sentence really struck me; I was lost for words.

The past century has seen more upheaval than any other time in the 5,000-year-old history of Chinese civilisation. The ways in which people show love for each other have also changed in the face of war and cultural development. Toby didn't mind my stalling at his first question; he simply moved on to another. We had known each other for more than twenty years, and in that time not only had his questions driven me into the boundless sea of questions on China, but also forced me into the furthest corners of my own knowledge.

At home that evening, I started to look into the Chinese term 'talking love', and how its meaning has changed over time.

In a culture that traditionally forbade physical contact between men and women, 'talking love' is a modern term, defined in the Chinese dictionary as follows:

'Talking love' is a type of social activity. It is the process of cultivating love or interacting on the basis of love. It is mainly an exchange between two parties. Generally, if the exchange is successful, you will marry, live together and raise the next generation. The moral requirements for 'talking love' are as follows: First, respect human equality; second, consciously assume responsibility for it; third, love each other with humility.*

This impersonal Chinese definition left me with a cold, empty feeling. The foundation of 'talking love' is romance and the feelings it generates are invigorating, so how could this official annotation reduce it to something so completely void of emotion? I had a daydream in front of the computer: like a magic wand, the term 'talking love' opened a mysterious cave in my mind. The cave was clouded by history, full of its silent cries and the tragedy of countless weeping spirits – four generations of Chinese over the past century, their love and affection cut off, passed by, forgotten, gathering dust.

Over the next few days, while out walking in the park, Toby and I discussed at length the love affairs of our own ancestors. Toby is very familiar with his family history, whereas my understanding of my parents and grandparents is almost a blank page. Toby's mother, the author Mary Wesley, wrote about her family for all to see, sharing her upper-class bohemian romance with honesty and courage, leaving behind the evidence for later generations. I, on the other hand, am completely ignorant as to how my grandparents got married, how my parents met, and so many other things. The few details I do have are taken from my political file – something every Chinese must keep. The only personal stories I have belong to other people, because in more than thirty years of interviews and research into Chinese women I have accumulated a lot of 'unique' Chinese materials. Many of these stories I still find hard to believe, even after my own investigations have confirmed them to be true.

---

* This definition is taken from the *Hanyu Da Cidian* (literally 'Comprehensive Chinese Word Dictionary'). It is the most inclusive Chinese dictionary available, comparable to the *Oxford English Dictionary* in scope.

Toby seemed to have read my mind: 'My mother's books taught me a lot about my own family history, but they also showed me that many people shared and sympathised with the loneliness and family silence they found in her books. You should help bring these stories of Chinese love and emotion out from under the dust of obscurity, and shine a lamp on history. Only then will young people in China and the world see this unexpected and beautiful side of humanity.' As always, Toby spurred me on: 'The world needs to know the emotional side of China, not just the rise of its economy or the hard facts of its politics. You should do your best to record these stories before your mother's generation disappears.'

After I finished writing *Buy Me the Sky* in 2012, I could hardly wait to get started. Little did I know then that the process of writing this book would not only take me deep into that mysterious cave, but also reveal to me something of the life my mother lived without ever telling me or my brother. Whenever I called my mother, in near-shock, to confirm the latest story I came across in my interviews, she would reply flatly:

Yes, it's true. That was our youth.

It's nothing to get worked up about. If needed, we could give up everything for the greater good of our ideals: family, lovers, children, even our own lives.

Just because you didn't know, it doesn't mean that it didn't happen. In our day, many people got married not for love or affection, but for their revolutionary compatibility.

Our understanding of sex, emotions and love is very different from yours, and from young people now. Many couples only talked about love; they never had experienced it or did anything about it.

My mother's words make me speechless once again.

I had published seven books based on interviews with more than 300 Chinese women, but I had never before realised just how much Chinese women have changed in their understanding of the difference between sex, emotions and love. Could it be that in the space of only two generations, a collective cultural understanding had completely turned on its head? China may have experienced war and political turmoil throughout the past century, but we still share the same culture, roots and ancestors. So how could the times we live in have reconstructed an entire cultural awareness of sex, emotions and love in such a short period?

In 2013, I brought my doubts, curiosity and deep concern with me to Beijing and started writing this book. After four years of hard work, I finally walked away with a story of four generations of one Chinese family. When I finally put down my pen, I also felt that this book had brought me much closer to my mother. I may still be on the other side of the riverbank, but I can see, more clearly than ever before, the silhouette of her life. She had been led astray by the promise of her political beliefs, and she had never known true love.

And let me tell you, since that trip to China, I have seen more and more young birds hopping about among the shoots budding by the path we still walk along.

Xinran, May 2018, London

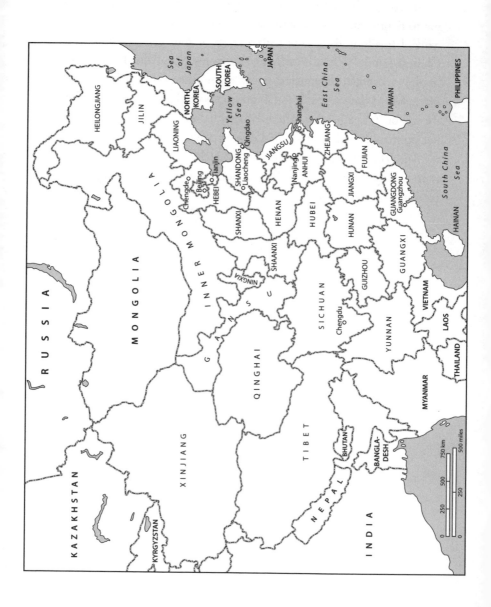

Key Dates

(Although historical sources are not always in agreement, the years given below are as they appear in the online version of the *Encyclopaedia Britannica*, which can be found at www.britannica.com.)

CHINESE TWENTIETH-CENTURY HISTORY		HAN FAMILY HISTORY	
1911/12	Fall of Qing dynasty and establishment of Republic of China		
1916–28	Warlord Era	1919	Red's parents marry
		1920	Red born
1928	Kuomintang (KMT – Nationalist Party of China) comes to power		
1927–37	First stage of Chinese Civil War, between KMT and Chinese Communist Party	1930	Orange born
		1932	Green born
1937–45	Japanese occupation of China before and during World War II, known as the Second Sino-Japanese War		
1945–9	Second stage of Chinese Civil War, between KMT and Chinese Communist Party		
1949	Mao Zedong declares founding of People's Republic of China	1949	Red marries Bao Gang

CHINESE TWENTIETH-CENTURY HISTORY		HAN FAMILY HISTORY	
		1951	Orange marries Mr Pan
		1952	Orange's daughter Kangmei born
		1953	Green marries Meng Dafu
1958–60	Great Leap Forward	1958	Green's daughter Crane born
1966–76	Cultural Revolution		
1972	US President Richard Nixon visits Beijing to re-establish US–Chinese relations		
1976	Death of Chairman Mao		
1978	New leader Deng Xiaoping adopts policies of 'Reform and Opening Up'	1978	Kangmei marries
		1980	Kangmei's daughter Wuhen born
		1984	Green's granddaughter Yoyo born
		1987	Crane marries Tang Hai
		1988	Crane's daughter Lili born
1989	Tiananmen Square incident		
1997	Hong Kong returned to China after 156 years of British rule		

Han Family Tree

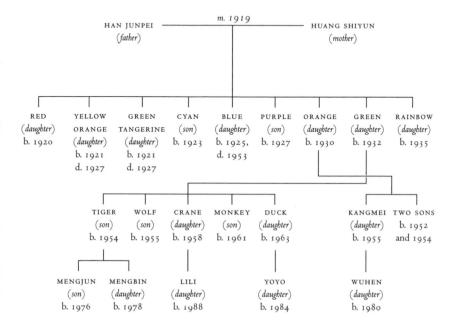

HAN JUNPEI
(father)

m. 1919

HUANG SHIYUN
(mother)

RED
(daughter)
b. 1920

YELLOW
ORANGE
(daughter)
b. 1921
d. 1927

GREEN
TANGERINE
(daughter)
b. 1921
d. 1927

CYAN
(son)
b. 1923

BLUE
(daughter)
b. 1925,
d. 1953

PURPLE
(son)
b. 1927

ORANGE
(daughter)
b. 1930

GREEN
(daughter)
b. 1932

RAINBOW
(daughter)
b. 1935

TIGER
(son)
b. 1954

WOLF
(son)
b. 1955

CRANE
(daughter)
b. 1958

MONKEY
(son)
b. 1961

DUCK
(daughter)
b. 1963

KANGMEI
(daughter)
b. 1955

TWO SONS
b. 1952
and 1954

MENGJUN
(son)
b. 1976

MENGBIN
(daughter)
b. 1978

LILI
(daughter)
b. 1988

YOYO
(daughter)
b. 1984

WUHEN
(daughter)
b. 1980

Introduction

谈 *tán*　　to talk
恋爱 *liàn ài*　　(romantic) love
谈恋爱 *tán liàn ài*　　to be dating; to fall in love

This is the story of the love lives of Chinese women, told through four generations of one family. Out of this story emerge six voices, told through their own words, all shaped by the shifts in politics, society and culture that defined and continue to define their lives.

All these stories are true, but the family names have been changed in order to protect the people concerned.

Note on the Text

All transliterations of Chinese into English are in Pinyin. The translations from Chinese to English in the text are my own, including the poems quoted, unless otherwise stated.

PART I

A Love Coloured by Wars and Political Movements

First Sister

RED

· born 1920 ·

Not long after *China Witness* was published in 2010, I received a quite unexpected call from a family friend.

'Xinran! I've just started reading your new book, and there's something I simply have to tell you about . . .

'For the past year, I've been working at a retirement home looking after elderly cadres and their families. Not long ago, one of the old officers I look after fell gravely ill. Knowing he didn't have long left, he made two final wishes: one was for us to go and visit his house; the other was to grant his wife one simple request.

'And so, after he died, another member of staff and I ended up visiting his widow in the home they had shared for Lord knows how many years. My colleague was grumbling the whole way over, saying that in the ten years he'd worked at the home, he'd never been invited into the old couple's house.

'But, in fact, no one had been. People who came to deliver letters or Chinese New Year gifts were made to leave them at the door. Even when one of them needed medical attention, they'd always wait for the ambulance outside. Behind their backs, the younger members of their work unit would whisper about them.

'When we walked in, we were the first visitors for many years. There was literally nothing in the house, apart from the old lady. We didn't dare stay too long, and after a few minutes of polite small talk we got ready to leave. On our way out, the old lady thanked us for granting her husband's dying wish, before very subtly slipping a pink envelope into my hand. "His other wish is written inside," she said calmly. The envelope was sealed.

'On the way back, my colleague spoke of nothing but that envelope and what it might contain. But on its front, in the most beautiful handwriting, were written the words:

Unless the spring has sprung, the flowers will not bloom.
Unless you received this letter, you must not open it.

'It wasn't until I got home that evening that I finally found myself alone. Inside the envelope was a single sheet of writing paper, beautifully emblazoned with a pattern of golden-red roses. On the page itself there was just one sentence: "Please arrange for me to have a virginity test." The letter was signed "Han Anhong".

'A virginity test?! I thought I must have misunderstood the message, so I went and found the internal phone book and dialled the old lady's number. On the other end of the line, her voice was adamant: "Yes, that was my husband's other dying wish."

'"And do you want to have the test?" I asked, because it was, after all, her body and not her husband's.

'"Yes, I do. I want for us both to have some sense of closure. Please make the necessary arrangements, and after that we can speak again. Thank you, and goodnight." With that, she hung up.

'Not long after, in accordance with her husband's wish, I took the old lady to the General Hospital of the People's Liberation Army (PLA) for a gynaecological examination. When I saw the results, I could barely believe my eyes.

'She had never had sex with her husband.

'Xinran, we all knew the old couple had no children, but I just can't understand why, in sixty-one years of marriage, they had never had sex. Would you agree to interview her? I can help make the introductions. You should know, though, that the old couple were somewhat eccentric; they were never ones to join in any community events or talk to their neighbours, let alone invite people into their home. So it's hard to say whether the old lady will agree to this or not.'

Since I became a radio talk show host in 1989, I have interviewed more than three hundred Chinese women, exploring the ways in which their lives and loves have been defined largely by external forces. It didn't take long to notice a clear pattern in how these forces changed according to their age – women from my grandparents' generation were often forced into arranged marriages by their parents, while it was political turmoil that shaped the love lives of my parents' generation. As for women of my own generation, money seemed to be the main driving force behind their search for a husband.

Many of their stories ended in tragedy – I'd even heard of women in the countryside who had killed themselves in order to help their families – but I had never before come across a story like the one just recounted to me. Without a moment's hesitation, I asked my friend to do everything she could to help put me in touch with this enigmatic old lady.

I started planning my visit the day I arrived back in China.

Our initial contact, however, was far from smooth. Our first telephone call lasted less than two minutes, with the old lady politely but firmly refusing to speak to me. It seemed completely out of the question that she would invite me into her home.

In my book *China Witness*, I explored the lives of the first two generations of modern China – those born before 1950 – and found the majority of them to have been silent, passive bystanders to the world around them. This was not just a result of the turbulent times they lived in, but also a remnant of ancient Chinese legal customs.

The concept of guilt by association was one of the most notable features of ancient Chinese law. Relatives and associates were held accountable alongside the criminal themselves, which not only led to fierce loyalty among individual factions and families, but also gave rise to a kind of 'clan consciousness' – no one would dare speak out for fear of being implicated themselves. This became so ingrained in Chinese culture that it had a profound and lasting effect on the way Chinese people behave, making them inherently cautious and reluctant to take assertive action for fear of the consequences.

This 'clan consciousness' withstood the great social and political upheavals of twentieth-century China – the collapse of the Qing dynasty, the chaos of the Warlord Era, the Sino-Japanese War, the Civil War and the Communist Revolution – because in the unspeakable chaos of these times, China never gave its people the chance to learn how to be 'conscious' of themselves as individuals, or how to talk about their own feelings.

Only after the 'Reform and Opening Up' programme of economic reforms spread through China in the 1980s did these people sense that the doors were slowly creaking open – between China and the world; between China's past and its present; between individuals and the government; even between family members.

But this does not mean Chinese necessarily think and act like others do. Caution and restraint have governed Chinese public expression for so long that forty years is far too brief a time to bring about any meaningful change, and freedom of speech in China continues to be hedged by ignorance and fear.

The traumas that Chinese people have lived through over the past few generations have been caged in their memories. To get them to talk about what they have witnessed, one must first find a way to help them open those cages. No easy task, but thirty years of interviewing, listening, studying and understanding have strengthened my resolve. If they can record a lifetime of Chinese history, then why can't I wait a few more days, months, or even years?

After numerous requests over the telephone, the old lady began to relent ever so slightly. 'Let me think about it, OK?'

'Of course,' I told her. 'I come back to China twice a year, and I'm happy to wait until next time, or the time after, or even the time after that. I gather these oral histories for the sake of our younger generations, so that they can better understand both the lives of their ancestors and the history of modern China. After a hundred years of chaos and upheaval in our country, historical records are lacking and subject to the government's own distorted view of the past. Every person is part of the heritage of their race and their country. We should leave behind a 360-degree view of history, one that is both colourful and complete.'

When I had finished speaking, the old lady said softly, 'It takes great strength to open such a heavy door.'

I understood straight away what kind of strength she was speaking of. It is a form of courage that has become part of the everyday lives of elderly Chinese, the thoughts that fill their heads by day and their dreams by night – the courage to face up to oneself and one's own place in history.

The following morning, at around half past eleven, I received a phone call from the old lady. She arranged for us to meet for tea at two in the afternoon that very day, on the top floor of a shopping mall near her home.

In my years of carrying out these sorts of conversations, I have established for myself a set of basic rules. Firstly, I have to arrive at the location beforehand in order to familiarise myself with the surroundings. Secondly, I look at what food and drinks are on offer. And thirdly, I choose – or wait for, if necessary – an isolated, hidden-away table so that the person I'm talking to feels completely comfortable, without any worry about what's going on around them.

The vast majority of elderly Chinese have never had the chance to live in freedom, at ease with themselves, because all they have ever known is self-sacrifice and fear. They cannot bear for strangers to see them express any undue or outward display of emotion, because they know that this could be used against them as evidence of an unsteady, disrespectful, and even dishonest character.

That day I was very fortunate. In the teahouse we had agreed to meet at, the two middle-aged women sitting at the table I had my eye on left shortly after I arrived. I sat down, ordered a *biluochun* tea and began my wait for the old lady. Observing and getting a strong feel for my surroundings is, for me, another way to explore and analyse how society works. China has developed at such an astonishing pace that when I return there twice a year, I am often made to feel like an old woman chasing after her little grandson.

From my vantage point in the teahouse, I could see at a glance the great stream of people filing in and out of the surrounding shops, the kind of throbbing crowd that can be found in big cities all over China.

There are always car parks big enough for a thousand vehicles. This is important, because in today's China, city folk who don't drive are looked down on. Even if their office is half a kilometre away, they will still drive to work for fear of 'losing status' or 'losing face'. Three-person households will drive three different cars.

Levels three to five of these malls are for shopping, where the sky-high prices of foreign brands entice the *fuerdai*, the second-generation rich, to keep up with the latest international fashion trends. At the same time, they also offer ordinary people – who can admire but never afford their goods – the chance to sample a flavour of what life is like outside China.

Linking these floors are sets of gigantic elevators that, like great veins, transport the people and the money that make up the very lifeblood of these colossal malls.

I watch the restless rush of people in front of me. They come from all walks of life, and in this great crowd they enjoy an equality that eludes them in their everyday lives. Their passion for shopping is stirred like some great tide by the rhetoric of advertising and the distorted vision of 'Going Global' presented in the media. This might manifest itself in something as simple as buying Japanese kitchen utensils or bathroom products, or, more significantly, purchasing land and property in major cities throughout the Western world – a phenomenon which has led to a growing identity crisis in Chinese living abroad.

I had lost track of how much time had passed when all of a sudden an old lady wearing a tan-coloured velvet jacket caught my attention. With her upright posture and short silvery-white hair, she appeared like a goddess amid such noise and disorder. Closely following her up in the elevator was our mutual friend. So this was indeed the honoured guest I had been waiting for.

Our friend began by introducing me. She turned and said, 'Xinran, this is Mrs Han Anhong – Red.'

I could barely take my eyes off her, thinking to myself, is she really over ninety years old? But then, as if in response to the question, my gaze fell to the old lady's aged, liver-spotted, trembling hands.

After I sat down, we took up the old lady's suggestion of ordering a pot of *pu'er* tea with three cups. She said, 'Xinran, I believe what you're drinking is *biluochun*, correct? For those of you who work in front of a computer all day, it's good for your health. But we Chinese drink tea according to the season – flower tea in spring; green tea in summer; oolong tea in autumn; black tea in winter.'

In the talk that followed, it was more like she was interviewing me. The old lady asked about my work, my views on Chinese society, and the books I had written. When I then began telling her about the female general I wrote about in *China Witness*, the old lady's eyes lit up in delighted surprise: 'So you know Phoebe?!'

'Yes,' I replied. 'General Phoebe is an old family friend.' She watched me grow up, and in many ways acted as my mentor. When I started recording these oral histories in the 1990s, General Phoebe was a source of great encouragement, and we would speak regularly on the phone. 'She said that so many records of Chinese history had already been destroyed, through the chaos of war, man-made fear and ignorance. Unless we move now to take a record of these personal stories and oral histories, a fracture will appear between China's future and its past. Our children will be bound to repeat the mistakes of the past, and our future descendants will succumb to the turmoil and chaos we struggled through. This—'

'Yes! Yes!' The old lady's eyes had started to well up. She seemed genuinely moved. 'Exactly, exactly. Many of our generation try and avoid the memories of what they went through, while some even try to forget altogether, creating for themselves a brand-new past. But those people have no sense of historical duty – they don't have the courage to confront their own history. They don't even have the courage to answer questions from their own children.'

Hearing this self-assurance and composure in her voice, my friend stared at the old lady's face as if she was looking at a stranger, barely able to contain her astonishment. That evening, she rang me and said, 'Most of the time the old lady's practically mute, using expressions and gestures to communicate, rarely giving more than one-syllable answers. But today she was completely different.'

In fact, I thought, the old lady had barely spoken at all that day – not about herself, at least.

Two days later, she arranged for us to meet in a park next to her retirement home. As it happened, General Phoebe and I used to meet there once in a while for a stroll. I remember fondly how we used to make small talk about the seasonal changes we noticed in the trees, simply to ease us into other, more serious topics of conversation.

Sure enough, as we ambled along a winding path by the lakeside, the old lady began to open up to some of my questions. Although these were just enquiries into small details of her family history, I could tell I was gradually starting to earn the old lady's trust as she slowly unravelled the memories of her past. But as I tried, with utmost caution, to steer the conversation towards more sensitive topics, the old lady interrupted me. 'Let's talk again next week. I need a little more time to clear my thoughts. My experience has not exactly been what most people would call "normal". Come and see me next week – I'll tell you my story then. OK?'

That week seemed more like a year. In my interview diary, I wrote down a list of things people of this nonagenarian's generation had lived through: the incessant fighting of the Warlord Era, the Sino-Japanese War, the Civil War, the Korean War (or, as the Chinese call it, the War to Resist US Aggression and Aid Korea), the Great Leap Forward and the Cultural Revolution. It seemed that at no stage had they known peace.

When the next week finally arrived and I called the old lady, I didn't get the reply I was hoping for.

'Wait a little longer. OK?'

I had to press her. 'I'm going back to the UK next Friday. After that, can I call you to talk?' The other end of the line was silent for a moment, before the old lady said, 'How about next week? Or maybe the weekend? What about Monday? Let's say next Monday. You can come to my home.'

The military retirement home where the old lady lived was in Beijing – a place where many unexpected wonders are to be found. In many ways the home seemed more like a cross between a luxury hotel and a botanical garden. When I walked through the front gate, which was surrounded by fresh flowers and green trees, I felt a special kind of atmosphere quite unlike that of the great swathes of skyscrapers to be found in the city's residential areas. I suspected that birdsong filled the air both day and night.

Standing in front of the huge doorway, I felt as if I was preparing to enter some stately palace, and before I rang the bell I couldn't help but check to see if my hands were clean enough to come calling at a place like this. The door opened slowly to reveal the old lady, standing there with a smile on her face. That day, she was dressed impeccably from head to toe in a light grey that perfectly matched her silver, silk-like hair. She moved with a slow elegance that made me feel I was in the presence of nobility.

Passing through a corridor whose walls were covered in military awards and certificates, I followed the old lady into her living room. The moment we entered, I did a double take. The home, which looked so luxurious from the outside, was empty. It was as if the family were completely destitute.

Standing in the middle of the living room, I could see into all the other rooms. I noticed two bedrooms, both empty other than two single beds; a big study with nothing but a chair and a desk, on top of which was a pile of what looked like manuscript papers; and a spacious kitchen that appeared to be used as another study – apart from a small teapot, the room seemed full of cultural and literary artefacts. I also noticed two bathrooms.

The living room itself was spacious. It was empty but for a fraying old wicker chair keeping lonely guard over a small tea table in the centre of the room. Opposite that stood an ancient-looking 9-inch black and white TV set – the kind I used to know so well – balanced on top of three cardboard boxes.

For me, the most interesting part was the way the bedrooms were set up. Each had two single beds, and two separate bedside cabinets. It looked for a moment as though there might also be two sets of cupboards, but in fact they were just old military-style bookshelves, on top of which the old lady's clothes were neatly piled. Aside from some underwear, it seemed that most of it was vintage army uniform. Facing the two beds was a wicker chair similar to the one in the living room.

It felt like those bedrooms were from another world, cut off from our own.

The old lady poured me a cup of hot water, while she herself drank from a flask with a glass case. I knew that type of flask well: it was from the latter half of the Cultural Revolution, when Chinese people had been so poor that they had relied on coupons to survive. But for those families lucky enough to have had one, that flask had been even more precious than the food you might put inside it.

I used to dream of having a flask like that, and of the jealous looks it would inspire in my classmates. But by the time I had made my own, everyone around me already had a new thermos – once again had I failed to keep up with the times. Anyhow, when I saw that flask in the old lady's hand, a strange feeling came over me: was I being transported back into the past? Or was the past finally catching up with me?

The old lady signalled for me to bring the other wicker chair forward. We sat down, and without waiting for me to speak the old lady leaned backwards, slowly tilting her head to gaze up at the ceiling.

'We can talk here, but don't interrupt me. My memory is stored away in an old part of my brain. I fear that as soon as it stops, it won't start moving again.'

Before I could say a word, the gentle stream of the old lady's story began to flow.

My given name is Anhong, but my nickname is Yaohong. *Yao* means rock, as in to rock the boat; *hong* means red, as in the colour. Most people just call me Red. When I was only nine years old, my father arranged for me to marry his friend's son, who was thirteen at the time. His name was Fang Baogang. People would say he was something of a child prodigy, able to recite the classics, write beautiful calligraphy and create rhyming couplets on cue.

The Fang family ran a highly successful shipping business in south China, mostly dealing in weapons and ammunition. During the chaos of the Warlord Era, which began in 1911, the Fangs made a small fortune by issuing a number of 'war bonds'. When Japan later invaded China and seized the family's fleet of ships, the Fangs sold off the rest of their assets and moved to Beiping.* There, they became one of the main suppliers of arms to the warlord Feng Yuxiang as he resisted the Japanese in northern China.† Later, the family sent three of their sons to enlist in the army of the Nationalist general Fu Zuoyi in his fight against the Communists.‡

In late 1948, General Fu began negotiating in secret with the Communists' Fourth Field Army. By 22 January 1949, they had reached an agreement for the peaceful liberation of Beiping, whereby Fu would withdraw his troops to the outskirts of the city and integrate them into Communist forces. When the PLA formally entered Beiping on 31 January, Baogang took the opportunity to take leave and visit his family.

The Fangs sent for my father straight away. It was agreed that the two of us, whose lives had been suspended in time for so many years,

---

* The city of Beijing was known as Beiping (or Peiping) from 1368 to 1403, and again from 1928 to 1949, when the Chinese capital was at Nanjing.

† Feng Yuxiang (1882–1948) was a renowned warlord who also served as Vice Premier of the Republic of China from 1928 to 1930. A strict Methodist, Feng was also known as the Christian General for his efforts to convert his troops.

‡ Fu Zuoyi (1895–1974) was a Chinese military leader who rose to prominence for his role in defending China from the Japanese.

would finally be wed. I was already twenty-eight years old. According to the old customs my family still adhered to, engaged women were seen as having already 'bound their hair',* meaning they could never be betrothed to another man.

We had not yet recovered from the war by then, and our families didn't go to any great lengths for our wedding. They didn't even follow the old series of rituals known as the 'Three Letters and Six Rites'. That's not to say there weren't any traditional elements to the ceremony; we did follow some of the rules passed down to us by our ancestors. These included: using a sedan chair to carry the bride to the groom's house; holding a ceremony to greet the bride at the gateway of the groom's house; kowtowing at the graves of our ancestors; paying due respects to the elders of both families; drinking a toast to the health of both families; visiting the new in-laws after the marriage; and placing peanuts, dates and other foods considered auspicious under the mattress of the bridal bed – these symbolise good luck and the hope that the bride will give birth to a boy soon (*zao sheng guizi*).†

We didn't have any friends to speak of, and nearly everyone in our families had already emigrated. Those left behind were mostly domestic servants who wouldn't dare cause us any offence. I suppose that's how we managed to avoid the infamous *nao dong fang* – that series of pranks that newlyweds fear most.

Baogang never came into the bridal chamber on the night of our wedding. He excused himself by saying he had drunk too much wine and had a lot of work. The next day, we had to move into the marital home assigned to us by the army, located outside the front gate of the barracks. Meanwhile, our fathers were busy packing their own suitcases, preparing to set out for Hong Kong to make a fresh start for the family business.

In those days, the political situation was a complete mess, rumours flying around everywhere and people running scared. According to my

---

* A Han Chinese wedding custom, whereby the woman would style her hair in a special way from the day of her engagement until the wedding night.
† In Chinese, the word for date ('*zao*') is almost a homonym for 'soon', while the word for peanut ('*sheng*') is similar to that for 'birth'.

father, of those merchants who had shown support for the Nationalists, very few dared stay on in the Communist-controlled north. The lucky ones had been able to take their families to Hong Kong or other parts of the Nationalist-controlled south, while those less fortunate were now doing everything in their power to emigrate. People were terrified that the Communists would come and steal their family property for redistribution to the poor.

You know, you can't let a wedding, no matter how big an occasion, get in the way of fleeing for one's life! Besides, it is the fate of a daughter to live by the whims of her family elders. I'm just glad that my mother had already passed away, so she didn't have to worry about her children.

Red's story came to an abrupt halt. She paused, composed herself, and spoke again in a gentle whisper: 'My marriage sentence began that day.'

On the second day of our marriage, when we moved into the barracks, Baogang arranged for two orderlies to help me settle in. At that time I had no knowledge of China's political parties, his army's background or what was really going on. For me, the army base was so fresh it was like another world. Everyone was so kind to us; they had even decorated our new apartment with all kinds of festive touches. Inside, the place was very simple – a bed with some bedding, a kind of clothes rack and a small wooden table with two wooden chairs – but everything was brand new.

Baogang said that we didn't need much furniture because it was the life of a soldier to always be on the move, and that we had no need for a kitchen because the mess hall was just around the corner.

I remember being very curious about my new surroundings. Everything felt so different. I had grown up in a compound surrounded by high walls, where the stark realities of the outside world had seemed like nothing but the fantasy stories I came across in my books. I hadn't given any thought to how I would build a home with this man. Times of war are like great mazes – impossible to find a path on which you feel in complete control of your own destiny.

Baogang spent the day working in the office next door. Later, he took me to eat supper in the mess hall. The taste didn't compare to home cooking, but sitting there among that group of bright-eyed young soldiers, bursting with energy and optimism for the future ... it was so uplifting! It's just a shame none of them came and spoke to me.

After supper Baogang went straight back to his office, which I took as a sign that he was giving me some space to wash and get ready for bed.

When I was ready, I lit a pair of special red candles, both with my nickname, Yaohong, carved into the side, and placed them by the head of the bed. I had found them in the jewellery box my mother left me.

The box itself was set with ivory, with the image of two wild geese flying side by side carved into the top.* Inside, apart from a few items of jewellery, I found a small vial decorated with the traditional *baizitu* imagery of one hundred sons and filled with a kind of opiate powder. There was also a page of hand-drawn images, like those you would find in the *Kama Sutra*, and a pink silk handkerchief on which two lines of poetry were embroidered in golden-red silk threads:

Following nature they fly south, never leaving their beloved's side.
The yin to his yang, loyal to the very end.

In the shy flickering of candlelight, my heart cried out to my mother in heaven: 'Yes, your daughter is finally somebody's wife!' I undressed slowly and lay down on the bed. Smoke rose from the two candles, casting shadows on the ceiling that appeared to me in an endless stream of erotic images, men and women locked in writhing embrace.

---

* Wild geese are an important motif in Chinese poetry. They are considered to be lovebirds, because of their tendency to fly together in pairs, and for the fact that they are known to mate for life.

My mind raced, my cheeks burned and my body seemed to tremble with waves of excitement as Baogang softly entered the room. I closed my eyes and listened as he moved towards the window. I could feel his heavy breathing, and those visions on the ceiling, which I could still see through my closed eyelids, writhed once more. They vanished when Baogang blew out the candles.

In that still darkness, my heart beat wildly as I waited to become a woman.

That wait lasted for a long time. So long, in fact, that my mind drifted dreamily into another world, where the voices of angels rang in my ears, reciting beautiful, beautiful poems:

No powder can conceal the bride's blushing cheek,
Red as the dress that slips smooth upon her delicate skin.
Enchanting, unreal, her life seems but a dream,
Made real by him who tomorrow she will wed.

You've never heard that before? Really? Well, how about this one?

Thinking of her, sleep shall not visit me tonight,
Her deep red dress, her hair adorned with jade,
Visions of bridal carriages flash across my restless mind,
Dreams of the past bring with them troubled thoughts,
And a longing so dark and deep.

As I lay there in bed that night, it was as if my mind was working like a projector, flashing these poems one by one across the blank sheet of my mind. You may laugh, but it really felt as if I were floating on air. I couldn't tell where the earth ended and heaven began.

Suddenly, a soft thud brought me back to reality. In the cold and lonely moonlight, I saw a figure kneeling beside the bed – the outline of the man I had just married.

'Baogang? Is that you? What's going on?' I had no idea what was happening – I had never heard of a man kneeling before a woman.

'Miss Anhong ... No, wait ... You want me to call you Red. Red,

I . . . there's something I need to tell you. There are two engagements in my life.'

As I raised my body to face him, my tongue, lips and fingers went numb.

'The first is the one my parents arranged for me when I was only a child – you. The second is with the woman I fell in love with, the woman of my heart. I can't give up either of them. I can't disobey the will of my parents, nor can I turn my back on the woman I love. I . . .'

Baogang could barely speak. His body was bent over so far that his head was nearly touching the ground, his face hidden.

It was like being struck by a bolt of lightning and smashed into a thousand tiny pieces: two engagements? 'The woman you fell in love with, the woman of your heart? You mean that's not me?'

Oh, I was so confused! My whole body went cold, a feeling I can still remember to this day – blood frozen, stricken breath, and the sense that I was falling into a bottomless pit.

I lay there in silence, too overwhelmed to react, as Baogang knelt motionless beside me.

For three nights in a row it went on like this – three nights! He would go to work as normal during the day, then come home and kneel by my bedside in the darkness. Neither of us knew what to say. It felt like I had nothing left to live for.

In the moonlight I could see him kneeling there, bent double, sometimes to the point where he was virtually lying on the ground. All the while I could feel the strength of his will, and knew that he was waiting for my forgiveness.

But how could I forgive him? This marriage had been arranged for us by our parents, and we couldn't disobey them, especially while they were still alive. Besides, the whole country was in turmoil, turned completely on its head, and breaking any of the new laws was a matter of life and death. I was completely lost.

Red stopped. Her eyes scanned the ceiling as if searching for something.

The helplessness I saw in those eyes was all too familiar to me. In more than thirty years of interviews, I had seen it in the eyes of many Chinese women. Divorce as we understand it today is a product of modern Chinese society. Up until the overthrow of the feudal imperial system in 1911, a man could disown his wife, but a woman had absolutely no right to end her marriage. Then, with the violent upheavals and political turmoil of the twentieth century, divorce (and remarriage) came to be regarded as a way of climbing the political ladder to a better life. No one would admit that the reason for their divorce was to escape from a loveless and unnatural marriage.

It was not until the 1980s that Chinese people were truly able to decide freely about marriage, to make up their minds and look for the kind of family that they really wanted. From that point on, the word 'divorce' finally became a topic which people talked about openly. Some young Chinese are even trying to persuade parents who married for political reasons to divorce and find the true love that was denied them in their youth. But what these children can't understand is that it is too late for many of these tired and weather-beaten souls. Red, I believe, is one of them.

I could see that Baogang had lost a lot of weight. Some people said that his feng shui had been upset by his life in the military, others that intellectuals like him always suffered worst when the country itself was in pain. Some even blamed the 'burden' of being a newlywed. But I knew all along that it was heartache, insomnia and a guilty conscience that weighed so heavily on his mind.

After supper on the fourth night I made Baogang a cup of black tea. I composed myself, looked him directly in the eye and said, 'Since you have such a stubborn will, such undying loyalty to your beloved, and seeing as how we can't split up … well, I think we should wait and see if she comes back. If she does, then I can just make up some excuse to leave, and you two can be together. For now, we can share a bed the way brothers and sisters do. You sleep on the left; I'll sleep on the right. OK?'

Baogang's eyes lit up at this unexpected surprise as he stuttered, 'Thank you! I won't take advantage of you, I promise.'

That night, Baogang was so exhausted that the moment his head touched the pillow he fell into a deep, deep sleep. Hearing the sound of his gentle snoring and seeing the outline of his body lying next to me under the blanket, I felt a mix of anger and grief rise up in me. Nine long years I had waited for this. For this! I couldn't help but think of the lines written by Li Guan in his work *Butterflies in Love with Flowers*:

> There are ten thousand ways in which I miss you,
> But even these are lost in the vastness of the universe.

Later, as I tossed and turned in bed that night, unable to sleep, three words drifted over gently from the other side of the bed: 'Are you asleep?'

'How can I sleep?'

'You must be tired. Get some rest.' The sound of his voice seemed to come down from the ceiling, and left me wide awake.

Without even realising what I was doing, I blurted out a question that had been eating away at me for days. Addressing the ceiling directly, I asked, 'How did you meet her?'

'Her name is Lin, and we met at work. We weren't in the combat unit, but worked gathering intelligence for the army, passing on information about battle commands, writing military reports, that sort of thing. Our department only had three people, all in one office, supporting the headquarters.'

'Well, what about your other colleague?' I added.

'A guy called Luo Wen, just a couple of years older than me. He also liked Lin a lot.'

'Then how—'

Baogang interrupted me before I could finish the question: 'Then how did I end up with her? Luo Wen was the head of our department. A hugely talented man, he could understand English, German and Russian, play several instruments, write beautifully, paint well. He was quite introverted, but always very good to us.

After Lin's father was killed in battle during the Civil War, fighting for Kuomintang forces against the Communists, her uncle arranged for her to work alongside Luo Wen in Fu Zuoyi's intelligence division. Lin always said that it was the experience that he passed on to her, and the way he looked after her so well, that allowed her to finally go back to being the happy, open person she had been before her father's death. Before I joined the department, they had worked alongside each other like brother and sister.

But Lin and I are the same age, and we ended up spending a lot of time together outside of work — it wasn't long before we fell for one another.'

That was our first night of ceiling-gazing together. Lying in bed, looking upwards. One of us asking the questions, the other answering. I'm not sure if it was that we ran out of questions, couldn't find the right answers, or maybe even that the ceiling just got tired of passing on our messages — but eventually we both slipped off into our own separate dreams.

Over the next few nights we would gaze up at that ceiling together, introducing ourselves to one another.

Not long afterwards, Baogang said to me: 'I'm taking part in a training exercise to incorporate our troops into the PLA. I might be home very late. An orderly will help you get food from the mess hall and take care of the chores around the house. Oh, and I've also arranged for us to be sent another blanket, so you needn't worry about me getting cold.'

That night he really was late getting back. While I pretended to be asleep, he slipped very quietly under the new blanket that the orderly had sent us.

Staring up at the ceiling above me, the words that had been stored up in my heart for so long came pouring out.

'You know, Baogang, when we got engaged I was too young to really understand what was happening, and didn't feel anything. Then, when I was fourteen and in the prime of my youth, all it took was for someone to say your name and my face would go bright red. I suppose it was around then that you really came into my life. By sixteen I could barely wait to meet you, especially when my father started talking about my brothers and sisters getting married. I couldn't wait until it was my turn.

Later, when I heard that you'd enlisted in the army, I started listening to news from the front lines. I would keep guard over the family radio every day, praying that I would hear news of the war ending. I had never left the boundaries of our family compound, but my longing for you carried me into the outside world, onto the battlefields of the Civil War.

I missed you in the day watching the seasons change, I missed you at night watching the stars shift in the sky. The most precious years of my youth came and went in those nine years of waiting. Finally, you came back. But ...'

'But? But what?' Baogang's voice came suddenly out of the darkness.

I was silent, embarrassed. After a while he said:

'I'm also talking to the ceiling. It's the only way I can talk to Lin; I'm waiting for good news.'

'Really? Well no one has news to pass on to me.' My tone was defensive. 'I'm just talking to myself.'

'Talking to yourself can be very self-comforting, very liberating.'

I think he was probably trying to console me.

'Do you still want to hear Lin's story?' he said.

'Go ahead. I'm sure it's very *comforting* for you, very *liberating*, right?' In fact, it was exactly that for me too.

He didn't reply straight away, making me wait in silence for some time before starting Lin's story. He spoke to the ceiling, of course, and I listened as the words rained down from above, showering my heart.

Over the coming years, I learned all about Lin.

She was from the south. Having lost her mother at an early age, her father sent her to study in Britain. As soon as she graduated, she returned to her homeland with a band of hot-blooded and patriotic young Chinese to join the War of Resistance against Japan.

Just after they got back, however, the Japanese surrendered, and Lin ended up helping her father and his troops reclaim areas previously under enemy control.

Soon afterwards, the dispute between the Communists and the Nationalists turned north China into a battlefield, and the families of many Nationalist officers were sent to Sichuan Province or other parts of the south. Lin, however, refused to leave her father, who entrusted her to work under his elder brother in the intelligence division.

As PLA troops in the north-east marched victorious down towards the central plains, Lin's father was tragically killed in battle. Chiang Kai-shek's main army were forced to retreat south. Even the Thirty-Fifth Army – General Fu Zuoyi's trump card – were annihilated by the PLA. With no one left in charge, the few Nationalist officers left in the central plains took fate into their own hands: some stayed on to fight to the death with against the PLA; some followed Chiang in fleeing to Sichuan; others were caught somewhere between the two.

At the time, Chiang still believed that he could use Sichuan's unique geography as a protective screen while leaning on the support of local warlords, just as he had done in defeating the Japanese invaders just a few years previously.

Lin was taken by her uncle to Chengdu, a city in Sichuan that acted as a meeting point for important Nationalists, while Baogang obeyed his family's wish for him to stay with General Fu's dwindling army in the central plains. Neither of them believed they would be apart for long; after all, the Nationalists had the backing of the United States and would surely suppress the 'rebellion' in no time! No one, Baogang said, could have predicted what would happen next.

In the weeks and months that followed, news poured in of crushing defeats and humiliating retreats for the Nationalists. But even then no one sensed that Chiang's army would eventually be forced to flee the mainland across the strait to lonely old Taiwan.

Radio stations from both sides would broadcast news of 'resounding victories': the Communists claiming to have liberated the south from the tyrannical Nationalists; the Nationalists that they had purged the north of the rebellious Communists. Newspapers were even worse, spreading endless rumours to gain the upper hand for whichever side controlled them.

By the time Baogang realised that the PLA was sweeping across the central plains like wildfire, it was too late to leave; Fu Zuoyi's army had already been surrounded, with no chance of escape.

Baogang and Lin spoke for the final time via telegram at the end of January 1949, when he found out that her uncle had decided to move with Chiang Kai-shek even further south, to the island of Hainan.

According to Baogang, Lin's uncle was involved in an undercover operation to withdraw funds from state reserves and relocate national treasures from the Forbidden City to Taiwan. If that was the case, it reveals that Chiang and his high-level supporters knew of their impending defeat. It seems a pity, then, that men like Lin's father had laid down their lives for what was already a lost cause.

I never expected Baogang to have such passionate feelings towards Lin. For several months, he could barely hold back the tide of longing that swelled inside him. Somewhere along the way, I forgot my role in all of this and why I was lying there next to him in the first place. All the while, Lin was there between us, whispering sweet nothings into the ear of the man I had just married.

Baogang was in a foul mood over the next few months while he completed his PLA integration programme, but he never wanted to talk about it. He clearly felt he was betraying his Nationalist origins and beliefs by wearing the uniform of the 'enemy'. The night he came home wearing his new uniform, he didn't sleep at all but just lay there, sighing deeply.

'Many people get to go home during the programme, but the PLA won't let me because I'm in the intelligence unit,' he said, letting out another sigh. 'They say I'm crucial to their research into the Nationalist army. But anyway, now I'm wearing this uniform, would Lin ever come back for me? I mean, who am I? Am I on her side or theirs? Will the Nationalists fight back? And if they do, what should I do?' Baogang's voice was full of pain and uncertainty.

'I hadn't thought of that either. I've only heard that Chiang Kai-shek might try and retake the central plains. But Beijing? It's so far from Sichuan and Hainan. Even if he does come back here, I don't think it'll be for some time yet.'

As I spoke, a thought suddenly occurred to me: what if Baogang tried to flee? What would happen to me? Then another thought came, just as suddenly: that might actually be a good thing! If he were to leave, our marriage would be over and we would both have our freedom. We wouldn't need an excuse; people would just put it down to the tumultuous times we lived in.

As if he had read my mind, Baogang said, 'Relax, I'm not going anywhere.'

'Why?' I asked.

'Lin and I parted ways in Beijing, promising each other that we would reunite here too. If I go south, and she comes north, we'll pass each other like ships in the night. Everything's a mess at the moment, and with no way of contacting each other we can't make any rash decisions. There may be no turning back – we might lose each other forever!'

I stared up at the ceiling, concentrating hard. 'I can wait here with you. When Lin comes back to find you, I'll be able to leave.'

I couldn't help stealing a glance at Red when I heard this. I was used to hearing such things from women living in the countryside, who had grown up in poverty and without education, women who blindly followed their elders' advice on the so-called Three Obediences and Four Virtues.

These were a set of moral principles that dictated how a woman should act, begun in ancient times and continuing right through until 1949. Confucian in origin, they set the moral standard both for how women were required to act and how men must choose their wives.

The Three Obediences dictated that a woman must obey her father as a daughter, her husband as a wife and her sons as a widow. The Four Virtues were feminine morality, physical charm, propriety in speech and efficiency in housework.

These 'life principles' allowed no space for women to be themselves or have control of their own lives and needs. I always believed that love, true love between Chinese women and men pre-dating my parents' generation might have only have existed in art, in those beautiful paintings, statues and works of fiction. They could only 'talk love', and never display their feelings physically, educated as they were according to the Three Obediences and Four Virtues. Red had been educated in this way too, but also by the Revolution. As a daughter of the new China, how could she settle for a life void of passion and meaning? How could she be happy to live under the same ceiling with a man she did not love?

Red could obviously sense that I was studying her face, but she paid no attention and continued her story.

In those early days, when we had just moved in, Baogang would spend almost all day at work. He never wanted to talk to me about any of it, though. This was back when the barracks were almost empty; hardly any soldiers had their families with them. But then, around 1950, the place started filling up as families who had been scattered by the war began to reunite.

Some soldiers had three or four wives come looking for them, each with children in tow. Without DNA testing or anything like that, we had to rely on witness testimony or some other form of material evidence to determine who the father was.

Due to the low rates of literacy in the army — and the need for women to look after all those left-over children — Baogang put in a recommendation for me to join. I was, of course, delighted. China was being rebuilt and in desperate need of talent, so the application process was very simple. Written on the front of my very first personnel file was the title PERMANENT COPY CLERK — ANSWERING TO MILITARY STAFF. From that moment on, I was a member of the PLA.

Around the same time, work gradually became an important part of our ceiling-gazing, and we discovered that we had more in common than we'd first thought. We mourned together those families torn apart by war, the historical events that had led us here, and the indelible imprint these times would have on the future. We rejoiced together, and grieved together. Sometimes we laughed, sometimes we cried. But we rarely argued.

It goes without saying that we avoided talking about our future, as that was still shrouded in uncertainty. Rumours of Chiang Kai-shek's counter-attack on the mainland had gradually gone quiet, and PLA troops were no longer being readied for an invasion of Taiwan.

'Why didn't you argue much?' I asked Red.

Her gaze dropped from the ceiling and fixed on my face. 'It wasn't that we were trying to avoid confrontation — we just happened to agree on most things.'

It wasn't the answer I had been expecting.

'Well, what was it you argued about, then?' I asked again, eagerly.

Red's eyes once more climbed the wall. 'The first big argument ... I think was to do with the Korean War.'

One day I brought home a copy of *Volunteer Army Daily* – in those days there was no *Liberation Army Daily* – with the headline 'American imperialists invade Korea – trying to knock down China's north gate!' Speaking to Baogang later that evening, I could barely hide my anger. 'Why can't those Americans let us Chinese have any peace?!'

He said: 'You can't always trust what you read in the paper. The UN has made the decision to send troops to prevent the north invading the south.'

I fought back: 'I know you get to read foreign newspapers through your work, but are you really claiming that the *Volunteer Army Daily* is wrong?'

'The media should be reporting facts, not making them up. When newspapers start spreading lies, it messes with people's minds and distorts their sense of right and wrong. It can lead to the downfall of a country or even a whole race.' Baogang's tone was deadly serious.

'That's a bit excessive, isn't it?' My voice was full of scorn.

Facing the ceiling, Baogang let out a sigh: 'The news is the news. It shouldn't be moulded into something it's not.'

I forget how the conversation went after that, but it wasn't long before I began noticing how many of those 'facts' he dismissed as lies were indeed proven false. I couldn't take my argument back, but I had learned a lesson I would remember for the rest of my life.

I can only think of one other serious disagreement between us ...

In 1951, China took its lead from the Soviets in carrying out a series of internal purges. People would use the Three-Anti and Five-Anti campaigns as a pretence to steal from each other and pursue personal vendettas. Newspapers and radio broadcasts were crammed with stories of class struggle. Every day brought a new, seemingly earth-shattering headline, while many of our colleagues were persecuted by the government. We only found out much later that we had come very close to being purged ourselves, thanks to Baogang's history in General Fu Zuoyi's army and my family background, including my relatives abroad. Baogang's communication skills and his proficiency in foreign languages kept him in his high position; the military's desperate lack of talent was the only thing that kept us from being swept away by the great political storm swirling around us.

Still, this atmosphere of fear caused me no end of stress at the time. Where had all these terrible people come from? Why hadn't I known anything about them? How could they betray their country – taking bribes and breaking the law like madmen!

At this, Baogang would always let out a long moan: 'You just don't see, do you? You're confusing what's real for what's fake, what's right from what's wrong. You're giving in to ignorance and fear.'

Whenever we argued before bed, no matter what the topic, I would always end up the victor. And yet when I woke the next morning it was always with the overwhelming sense that he had let me win; not only that, but more often than not, whatever he had been arguing would later be proved right.

Before he died, when I thanked him for this gesture, he said gently: 'A teacher once told me that a gentleman doesn't fight with a lady. Letting you have a good night's sleep was perhaps the only kindness I could give you.'

When the 1960s had passed, and the subject of Lin had been all but phased out of our night-time chats, Baogang would every now and then find some excuse to bring her back into our lives. Although I was so used to talking about their love by that point – I had even begun to quite enjoy it – I was basically living the life of a widow while my husband was lying next to me. My so-called marriage to him was nothing less than a spiritual and physical jail.

Every night we didn't talk about Lin was like a breath of fresh air, a holiday, a day with blue skies in which I could get some sort of enjoyment from my marriage. The longest holiday I had during the 'life sentence' of my marriage was probably from 1966 to 1976, during the Cultural Revolution.

What did we talk about at night during that period? Well, China had previously gone through a long, uninterrupted period of turmoil. Great political and economic storms had virtually wiped out all families with any kind of land or wealth; the Three-Anti and Five-Anti Campaigns brought chaos to all corners of the country; the reorganisation of the agricultural industry was a disaster. Then there was the madness of the Great Leap Forward, the split of the Communist leaders at the Lushan Conference, and the decline in Soviet-China relations which culminated with the Zhenbao Island incident.

However, because our work was mostly focused on analysing foreign trends and collecting information from abroad, we were part of the 'Shangri-La' of state security, a kingdom within the army: the intelligence division.

Baogang used to say that although our country had been through a century of chaos, at least Communist China wasn't a slave to any other nation. But why was this? Well, firstly because the peasants, who made up the majority of the population in this huge agricultural nation, had been devastated by the Civil War and were left with no energy to revolt. Secondly, this was an oppressive and autocratic ruling party that wouldn't allow its state security to be compromised by having any other political parties on the scene, thus avoiding civil war. Thirdly, China's deeply patriarchal culture naturally suppressed any kind of religious belief or extreme behaviour.

But what happened in 1966 was completely unprecedented. To make matters worse, all our domestic fears were underscored by concerns over the Soviets' nuclear testing. Even our team from the core of state security was sent down from Beijing to Daxing County in Hebei Province, in the foothills of the Great Wall. It's actually a part of Beijing these days.

The barracks we stayed in had been around for a while, and there was a fairly well-established structure to the place by the time we arrived there. I heard that in 1985, when the military withdrew from the area, the buildings were left vacant. It's a great pity. Sometimes I think about going back and having a look around.

Anyway, when we were there the living quarters were allocated according to rank. Although Baogang and I were never physically attacked, we had been demoted because of our suspect 'political backgrounds' and 'overseas connections'. That's why we were put in a very basic residential area made up of a series of bungalows.

A single ventilator duct ran from one end of the row of bungalows to the other. Its main purpose might have been to prevent gas poisoning, but it would also pass on news from our neighbours – elderly people scorning their juniors, couples squabbling, children throwing tantrums. Other sounds travelled too – things breaking, food being cooked, even the sound of the bedpan being used in the middle of the night. We could hear it all perfectly! Baogang used to joke that he never imagined we'd be living in a real-life radio drama.

The political infighting of the Cultural Revolution began soon afterwards, and the volume of the radio drama was turned down several notches as people's ears grew longer, searching for any excuse to condemn others' behaviour. Baogang and I stopped airing our views on current affairs and began talking more and more about our families, and how we missed those no longer with us.

Baogang absolutely loved hearing stories of my family. Why? I suppose my artistic heritage appealed to the poet in him. Baogang had started practising calligraphy when he was just three, and he wrote beautifully too, letting his mind roam. Sometimes, as a child, he would innocently explain which individual words he liked most to his family elders – to their great amusement!

Later, at private school, the old teacher would scold him: 'Poetry is not about words alone. It's about rhythm, length, context – the whole is greater than the sum of its parts! You can't analyse poetry by simply taking it apart.' But he soon realised that the young boy was fearless – like a newborn calf willing to stand up to a fearsome tiger. Baogang took his teacher's words to heart, and became obsessed with reading and analysing classical poems, sometimes translating them into vernacular speech.

And that was pretty much all we spoke about when ceiling-gazing during the Cultural Revolution, those main forms of classical poetry – *ci*, *fu* and *shi*. As I was saying, that's why the Cultural Revolution seemed like something of a holiday from my marriage jail-sentence, because Baogang didn't dare speak but one syllable of Lin's name, let alone talk about her. At that time, she certainly wasn't sleeping between us.

'It sounds as though you may have quite enjoyed the Cultural Revolution?' I asked Red.

She seemed somewhat taken aback. 'Why do you use the word *enjoy*? Is it that obvious? Could you tell from my expression?

Well, yes, I really did enjoy our ceiling-gazing in those days. Maybe I shouldn't say that – it was after all a time of great suffering.' Red's voice sounded almost giddy.

Perhaps only we Chinese are capable of finding such consolation in the small space between life and death. I thought this with a dull ache in my heart as I watched Red.

Red carried on gazing up at the ceiling, speaking in a way that seemed almost drunk.

Red's parents: the colourful poetry of love

Before then, it had always been Baogang who would initiate our talks. I suppose this was because I had been brought up on the notion that women should always sing to their husband's tune. Nowadays? I don't know – it's a whole new world. We grew up behind closed doors, rooted in the values of our own respective families, with our own particular rules and outlook on life.

Baogang didn't really do small talk. Apart from Lin, all he wanted to discuss were events of great historical significance – international current affairs, domestic news, ancient parables, the natural world. Never anything about everyday life.

There was no real plot to our lives, though. Besides being forced into lying in bed together and acting as if we were husband and wife, most of our days were spent in our work units. Did he talk about his family? Not at all, really. Before the Cultural Revolution, we'd never spoken about either of our families. I think maybe he was trying to show that we weren't related in any way, or maybe he was just trying to prove that there was only space for one woman in his heart.

But the first time he asked me about my family, it was as if a magic wand had opened up some secret well. After twenty years of missing home, and the twenty years before that of simply waiting to get married, suddenly the water began to rise up in a relentless stream from my heart, my mind, the very depths of my being. I spoke the whole night, reeling off memories one by one, with Baogang hanging on my every word.

Was this the first time he realised I had so many stories to tell? Maybe. And no, I never found out why he only wanted to listen and not speak. It never occurred to me to ask. Eventually, he began to let me take the lead in our discussions, especially when I spoke about my parents' love of poetry. That was probably the first time he showed any hint of interest in me.

My parents both came from reputable families: one from the world of officialdom, whose fortune rose and fell; one from the world of business, who also experienced many hardships.

My mother could trace her lineage back to a powerful official in the south who had been given land and title by the emperor himself. Another of her ancestors had been less fortunate – a gifted scholar who was banished to the remote mountains of Guizhou for offending the Imperial censors.

My father came from a family of merchants who made their name during the Ming dynasty for their role in building the Beijing–Hangzhou Grand Canal. From then on, all family descendants would follow a set path – accompanying their fathers on the boats in childhood, steering the rudder in their youth, before finally taking over the business when they grew up.

After the Opium Wars ended in 1860, a bitter conflict arose between two opposing factions – those who promoted foreign influence and those who opposed it. My mother's grandfather was in the opposition camp, and was forced by influential foreign supporters into exile to a granary in Shijiazhuang, Hebei Province. From the moment Western ships sailed into Tianjin harbour, the opium trade became part of the canal business, which in turn led to a huge number of merchants becoming opium addicts. What started out as simple curiosity about a new, exotic import ended up destroying so many families. The network of connections that my father's family had built up in the shipping industry fell apart.

The abdication of the last Qing emperor in 1911 gave way to the anarchy of the Warlord Era. With no recognised leader, power was divided among several rival factions splintered across the country, all constantly looking to raise money in order to buy more arms, which they did by taxing the common folk.

Political power was constantly shifting, and businesses suffered heavily as a result. My parents' grandparents were old by then, and worried constantly that the men in the family would be conscripted against their will and sent to some faraway battlefield. Their families were hardly wealthy, but each of them owned property and had some modest form of income they didn't want to lose.

Then the Civil War between the Communists and Nationalists began – so soon after the end of World War II – and dashed any last remaining hope that people had for peace. Many began to question whether it was worth staying on the mainland, with the situation as volatile as it was. My father's family began moving their business down to Hong Kong and expanding their presence in southern China. Meanwhile, my mother's family emigrated to the safety of the US. That's why I have hardly any relatives left on the mainland, only two younger sisters.

Perhaps this is the collective fate of the Chinese people. When you think that every person, man or woman, has their own personal character, then the same could also be said of every family – they all have their own unique DNA that determines their behaviour. My family's genes carry a deep love of poetry. I think that's what brought both lines of my heritage together in the first place.

In the spring of 1919, my father took my mother in a sedan chair from Shijiazhuang back to the family's mountain town in Chengde, which is in the north-east of Beijing, well-known as a summer residence of Qing dynasty emperors. About a kilometre from home, my mother looked up and saw that the tree trunks on either side of the road were wrapped in brightly coloured ribbons, fluttering softly in the breeze. Curious, she asked to be let down to take a better look.

My father, who had been travelling in the carriage in front, got down to help my mother. With great care, he took her by the arm as she hobbled over on her bound feet. Later, my mother would tell me that she was so enchanted by those ribbons that she completely forgot about her own 'three-inch lily feet' and the uneven ground she was walking on. Swaying heavily, she rushed between every tree. If my father hadn't been there to support her, she would have had great trouble staying upright.

Why was she behaving that way? Well, because on every ribbon was written a poem!

Upon entering her new home, my mother looked around and saw scroll after scroll of poetry pinned to the walls, with several inkpots and brushes scattered around the place. At that time, my father had only just taken over the family's shipping business, which took him away from home for long periods at a time. Not only did he feel guilty about this, but he was also terrified that his wife would feel lonely or bored in her new life, or, worse, that she might regret marrying into an uncultured family who could work an abacus but not an ink brush.

That's why my father went to such great lengths to decorate the house in a way my mother would like, in order that she might feel the warmth of her new home and the love of her new husband.

This was during the height of the Warlord Era, before the revolution, when it seemed like the fighting would never stop. Big cities like Nanjing, Shanghai and Beiping were also dealing with the fallout from the New Culture Movement, a spiritual, cultural and literary movement started by a group of Western-educated students that was anti-tradition, anti-Confucian and anti-classical Chinese.

Because the New Culture Movement opposed feudalism, it sought to rebel against anything from traditional Chinese culture. To this day, I still believe that the New Culture Movement was the first Chinese Cultural Revolution, for the way it destroyed great swathes of our classical culture.

As a woman, my mother wasn't allowed to venture far from the family home or have a say in making important family decisions. News from the outside world was therefore hard to come by, and usually only available from the guests who would occasionally pass through the house. My mother, however, soon became the news hub for the women in the family, because of the endless stream of letters my father would send her.

At a time when most people couldn't tell the difference between *shi* and *fu* poetry, my parents came up with an ingenious system for embedding secret messages in the poems they would write for each other. The real meaning of each letter was hidden either in the first word of each line, or the last word of each line of the poem. Sometimes the meaning was hidden in a zigzag line. Fascinating, no? So their love letters were also reports on what was going on elsewhere around the country!

Sometimes, I really want to ask the young people of today what's so interesting about their love lives. To me, modern relationships just seem like a series of glorified trade-offs, as if people see love as a means to gain the upper hand in some way. I can't make sense of it anyhow; I thought the human race was supposed to have advanced.

Seeing her in this agitated state, I started to worry that Red might be getting tired. I politely suggested we take a break for some food.

Perhaps not expecting to be interrupted, the old lady looked at me with an odd expression. 'Am I hungry? Well, yes, I suppose I am. I should have something to eat, and maybe take a rest too. Let's talk again tomorrow.'

I went back to visit Red the following day. I sat in that bedroom once occupied by this mysterious old couple, under that ceiling which stored so many memories of love and family, on that old wicker chair whose fraying strands in some way echoed the hardship of their lives. All the while, I continued to listen to Red telling the story of her life.

Out of nine brothers and sisters, I'm the eldest.

My mother fell pregnant with me the same year my parents were married. As soon as my father's family heard she was expecting, they invited a fortune teller to come and find out if it was a boy. In those days, people really believed that the power of feng shui could help families have a son and keep the candle of their ancestral line burning bright.

A month before my mother was due, my father returned home to Chengde from the salt docks of Tianjin to greet the arrival of his son.

Alas, in 1920, I was born, much to the disappointment of the family elders. I heard that when I let out my first cry, they just sighed and turned away. Their silence said it all, though – my parents had failed in their filial duty.

On the night of my birth, to console my mother, my father took her silk handkerchief and wrote out a poem written by Bao Zhao during the Liu Song dynasty. It's from a collection of eighteen poems called *The Winding Road*, which my mother used to read to me so often they are all practically imprinted on my brain:

I present to you, dear friend, a golden goblet of vintage wine,
An engraved zither set in jade, a feathered veil of dazzling rainbow silk,
And a silk blanket adorned with colourful flowers.

But as winter draws near, and the light begins to fade,
As you shed your beauty, as you shed your youth,

I wish my dear friend could hear, not echoes from the past,
But the beat of this song.

Do you not hear music in the wind?

Baogang was a little surprised at my father's choice of poem, given the decadence of the opening lines and the melancholy of its ending. He said he thought that life was supposed to get better as you got older! But my father really loved the image of 'a feathered veil of dazzling rainbow silk' – so much so, in fact, that my youngest sister got her nickname from it.

The morning after I was born, my father found on his breakfast tray a sheet of beautiful writing paper. As a return gift, my mother had written out the poem 'My Dear Friend', by Wang Shen:

The red candlelight flickers in the dead of night,
I awake from my drunken slumber with a heavy heart,
The song I sang for you as we parted is now but an echo,
And you are far far away.

All hope is lost, scattered like the clouds,
I lean on the railing and stare into the distance,
An easterly wind blows the tears from my face.

The crab apple tree is withering,
The swallows are flying back to their nest,
As the weary dusk descends on my courtyard.

It had a profound effect on my father, who rushed to see my mother while she lay recuperating as part of the *Zuo Yue Zi* period:* 'Our daughter's name may be decided by family elders, but let's give her the nickname Yaohong [Flickering Red].'

---

* *Zuo Yue Zi* is a Chinese custom that sets out various rules to optimise recovery after childbirth. It can be traced back to the *Book of Rites*, which became famous during the Western Han dynasty (206 BC–AD 25).

From then on, all my brothers and sisters were named by the family patriarch, according to family tradition, but always known by the nicknames my parents gave them. Baogang said the children in his family were also named in the same way.

Red's siblings: dreaming of love in colour

Late in the autumn of 1921, my twin sisters were born six weeks early. They were given the nicknames Yellow Orange and Green Tangerine.

Their birth was met with mixed emotions by my father's relatives. They were upset that their ancestral line was lacking a male heir, but happy with what the feng shui masters called the highly auspicious birth of twins in late autumn.

My mother must have known that she was having twins, as she'd already sewn two special handkerchiefs — one yellow and one green. When my sisters were born, my mother got some relatives to sew each handkerchief onto their swaddling clothes.

Only when my sisters were nearly a month old was my father able to come home and see them. When he heard my mother had given them the nicknames Yellow Orange and Green Tangerine, he asked her if that was from 'For Liu Jingwen', by Su Shi? Without even replying, my mother wrote out the passage they were both alluding to:

The exhausted lotus folds its canopy in two,
The chrysanthemum branches are dusted with frost.
But you must remember, dear friend,
That this is the sweetest season of the year,
The time of yellow oranges
And green tangerines.

Baogang reflected on this: 'What your mother meant was that, without a son, the family thought that nothing could ever come to any good. But life moves with the seasons, and what comes after spring and summer is not decay, but a beautiful time of yellow oranges and green tangerines!'

He was right, of course. As summer ends and autumn begins, the lotus leaves start to wither and lose the grace and elegance they once had, while the stiff and bare branches of the chrysanthemum trees are already coated in the first frost of the year. But that doesn't mean the beauty of life is confined to spring and summer – the most beautiful time is in fact late autumn and early winter. Thinking about it now, I'm sure my mother chose our nicknames based on the seasons we were born in: Red, Yellow, Green.

First brother was born in 1923. Along with the name An, which was given to everyone of our generation, the elders named him Qing, meaning high official, in the hope that he would one day grow up to be a man of great influence. So his full name was Han Anqing, and his nickname was Cyan.

Although his great-grandfather fulfilled his long-cherished wish to see the birth of his great-grandson, he passed away soon after. And so once again the family greeted the birth of a new baby with a mixture of joy and sadness – joy for the boy who would carry on the family line, sadness for the death of the old man.

The nickname Cyan was my father's choice. He had decided beforehand that his next child, boy or girl, would be called Cyan, keeping with my mother's wish that all her children would be nick-named after colours. Actually, my mother told me that ever since my father had given her *The Winding Road*, the line 'a feathered veil of dazzling rainbow silk' had been etched into her heart as a symbol of her love for my father. She wanted to give birth to seven beautiful children – all the colours of the rainbow – to bring honour to him and his ancestors.

Because he had been born in early spring, Cyan had seemed like a good choice of name. My father had also found it in a poem by Su Shi called 'Pear Blossom by the Eastern Fence':

Pear blossoms pale, white against the cyan willows.
Catkins twirl in the air, flying towards town.

By the eastern fence stands but one solitary pear tree.
How much of life do we truly see?

My mother said that when my father was reciting this poem, she was staring down at my infant brother as the sounds of people grieving his great-grandfather drifted through from the next room. She couldn't help but sigh; sigh for the passing of spring, and the transience of life.

But wasn't that the whole point of the poem? When the pear trees are in blossom, everything is white; the willow tree is so white it looks like it's covered in snow. Then there's that one solitary pear tree. Life is full of sadness, but that tree will still grow despite all those troubles.

Fourth sister was born on an autumn day in 1925, while an old friend of my father's was staying with us. The two of them would stay up drinking late into the night, reciting poetry and making up rhymes together in the clear autumnal moonlight.

In those days, people usually started showing signs of age around forty, and by the time you reached fifty you were considered old. Well that friend was already over sixty! When he heard fourth sister would be given the nickname Blue River, he piped up, 'Blue River? I know the perfect accompaniment to that name! A poem by Du Fu called "At Cui's Villa in Lantian on the Double Ninth Festival"':

Though I grieve the coming winter of my years,
I am happy to have shared this day with friends.

My hat comes loose from thinning hair and drunken step,
A fellow guest must help me fix it back.

The Blue River comes from afar,
                 descending from a thousand distant streams,
The Jade Mountain is high and its twin peaks cold.

This time next year, who will still be here among us?
Drunk, I let my mind wander into the future.

Baogang loved that poem, so much so that he even wrote it down in his notebook to send as a gift to Lin, joking that perhaps when they finally met again, he too might be so old that his balding head would have trouble keeping a hat on.

Hearing that Lin was still so very much on his mind, I couldn't help but let out a sigh. Perhaps, I thought, they will still be waiting to meet in their dreams when the clear blue water of those mountain streams has dried up.

That's how fourth sister got the nickname Blue River, or sometimes just Blue. I still remember the time – she must have been around three – when she kicked up a huge fuss about wanting to see the actual Blue River. My mother pointed to the faint purple outline of a faraway mountain range and said, 'When you grow up, when your legs are as long as your father's, when you can walk a long long long way, then we'll go to that purple mountain to see the Blue River. How about that?'

Poor fourth sister. Her legs never did grow long enough, nor did she live to an age where she might have understood why those mountains appeared purple on the horizon.

In the summer of 1927, my youngest brother was born. My father asked his father, the family patriarch, if he would allow the name Zi, as in purple, saying that purple would go well with the cyan of his older brother, and that this cohesion would bring good health and prosperity to our family. His father agreed, and my little brother got the nickname Purple. This also meant that the names of both my brothers – Anqing and Anzi – were homonyms of their nicknames, Qing and Zi (Cyan and Purple).

This 'purple' in my brother's name came from 'Summer Quatrain', by Lu You:

When those red and purple flowers turn to dust,
And the cuckoo's cry heralds the arrival of summer,
I walk along this path between two rows of mulberry trees,
And realise that I am living in a world of peace.

My mother believed that the birth of my little brother would finally settle her husband's family's fears about their ancestral line. The seven colours and seven children were now complete – a full rainbow. She interpreted the poem as meaning that you can see the spring colours return to the earth, while birdsong reminds you of the happiness of summer. Walking through the bushes, you feel a sense that you have been blessed with good fortune and peace.

When I told Baogang this, he wasn't so sure about this good omen: 'I would have worried that your mother's wish may have been cursed by that word "dust".'

I couldn't believe it! I was so shocked that I turned and raised my body to face him. But Baogang didn't notice, and just carried on looking up at the ceiling. 'That reminds me of another poem,' he continued. 'I think it's from the first volume of *Dream of the Red Chamber**':

Unfit to mend the azure sky,
Long years a foolish mortal man of dust I lived.
My life in both worlds on this stone is writ,
Pray, who can I ask to pass it on?

I'd forgotten *Dream of the Red Chamber* had several poems in it; I even had to check for myself later on.

But he was right: the arrival of my little brother didn't bring peace into our lives. Not long after his birth, my little twin sisters – Yellow Orange and Green Tangerine – were struck down by a bout of chickenpox. On the day we buried them, they both had the silk handkerchiefs our mother made them braided into their hair. They were only six years old.

In the months after we said goodbye to the twins, my mother would spend days on end inside the house. When she did come out, it wasn't to play with us, but to take us to the temple to burn incense and pray.

---

* *Dream of the Red Chamber*, also called *The Story of the Stone*, is one of China's Four Great Classical Novels. Written by Cao Xueqin around the middle of the eighteenth century, during the Qing dynasty, the novel tells the story of the contrasting fates of four noble families while also acting as a record of the traditional culture of the time.

My younger siblings and I went there and knelt by my mother's side, but I would never follow the words of her prayers. I would instead plead with the gods to relieve the pain of my mother's suffering.

I don't know whether they heard me, or whether heaven was moved by my mother's devotion. Either way, not long afterwards, fate would bring my mother two more daughters.

To acknowledge this good fortune, fifth sister was given the nickname Orange when she was born, in the summer of 1930. That was my mother's choice, and my grandfather had no objection whatsoever. Of course, as girls wouldn't be carrying on the ancestral line, they weren't considered of great importance.

Orange's name also came from a poem – 'The Wandering Youth', by Northern Song dynasty poet Zhou Bangyan:

> A knife from Bing is sharp as water,
> Salt from Wu is white as snow,
> Her slender fingers cut for him a fresh orange.

> Behind the brocade curtain,
> The incense incessantly rises,
> As they face each other, tuning their pipes.

> Softly she enquires:
> Where will you spend the night?
> Darkness rises upon city walls,
> The frost is thick and the road unsafe.
> Don't leave me here,
> While so few souls walk the night.

Hearing this, Baogang said, 'Your mother chose this poem for your father, you know. Although it echoes her heartbreak over her lost daughters, it's also a message, a warning that he's not getting any younger and needs to stop rushing about all the time.'

He also told me that the ancient province of Bing was located around where Taiyuan is today, in the time before the Southern Song dynasty. It was said that the knives they made there were especially sharp. The province of Wu was where Lake Hu is now, and the salt found there was dazzlingly bright. Both places were famous in ancient China.

Fifth sister was closely followed by sixth sister, who arrived on a spring day in 1932. She was given the nickname Green, in place of our late third sister, but also from a poem my father chose, called 'The Girl Who Lived', written by the famous lyric master Feng Yansi during the Southern Tang dynasty of the turbulent Five Kingdoms period. Of course, it was also acknowledging my mother's wish for her new daughter:

At this feast,
On this spring day,
With green wine in hand, I bow to you and pray:

That you live many years,
And not one without me,
Like a pair of spring swallows, together we'll be.

Baogang liked that poem too. Since ancient times, he said, the Chinese people have lived through periods of great strife. While their poetry and music are full of inhibition and anxiety, their art reflects this suffering through endless shades of black and grey. The *fu* verse, therefore, relies on images of the four seasons and a range of other things to evoke feelings in the reader.

But this poem is easy enough to understand: a family go for a pleasant picnic in the springtime, and as they raise their glasses to toast each other, the woman has three wishes: that her husband lives a long life; that she too remains happy and healthy; and finally that they grow old together like a pair of spring swallows, two parts of one whole.

In 1935, Mother died while giving birth to seventh sister. Father was swallowed up in grief.

Out of respect, the family patriarch allowed my mother's family to choose the child's nickname – the first time this had happened, and of course the last. They chose Rainbow, in keeping with Mother's wish to give us all colourful nicknames.

Father later took in two mistresses. Young and beautiful though they were, neither of them inspired in him the same feelings he'd had for my mother. Although they lived with Father, neither managed to get close to him; although they spoke, their words never meant anything to him. In short, neither of them ever won his true love.

Red fell silent for a long time. She fixed her eyes on the ceiling as if trying to bring an image into focus, as if in that image was her parents' love, a love she had never had herself. I followed her every move, sizing up her serenity, noticing how her right and left hands stroked each other, very very gently. Perhaps that was what she'd been waiting for her whole life, love's touch?

When finally she spoke, it was with the gentlest of voices: 'Not one of us brothers and sisters ever found the kind of love my parents shared.'

When she looked up and saw that I hadn't reacted to what she said, she repeated, 'No, not one of us brothers and sisters ever found the kind of love my parents shared.'

Not only had I heard what she said loud and clear, it had touched my heart. I couldn't find any sort of reply, simply because her words were too weighed down with the burden of history. I have interviewed many Chinese, and whenever I encounter this kind of regret and sadness felt between generations it always casts me back into my own childhood memories, and to the longing I still feel for my family.

Red seemed to speak on my behalf. 'Every time I talk about my family, I feel restrained by those feelings of sadness and confusion. Baogang would try and comfort me by asking, "Which family could have avoided the storm of history? Which individual can swim against the current of the times they live in? What love is free from the influence of society?" The funny thing is, he never seemed to acknowledge that we were living in a sham marriage, where all we did was *talk* about love.'

There were nine of us brothers and sisters in total – of course, that's including poor little Yellow Orange and Green Tangerine, who didn't live beyond childhood – all born in perhaps the most chaotic period of Chinese history. Chaotic not just because of the fall of Imperial rule and the rise of a new regime, but because of the subversion of beliefs that had been at the very core of Chinese people's lives for thousands of years. Not having an emperor was like having no religion, no rules or sense of order. Nobody knew who was in charge.

That's why families started pulling together, because people believed that the only safety to be found was in the company of those with the same surname. Meanwhile, the separation of power into various different factions gave rise to the turmoil of the Warlord Era. Most of those warlords would claim that they were fighting on the side of justice: the justice of restoring the emperor; the justice of destroying the last remnants of Imperial rule; the justice of robbing the rich to save the poor.

Ordinary families paid a heavy price during that period; many lives were ruined. Sons were conscripted into the army against their will; property was stolen; much-needed supplies were allocated to troops. Women, children and the elderly were all caught up in the bloody mess of that so-called 'fight for justice'.

Compared with the vast majority of Chinese people, we were lucky. Our educated parents brought happiness into our home with poetry, music and love, all the while shielding us from the realities of the outside world. The home they built for us was like a paradise on earth.

Under their guidance, we learned how to read and write, how to paint, how to play chess and grow flowers. The boys would study the abacus, formal composition and business, while the girls would study embroidery, flower arranging and childcare.

My parents did everything they could to guard the gates to that paradise, but the chaos of war would eventually break down those walls, and the loss of innocence would force us out of the door. In the outside world, we were completely lost – lost between the gaps of faith and truth, good and evil, knowledge and ignorance.

There's an old Chinese saying: 'Men fear getting the wrong job, women fear getting the wrong husband.' Well, in the chaos of war, countless men and women lived out those fears. Why? There weren't any good jobs going, and the men were all off fighting.

My brother Cyan was the first son born into my generation of the family. As was always the case back then – and perhaps still is – the eldest son had no say whatsoever in his life choices. According to family tradition, he had to take over the family business from his father, while the woman he married would be chosen by family elders.

In 1948, the Nationalist cause was all but lost, and rumours spread thick and fast that the Communists were coming to 'share your property and share your wife', a common scare phrase used by propagandists. Members of the business community in China, who had assumed all along that the US would intervene to settle the Civil War, now began moving their assets and even their relatives down to British-controlled Hong Kong. Some even sent their children to live in the US.

Cyan had only just taken over the family business, and in order to evade the threat of war, coupled with a fear of the Communists, Father arranged for the then twenty-five-year-old Cyan to go to Hong Kong and marry the woman he had been engaged to since the age of sixteen. The marriage was more like a business deal, really. His wife also came from a prominent shipping family, involved in the increasingly lucrative business of transporting goods between southern China and other nearby countries.

But not everything had worked out so well for their family. Although business was booming, somehow not one of the three brothers had had a son. That's why they had begun making enquiries of the more prominent Chinese families in the region, looking for a son-in-law to help out with the future of the business, and that's how our families came together.

My father used to say: 'People who make their living on the water are bound together, as the rivers intertwine with the lakes and the oceans.' It wasn't long before a matchmaker introduced the two families, predicting that our futures would indeed be heavily entwined, and everyone was delighted when the engagement was announced.

Cyan's wife was a wise and compassionate woman. Although she had been born and raised in British-controlled Hong Kong and had studied for many years under the British style of education, she was also very traditional in her beliefs. She really took to heart the old saying that 'the more sons the better' — they seemed to just pop out of her in the years after their marriage! In 1985, when Cyan and I were reunited after nearly forty years apart, it was also the first time I met his wife. This bag of skin and bones told me that she had, somehow, given birth to fourteen children in just twenty years.

I asked my younger brother if he still liked to read poetry, to which he replied, 'I do. I read poetry as if reading poetry were a religion. If I didn't, I'd have drowned in Hong Kong's sea of business a long time ago!' Then he said with a sigh, 'My wife isn't interested in poetry; she just doesn't have any passion in her.' I thought to myself, wickedly, *with fourteen children, there must be some passion there!*

When she was eighteen, fourth sister Blue was married off to a rich and powerful shipping merchant on the Yangtze River. Before the wedding, the pair only knew each other's names and had never met. Only three months after they married in Shanghai, the husband's shipping fleet, his docks and all his sailors were commandeered by the Japanese army. In 1945, when the War of Resistance against Japan was won, the husband was marked as a traitor. If it wasn't for a group of my father's old friends in the industry vouching for him, he would almost certainly have been executed by the Nationalists. From that moment on, the couple eked out a meagre existence, always relying on my father's support.

After 1949, Shanghai became a hotbed of fighting between China and the West, both under cover and out in the open. Rumours were flying about in all directions, and there was no end to the acts of political terror carried out there. Poor Blue and her husband: they endured great hardships during the Communists' Three-Anti and Five-Anti campaigns, not least the death of their infant child. In the end, her husband was executed for being a Japanese spy, after which Blue fell terribly ill and died, depressed and alone, before she had even turned thirty.

Why didn't anyone help her? In those days it was every man for himself. No one would believe you if you tried to stand up for someone being accused of a crime; you'd probably just get in trouble yourself. As soon as you were labelled a traitor or corrupt, no one could save you. I remember, around that time, even Communist officials were being executed!*

In 1944, when he had just turned seventeen, my father sent second brother Purple to study in the US. Of course, it was also a way of getting him out of harm's way during the war. He would later marry an American woman, and it wouldn't be until 1989 that we would finally meet again. I don't speak English and she didn't speak Chinese, and having lived abroad for forty-five years my brother could barely translate for us. To this day, I still feel bad that I wasn't able to communicate properly with that foreign sister-in-law of mine.

While she was studying in Beiping around 1947, fifth sister Orange became inspired by the underground Communist movement, so much so that she even got a friend to deliver a copy of *The Ballad of Mulan* to our father.† She later fell in love with a revolutionary, and they married despite the fact our family knew nothing about the man.

---

* In 1952 two leading officials from Tianjin Municipality, Zhang Zishan and Liu Qingshan, were convicted of corruption and executed.

† Hua Mulan (AD 412–502), also known simply as 'Mulan' in the West, is a legendary female warrior from the Northern Dynasties period, first noted in the epic poem *The Ballad of Mulan*. In the ballad, Mulan takes her ageing father's place in the army. She was a beautiful woman, proficient in kung fu, and renowned for her swordsmanship. Mulan fought bravely in the army for twelve years, but she refused any reward and retired to her home town instead. The poem praises Mulan's brave and kind-hearted spirit.

All I know is that Orange wrote another letter home, this time to tell us that she and her husband were madly in love. Although they worked in the same building, they would send each other love letters constantly, or share little poems and inspirational quotes. She said that this experience made her appreciate the love my parents had felt all those years ago.

I heard Orange and her husband gained something of a reputation for their work covering the Civil War. At first, we heard that the man was a university lecturer, later that he was an underground Communist Party member. Either way, during the Cultural Revolution, the Red Guards told Orange that he was in fact a Nationalist agent working undercover on the mainland. Less than three weeks later, he was dead.

Orange never fully recovered from the trauma of losing her husband, and she's suffered from a form of dementia ever since. Of the couple's three children, the two sons were taken by their paternal grandparents to the countryside to carry on the ancestral line, while the daughter stayed behind with her mother. She's a mother herself these days.

Sixth sister Green was studying at a girls' school in Beiping when the city was liberated. She was a hugely talented writer, becoming more and more involved in the city's growing cultural and literary scene. Then, at the great ceremony held to mark the founding of the People's Republic of China, she met a PLA officer. I always thought he treated her more like a revolutionary comrade than a wife, but they seemed happy together. They certainly didn't waste time getting married. Their love was like wildfire.

Green's husband came from a poor family in Shandong Province, but he grew into a kind and considerate man. He would often take Green out with him to some of the poorest areas of the country, helping out the locals in any way he could. Those trips had a profound effect on Green, I think. She was shocked by the stark contrast between the countryside and the city, but equally touched by the warm hospitality of the peasants she encountered there. More than anything, she was incredibly proud of what her husband did. For Green, the spark of life she saw in this 'hero' of hers more than made up for his lack of education.

Our family weren't so keen to begin with, though. Those of us left on the mainland all warned Green that this gap in class and education could leave her regretting her decision later on, once she awoke from this fantasy. I gave her a long speech about the nature of fire: 'Yes, it's one of humanity's blessings, bringing light and warmth. But if you get too close, it could spell disaster!'

Despite all that, Green remained adamant that it was our fault for not being able to appreciate just how noble her hero really was. But my little sister, she's very Chinese. What do I mean? Well, we Chinese believed Chairman Mao when he said that 'man can conquer nature', and indeed, in just thirty years we went from being the laughing stock of Asia to one of the world's most powerful countries! And what did Green do? She turned that uneducated army officer into a poet!

'Actually, Xinran, I'd really recommend that you go and talk to Green. Although she's my sister, our experiences are more like those of two different generations. Besides, her story is much richer than mine, and filled with Chinese flavours.'

Rainbow is the youngest sister. She never met our mother, but was always Father's favourite while he was alive. In fact, he spoiled little Rainbow so much that she was never really able to adapt to life in the real world. Before the founding of the People's Republic in October 1949, Father sold our house in Chengde for very little money, and took little sister to be reunited with our brother Cyan in Hong Kong.

Not wanting to be a burden on his son, Father bought a small house in Kowloon, where he lived alone with his youngest daughter. Rainbow never married.

When Father fell gravely ill there was still a lot of tension between China and Hong Kong, and those of us on the mainland had no way of communicating with him. It wasn't until 1984 that we were finally able to get in touch with Rainbow, who informed us that our father had died in 1981. The only ones there with him at the end had been her, Cyan and Purple, who had rushed back to Hong Kong from America.

Apparently, before he died, Father had spoken of how much he regretted not bringing all his children with him to Hong Kong, because when he and Mother were reunited, he wouldn't be able to tell her about our lives. Of course, he didn't even know that his daughter Blue was already up there waiting for him with Mother.

Baogang had virtually no dealings with my family. The only one he ever spoke to was my sister Green, and the only reason for that was because she had been transferred to work in the Taiwan Affairs Office of the State Council in 1988. Baogang thought that her connections there might help him hear news of Lin:

'Have you found Lin yet?'

'No.'

It was a familiar exchange.

Baogang lived to the ripe old age of ninety-two. He wasn't what you might call a particularly healthy or robust kind of man, so maybe it was the hope of meeting Lin again that kept him going for so long? Or maybe he just had other ways of conserving his energy.

The long grey shadows of past promises

I couldn't help but feel that Baogang's infatuation with Lin had somehow clouded his judgement, allowing him to be tricked by the media on both sides of the Taiwan Strait. Part of his work had been to collect and analyse foreign media reports, so he would certainly have had ample opportunity to hear news from the island.

Up until the time of Chiang Kai-Shek's death in 1975, Taiwan had been circulating endless reports on how it had created an extensive network of intelligence on the mainland. At the same time, the mainland media had its own take on the unification process – first came the promise of liberation in the 1950s, then military threats in the 1960s and 1970s, then the increased trade of the 1980s, the revived postal service of the 1990s, right up until the relatively stable period of the 2000s. It was like the mainland was fishing, casting line after line into the Taiwan Strait, often using the promise of reunification with long-lost family as bait. It had been making good progress too.

I kept these thoughts to myself; the many interviews conducted with Chinese elders from my parents' and grandparents' generations had taught me that the pain of going down some paths of memories was so great that any disturbance could close the doors on them forever.

I carried on listening to the old lady's story.

In 1953, Baogang asked me to help him flee the country in secret. He wanted to use the excuse that I was in poor health and needed him to take me to visit my dying sister Blue in Shanghai. But as a former Nationalist soldier, he couldn't get permission to take leave. What's more, he was told that if he went of his own accord, he would be hunted down and executed.

Only later did Baogang tell me the real story.

At that time, the Nationalist Party were carrying out a series of violent purges in Taiwan, and Baogang found out that Lin's uncle was on the list of those waiting to be executed. Meanwhile, the Taiwanese military sent out a radio broadcast ordering the families of those soldiers who had tried to flee to the mainland to return immediately to their barracks. Baogang clung to the hope that this might include

Lin and her family. 'This might just be a fantasy,' he said, 'but it might just be true.'

One evening in 1963, Baogang turned up most unexpectedly while I was having dinner in the mess hall. We always made sure that we ate at different times – me early and him late – to avoid having to talk with other people there, for fear of accidentally revealing the secret of our sham marriage. Baogang would even claim that the confidential nature of his work prevented him from socialising. That day, however, he made a point of sitting at my table and making small talk with the other people there.

On the way home he suggested, very abruptly, that we go for a walk. My instinct told me that this definitely had something to do with Taiwan, maybe even something to do with Lin. He led me by the hand to the very middle of the training ground, which was the size of four full-sized football pitches. We were the only ones there, alone in that vast space.

Looking up at the sky, Baogang said to me, 'China is in great trouble. We need to make preparations.'

'What kind of trouble? What preparations?' I was a little shaken up by what he said.

'I can't really say for sure, but I've heard news from Hong Kong that many many people in our crop-growing regions have died. Henan, Shandong, Sichuan, Anhui, Hubei, Hunan – those places. It seems a great famine has taken hold, and to make things worse, people have been killing each other in fights over the dwindling supplies of grain that are left.'

Baogang's voice was deadly serious, but I still couldn't quite believe what he was saying.

'How's that possible? I heard those regions are producing more food than ever.'

'Listen to me. Taiwan's forces are gathering around Kinmen Island, using the excuse that if there's a famine on the mainland, it's their responsibility to come and "save" their brothers! It seems there really will be a war this time, and there's a strong chance I'll be transferred to the south.' Baogang was now looking right at me.

'Have they given you notice?'

'Not yet. But you know what they say, military orders are as rigid as mountains. If for whatever reason we don't have the chance to talk things through properly later on, there's something I want to tell you now: thank you for your company and your understanding over all these years. When I hear news of Lin, you'll be the first to know. After all, we're like brother and sister!'

Just two days later, Baogang took me for another 'walk'. This time, however, he was utterly deflated. 'President Kennedy just announced in a press conference that if Taiwan wants to launch a counter-attack on the mainland, it needs to talks things through with America first. In short, they've made their position clear – the US won't support Taiwan in attacking the mainland.'

'So we're not going back to war?!' It was a completely instinctive reaction; I was just so happy to hear the news.

'And it'll be even harder to find Lin.' Baogang's voice went so quiet I could barely hear it.

I tried to comfort him. 'Don't say that. With the way things are, who's to say what will happen next? Maybe another opportunity will come up soon.'

Baogang shook his head, but didn't say another word.

And then? Well, nothing happened with Taiwan, but China really did run into a great deal of trouble. When the bloody mess of the Cultural Revolution came around, Baogang and I were sent down to the mountainous region of Daxing County, just outside Beijing.

Thanks to the ever-changing political situation, we came across quite a few different types of ceiling in our time: plaster, wood, iron, mud. We even had a couple of weeks under the stars; in July 1976, when the great earthquake hit Beijing and Tangshan, the surrounding areas were also affected and we ended up sleeping outside. That was also around the time that Baogang's hopes of seeing Lin again started to fade, and his interest in the sad story of my life began to appear.

By 1981, we were both coming up to retirement. Our work unit was good to us, even including Baogang's time with General Fu Zuoyi in his pension, which was very generous. However, because he worked in intelligence, he wasn't allowed to leave the country. Once again, his hopes were thwarted.

In 1983, we moved into this house. It has three bedrooms, a studio, a drawing room, two bathrooms and a huge kitchen. The day we walked in for the first time, neither of us had any idea what to do with the place.

'How are we going to make use of all these rooms?' Baogang asked.

'Well, we can have our own personal ceilings now,' I joked, 'and the studio can be your study. All these years you've spent most of your time working away from home. Without a decent study, how will you manage?'

'Well, what about you?' Baogang had a guilty look on his face as he asked me this.

'I'll use the kitchen as my study. Neither of us can cook anyway, and we can still go to the mess hall for our meals.'

Baogang went into the master bedroom while I checked out the bigger of the two guest rooms. Looking up at the ceiling, he said, 'Looks big enough to store quite a few of our stories.'

'I think this one's soundproof,' I replied, and we both laughed.

But to tell you the truth, even after all those years the tears of my heart were not yet dry. I had simply become used to smiling on the outside and crying on the inside. I wouldn't have been surprised at all if he had suggested, with a big smile on his face, that we keep one room free for when Lin arrived.

That first evening, as we lay in our own separate bedrooms, I felt empty and confused. Almost every night for thirty years we had slept in the same bed, our heads on different pillows but our minds together in thought, soaked in the harsh rains of our times.

'Are you asleep?' Baogang's voice drifted through softly from the other room.

'How can I sleep?' It was true — how could I?

'This ceiling's too high! I'm worried you might not hear.' Baogang was now virtually shouting.

'The doors are open; we don't need to use the ceilings in this apartment.' I reminded him.

'Oh, yes, right. You were always quicker at adapting.'

'Oh *really*? I adapt quickly, do I?' At least that's what I asked him in my mind. Asking myself too, because for more than thirty years I'd been struggling to adapt to the jail sentence of our marriage.

But why couldn't I set myself free? I'm educated, I'm well read, I played my part in the revolution by working as a clerk. So why couldn't I escape from that jail cell? What was it that restrained my courage and controlled my freedom? In fact, I've been asking myself these questions ever since Baogang and I first married.

Do I know the answer? Oh yes, I've always known the answer. It's the contract that my father signed for me when I got engaged, and the set of values my mother passed down to me when I was young. Like some kind of spell, they've made it impossible for me to break free.'

That night, my mind racing, I couldn't sleep. Perhaps I was subconsciously waiting for the sound of Baogang's voice.

Early next morning, I woke up in a daze to that near-forgotten smell of *biluochun* tea: Baogang was standing by the side of the bed, holding a lunch box in his hands. Seeing me open my eyes, he said, with an awkward smile, 'Sorry, I couldn't find any cups, so I had to make do with this.'

In that moment, the tears that had been pent up in my heart for so long began to pour down my cheeks — Baogang had recreated the scene from our first morning together. It stuck me then that we had never broken the promises we'd made each other when we first married — he hadn't broken his engagement to Lin, and I hadn't broken the oath I made to my parents. What's more, we hadn't broken off our own engagement.

That night, I separated the two single beds and put two bedside cabinets between them. When we had finished watching the news — on that old 9-inch black and white television that had followed us for so many years — we entered our own 'special' bedroom.

Baogang said, 'We can face each other when we talk.'

'Won't the ceiling get lonely?' I teased him.

But had he actually given up talking about Lin? Of course not! When he found out in 1988 that Green was working at the Taiwan

Affairs Office, Baogang was thrilled. He even thought that it was some kind of sign from God that he shouldn't give up hope.

For four years, Green and her friends in Taiwan made inquiries into Lin's uncle and his family, but to no avail. Many historical records were under restricted access, and the only verifiable fact was that Lin's uncle had indeed been executed along with his wife during the White Terror era.

In the autumn of 1992, Green introduced Baogang to a Taiwanese businessman. From the leads he provided, Baogang found out that after her uncle's execution Lin had changed her name and married an academic. She had later died giving birth to their first child. This was around 1963, when she would have been thirty-seven.

In the week that followed, our night-time chats were put on hold. In the darkness, I could feel the depth of his despair. Night after night he would stare blankly up at the ceiling. Every so often the glimmer of a teardrop would appear in his eye and run gently down to his ear.

After that, Baogang barely mentioned Lin's name again. We still broadcast our words on the night breeze, but the ceiling was now our only listener — without Lin sleeping between us or nosy neighbours eavesdropping.

Yes, from that moment on, our night-time chats became unbounded, unrestricted; impulsive, even. We had reached the age when we had no need to care any more. Baogang had retired from the intelligence unit, and besides, all of those secrets he used to gather were now public knowledge anyway. As for me, there were no rules to follow or important things to remember.

We talked about the past, and all those things that the young people of today find so hard to understand. We talked about the present, and how we would never be able to get used to the modern ways of life. Young people's whole philosophy is lost on us, and everything they try and teach us we just forget in an instant. That's why society sees us as being 'surplus'.

I noticed a great change in our relationship once we stopped needing to worry so much. We no longer had this great weight hanging over us, panicking over other people finding out that our marriage was a sham. We just stopped thinking about it, stopped caring about how they might react. No, for Baogang and me this was a chance to follow our own free minds, at least in the context of our night-time chats.

What kind of free thoughts did we have? Well, you know that Baogang and I both come from families who were very strict when it came to our education, with countless taboo topics we were forbidden to study. On top of that, we both grew up at a time of complete chaos, when everything around us was in turmoil. After that, we both served in the ranks of the red revolution as part of the intelligence department. To top it all off, our own personal desires and impulses had been suppressed by the strange circumstances of our marriage.

Our instincts had been frozen by the political environment. Our sense of right and wrong was no longer black and white, it was blurred by forces beyond our control. After several decades, our own hearts' desires no longer had any kind of individual or personal characteristics to them. We had become part of the mass production of our age.

But I suppose if I have any free thoughts of my own left, they are still the memories of the paradise of my youth and the poetry I shared with my family back then. After all, that's in my genes.

Baogang's free thoughts? His obsession with Lin aside, there wasn't much else really. I never heard him speak much about his family. My father told me a long time ago – probably around the time he arranged our marriage – that Baogang was the youngest son of a family who owned a lot of land in Chengde. Later, I know they sold arms to warlords and also helped Feng Yuxiang raise funds for an attack on the Japanese. But by the time we were married, the family was all but bankrupt. I don't know anything about his family roots, or where the rest of his family live now.

In the months leading up to his death, Baogang had an uneasy feeling in the pit of his stomach. He said it felt as if his body was dried up, emptied, exhausted. One evening, he told me that it wouldn't be long now before he joined his ancestors in watching over the family tomb, where his two older brothers would already be waiting for him.

I tried to lighten the mood a little, saying, 'Perhaps they're still alive? We could try looking for them.'

With great effort, Baogang turned his body to face me, raising his head to meet my gaze as he did so. In the dying light, he looked right at me for several seconds, before saying, 'I've always wanted to tell you: you really remind me of Lin. The way you're so kind and pure. But really, Red, I'm the youngest in my family, and I'm over ninety! Do you honestly believe those brothers of mine, who were nearly ten when I was born, can have lived longer than me, through the chaos and uncertainty of these times? Anyway, even if they have, do you think they'd remember me now? When you lose your memory of someone, they are lost to you. When you lose your memory completely, then you're lost to this world.'

That was the first time I'd ever heard him go so far as to compare me with Lin. But I'm sure that after all those years of him missing her, pouring out his heart to the ceiling, living his life with me, all these things merged to form new memories. He may even have begun to see us both as one woman, like in a fairy tale.

Did he have any physical needs? Not really. I told you, he was faithful to the memory of his beloved. Once, when he was reading a *wuxia* novel by Louis Cha, he came across a passage about how remaining celibate can increase your vitality and prolong your life. I remember once hearing my family elders talking about this too, but I had been too young to understand. When I grew up, talk was all about work or politics, and I didn't dare bring up those more sensitive matters. In one's later years, it's much easier to find out from the newspapers and television about prolonging your life.

Me? Did I have any physical needs? It's hard to say. Before we married I often fantasised about things, sometimes to the point where my whole body would shake. I also had these strange dreams about men, that terrified me so much I wouldn't be able to face my family the day after. To tell you the truth, at the very beginning of my marriage, when Baogang knelt for three nights straight by my bedside, I think that's when I realised I would never be able to satisfy those particular needs.

After that, our night-time chats were mostly about work, and certainly never anything that could ignite any kind of passion between us. Besides, in those days we were working flat out, and never had enough sleep as it was. Later, when other members of our work unit noticed that we were married but didn't have any children, they just felt very sorry for us.

So no, Baogang never showed any interest in me physically. You have to remember we were husband and wife in name alone. In his heart, I wasn't part of his family, even less his wife. That's very hard for outsiders to believe, and perhaps our ceiling is the only one who could verify this fact.

Did we talk about what goes on between men and women? Not really. Maybe once, in a roundabout sort of way, when we were watching a television series about a eunuch who kept a secret family in the Imperial Court. Later, I remember saying to Baogang, 'TV these days is just too much! How could a eunuch have kept a family?'

He replied, 'Lots of imperial dynasties allowed eunuchs to have families of their own.'

I was surprised, 'But eunuchs are neither man nor woman! How could they possibly have a family?'

Baogang laughed. 'Eunuchs can have families, and they can have love lives too. There are plenty of examples of it throughout history.'

That night, Baogang did his best to explain the phenomenon to me.

During the Ming dynasty, there was something known as *Dui Shi*. Actually, it's even included in *The Book of Han*, as '*Dui Shi* of the Palace', referring to two concubines in a marriage-type relationship, what people today would call lesbians. Later, especially in the Ming dynasty, *Dui Shi* gradually became used to describe a relationship between a concubine and a eunuch. In fact, at the beginning of the Ming period, the palace strictly prohibited concubines and eunuchs forming a relationship. It's said that when Zhu Yuanzhang was emperor, if anyone was caught in this kind of illicit relationship they'd both be skinned alive. But later on, as eunuchs became more and more powerful and the emperor came to rely on them more and more heavily, *Dui Shi* gained more acceptance.

Why *Dui Shi*? Well, it had a lot to do with food, that's why. When eunuchs were on court duty, they had to prepare for themselves a whole day's worth of food. While rules of the court prohibited anyone but the imperial chefs from cooking inside the palace, the concubines would always keep hand warmers. Therefore, when those eunuchs wanted to heat up their food, they would do so by asking the concubines. As a way of thanking them, the eunuchs would often invite the concubines to dine with them. Eventually, *Dui Shi* became an established practice as eunuchs and concubines developed deeper relationships.

There's another phrase for *Dui Shi*, actually – *Cai Hou*. It was called that because when a eunuch was interested in a certain concubine, he would often go out and buy her some small gifts like fresh vegetables or needlework to win her affection.

But *Dui Shi* and *Cai Hou* aren't exactly the same thing. *Dui Shi* is more like dating, just a dinner for two really, whereas *Cai Hou* is more like a husband-and-wife-type relationship – sometimes they would even declare oaths of undying love for one another.

Have you heard of *Dui Shi* and *Cai Hou*? No? Well, that day, when I listened to Baogang's story, I asked him, 'I suppose we are neither *Dui Shi* nor *Cai Hou*?'

He just laughed and said, 'No, because I'm not a eunuch, and you're not a concubine!'

The last time I met Red, we spoke about Baogang's two dying wishes. Before broaching this final topic, the old lady let out a deep sigh.

When he was on his deathbed, I imagined Baogang would express some kind of gratitude for the sixty-one years of marriage we'd had. He might even go so far as to say 'thank you' to me. I had long known that he wouldn't apologise for anything, because regret just wasn't something he had in him. Perhaps he believed that we both had a hand in deciding our fate. But in reality, Baogang was the one doing the choosing. He was the architect of our marriage jail, and I its prisoner.

But I chose to follow him. And that, in the end, was the fate I was destined for.

As for his two dying wishes, they were left for Lin. Yes, in 1992, when the spark of life that had been sustaining him all those years finally died out, he began to age rapidly. His spirit had long been together with Lin anyway. In order to leave a mark of this unwavering love and loyalty on this world he left two dying wishes — one was for someone to come and visit the home of our fake marriage, the other to provide evidence that we had never had sex.

While Red was saying this, her eyes were fixed upon the ceiling, as if begging this witness to sixty-one years of her marriage sentence to offer some sort of evidence, even just the smallest hint of conclusive proof.

My gaze moved slowly back and forth between the ceiling and Red's face. I was trying to feel and understand that void — a space so distant, so vast, and so loaded with the history of Chinese families and their children.

'I think, perhaps, Baogang was scared that you'd get lonely lying there, ceiling-gazing by yourself. Maybe he wanted someone to understand and appreciate that because of his love for Lin, you were never able to be a wife, to be a mother. Perhaps he is here now, listening to those heartfelt words that you never dared speak to him before.'

'Really?' Red spoke softly, still staring up at the ceiling.

'Really.'

I thought I heard the ceiling's reply: 'Yes, that was the story of a man and a woman, talking love for sixty-one years.'

PART II

A Communist Family Tree

||||||||||||||||||||||||||||||||||||||||||||||||||||||||||||||||||||||||||||||||||||||

Second Sister

GREEN

· *born 1932* ·

On Red's suggestion – or should I say insistence – I got in touch with her younger sister, Green.

In 2014, I was back in China to take part in the South China Book Festival in Guangzhou, after which I accompanied my husband Toby to the China Literary Translation Forum in Qingdao. When we arrived, I tried calling Green again to arrange a meeting in Beijing. But as it turned out, she and her husband were in Qingdao as well, and she invited me to visit her in the convalescent home where they were staying.

On the day of our meeting, my taxi was blocked off at the main gate. The driver turned to me to explain.

'It's all government property in there; you can't go in unless you've got a proper notice. Cars like mine aren't allowed in, that's for sure. Nowadays all the Communist Party cadres live in these special neighbourhoods. They've really taken what Chairman Mao said about "serving the people" to heart, haven't they? That's not just another empty slogan now, is it?!'

There was more than a hint of irony in his voice as he handed me back my change.

I walked through the very government-style gateway and followed the long, curved path round to the main building. Rows of immaculately kept flowers marked each side of the road, so carefully arranged by shape, size and colour that they appeared like a well-drilled 'floral division' of the army.

From a long way off, I could tell that the lady standing at the front entrance was Green. She had the same poetic elegance as her elder sister Red – Chinese believe that women who read poetry are more sophisticated – and the thought crossed my mind that perhaps they both took after their mother in this regard.

But the way Green welcomed me, with arms outstretched and voice booming, couldn't have been more different from the woman I had met in Beijing a year earlier. If it could be said that Red was a refined and elegant lady, then Green could best be described as a frank and outspoken woman.

Over the next three years, I interviewed Green, her children and grandchildren on a number of different occasions in Qingdao, Beijing and Nanjing. Without them, this book would never have become what it is today — a collection of tales of life and love from four generations of one family.

As Green spoke, her stories rooted themselves in my mind and took on an irresistible power. Although the forcefulness of her personality had a part to play in this, her life experience struck a personal chord with me, not least because she is the same age as my parents.

A Communist seed

There are nine of us brothers and sisters in total. Three went abroad, three married into the Revolution, and three met death before their time.

To be honest, I was never that close to big sister Red. That's not just because of our twelve-year age gap, it's mainly down to the fact she cut off all contact with us younger sisters when she got married and started working in intelligence. Up until her retirement in 1981, the only news we heard of her was through my elder brother in Hong Kong. Most of the memories I have of big sister are from the time before I started school in Beiping, all those years ago, when we all lived together at home.

In those days, our father rarely came home, and when he did it seemed all he wanted to do was talk about poetry and art with big sister Red and my two elder brothers. He never paid any attention whatsoever to Blue, Orange and me, the three youngest sisters at the time. As I remember it, my mother was always rushed off her feet, and whenever she appeared in a room you could tell what mood she was in by listening to the sound of her voice. Sometimes it would be as gentle as the breeze, as she'd tenderly stroke our hair. Sometimes it was damp like the rain, as she'd take us all together in her arms in a big hug. Sometimes she would roar like a great gale, and our bodies would shake as if caught up in some terrible storm. But I was only young back then, and didn't understand the ways of the world. Much less did I appreciate how all my mother's efforts were focused on keeping our family affairs in order at a time of great struggle.

My two brothers began their training practically from birth, learning the ways of the family business so that they could bring honour to their ancestors. They had their own servants – not just men and women who would help out with chores around the house, but also young children hired to come and play with them. They started private school at the age of three.

Big sister was allowed to go and study with them too, which I thought was hugely unfair, but I was too young at that time to understand traditional Chinese rules for women, such as that Chinese girls didn't belong on the family tree, weren't allowed to choose who they married, and weren't even allowed to receive an education in most families. Now I often think this might be one of the reasons that, like many young Chinese women of my generation, I devoted almost my whole life to the Revolution and new China.

After Mother died giving birth to Rainbow, everything around the house changed. Father grew very quiet, and although he was at home a lot more, we rarely saw him. He was around at mealtimes, but even then he wouldn't talk to us. I heard that he often took little sister Rainbow out to look for small animals in the surrounding fields, perhaps searching for traces of the mother's love she never knew.

Big sister Red took over managing affairs around the house, but I don't remember her ever seeming as busy as Mother used to be. Perhaps that's because we sold off parts of the family business and let go of several servants, or maybe because Father's two new mistresses would help with things like cooking. Just as she had done before, big sister would teach us some basic life skills – reading and writing poetry, embroidery, flower arranging, that sort of thing. She'd often take us outside to pick vegetables from the allotment and weed the flower beds.

But we younger daughters – that is, Blue, Orange, Rainbow and I – we all knew that big sister was different. She was the only one allowed to go to school for a start, and the only one allowed into our brothers' study. The family tutor and the old man who did our accounts would go out of their way to greet those three, but seemed just as keen to ignore the rest of us.

The way I remember it now, my brothers were like the trees of our family, big sister Red and little sister Rainbow were the flowers, while Blue, Orange and I were the leaves – very much a supporting act. But having said that, those 'leaves' led some very colourful lives, and very different lives, too. Fate has divided us into three different realms – earth, heaven and hell.

After fourth sister Blue started school in Beiping in 1940, she would come home during the holidays with all kinds of wonderful stories. She'd tell us how huge the city was, how many people there were, how the wide streets were packed with horse carriages and all sorts of other vehicles. I heard about all the different types of buildings; the circus acts who came from all over the country to perform during Spring Festival; the mouth-watering local delicacies to be found on every street corner. My favourite was hearing about the weird-looking foreigners, whose eyes were a different colour to their hair. Some were beautiful, Blue told us, others terrifying.

That Beiping described to us by Blue seemed to open up a window to the outside world, a place so full of life and opportunity. Stranded in that fortress of a home we grew up in, surrounded by high walls, we would wait impatiently, counting down the days until Blue could come back and tell us more.

But good things never last. Less than three years later, Blue was called back from school by my father to get married to the boss of a shipping company in Shanghai. Because of the war that was still raging around the country, my father sent a number of servants to escort her down to Shanghai.

The memory that's stuck with me the most is how Blue cried for days before she left, saying she wanted to go back to school, not get married. The whole family urged her to accept Father's decision – after all, he was the head of the family, and his word was final.

Did Red tell you the tragic story of our sister Blue? I often wonder if I could have escaped the fate that befell her, had I been in her position. There were only a few years between us in age, but that's all it took for everything to change – a few years. For Blue, going against Father would have been seen as a disgraceful act of rebellion. For me, going against Father was just part of the Revolution, part of destroying the Four Olds.*

Her husband also got caught up in all that mess. When the Japanese occupied Shanghai, local businessmen had to submit to their rule or face the sharp end of a bayonet. Blue's husband's whole business – including his fleet of ships, his crew of sailors and his land on the docks – was taken over by the Japanese army. That's not to say he simply surrendered, nor that he was colluding with the enemy. The Japanese had robbed everything they had, left them without a penny to their name, so how then could society add insult to injury by accusing them of wrongdoing, even sentencing him to death? And just because they received a few small handouts from our family in Hong Kong, how could they have been accused of being traitors to the country? Not only did the government refuse to give them the help they needed to survive, but they wouldn't allow their own family to lend a hand either.

Poor sister Blue, fate was never on her side. Her child died, her husband was executed. She found herself trapped, with no real place to go or person to lean on. In the end, she never stood a chance.

Could I have helped her? I'm ashamed to say no, I couldn't. I never even saw Blue again after she went to Shanghai that time to get married. For one, I was very young, and hadn't grown up enough yet to really think about anything or anyone other than myself. What's more, China

---

* The 'Destroy the Four Olds' campaign was launched shortly after the start of the Cultural Revolution in 1966, aimed at bringing to an end Old Customs, Old Culture, Old Habits and Old Ideas.

between 1949 and 1960 was a suffocating place – you could barely breathe for the chaos swirling around you. The country had only just come out of half a century of fighting, people were just starting to build up a new country from the ruins of war, setting out on long and arduous journeys – both physical and mental – to pick up the pieces of what was left of their families and their homes. Everyone, no matter what class they were from originally, was waiting to see how they would be treated by the Communists.

Megaphone announcements rang through the streets to warn people that American imperialists were still banging on our door and Nationalist spies were still wreaking havoc up and down the country. This was also how they would announce the latest series of political purges, which came and went as unfailingly as the tide.

On top of all that, five hundred million people needed food, 95 per cent of the population needed an education and our leaders wanted China's economic strength to exceed that of the UK and US within twenty years. We worked so hard that I barely found time to sleep at night.

In those days, I took anything to do with the country very personally, obeying Party discipline and acting according to its needs at all times. In our eyes at least, the Party was the country and the country was the Party. Many people neglected their own families in order to fight in the Party's name, sending their children away to live with relatives so they wouldn't be a distraction.

That's why, out of all my brothers and sisters, I only stayed in touch with Orange. All the others went their own separate ways, and it wasn't until Reform and Opening Up in the 1980s that I managed to contact them again, one by one, through our brother in Hong Kong.

Why did I only stay in contact with Orange? Well, there were only two years in age between us, so naturally we had similar interests and followed a similar path growing up. But it wasn't just that; she strongly influenced my whole outlook on life and my political views. In fact, I even owe my marriage to her.

In 1945, Orange also went to study in Beiping. The stories she brought back were completely different to Blue's, though: they were all about her classmates, her teachers. She even shared the latest school gossip about boys. Having just reached adolescence, those stories sounded more appealing to me. I begged big sister Red – who was living at home waiting for her fiancé to return – to speak to Father on my behalf, so that he might grant his permission for me to start school earlier than planned, and to make sure it was the same one as Orange.

In the end, my wish was granted, and I arrived at school the following year, one grade below my sister. In those days it was called the Girls' Middle School Attached to Beijing Normal University, but now it's the Experimental High School Attached to Beijing Normal University. Founded in 1917, it is a true cradle of Chinese learning.

Since the founding of the People's Republic of China, it has cultivated many outstanding women – scientists, artists, even army generals. Most of our country's leaders sent their daughters or nieces there, including Mao Zedong, Liu Shaoqi, Lin Biao, Zhou Enlai, Chen Yun and Deng Xiaoping, among others.

But while it is undoubtedly one of the leading lights of Chinese education, the school is perhaps most famous for the black mark it left on Chinese history. On 5 August 1966, the deputy principal Bian Zhongyun was beaten to death. She died in a most obscene and inhumane way, at the hands of a group of supposedly warm, loving and innocent young students. As her corpse was trawled off in a rubbish cart, faeces leaked from the seat of her trousers. And the killers? To this day, nobody knows.*

When I was a student there, the school was located on Picai Hutong in Xidan, in the west of the city. In those days the campus was nowhere near the size it is now, but instead was made up of a series of courtyards. The students had to strictly obey the school rules. The girls, for example, were only allowed to keep very short, straight hair. Curly hair of any kind was forbidden, as were braids. The hair at the

---

* Bian Zhongyun is thought to have been the first person killed in Beijing during the Cultural Revolution. On 12 January 2014, former Red Guard leader Song Binbin apologised for her actions, which may have led to Bian's death, but denied the act of murder.

front wasn't allowed to grow beyond halfway down your forehead, around the same level as the hair at the back, which couldn't grow longer than the middle of your ear. Locals back then used to call us 'Little Japanese Tops' because of our resemblance to the Japanese students who wore a similar style.

The use of any kind of make-up or hair accessories was strictly forbidden as well, even hair clips. Some girls came back to school after the holidays wearing make-up, but before they could register for the new term they would always be made to wash it off with towels and soap provided especially by the school. School rules stated that in the ten-minute break between lessons, aside from using the toilet or fetching some water, each class was to remain in their own individual classroom area. Classes were not to mix together, and there was to be no running around or shouting in the campus area whatsoever.

As part of our studies, we also learned to behave in a civilised manner. We always carried a handkerchief with us, just in case we didn't have any tissues to blow our noses or spit into – something we were taught *never* to do onto the ground. If we used the handkerchief, we would wait until we got home to wash it and dry it outside.

Girls all wore the same sky-blue school uniform, with two red scarves sewn into the collar. As Orange used to say, you could walk down any single street or alleyway in Beiping wearing that uniform and there wouldn't be one head that didn't turn in admiration. It didn't matter if it was a high-ranking official, a rickshaw driver or a security guard: they all gazed at us with the same look of awe.

It was around then that I noticed a growing sense of change in the air. I may not have realised it then, but those were the first hints of revolution.

In all honesty, we young people back then saw this revolution as the latest popular trend – just something to get excited about. We were too naive to see for ourselves its bloody nature, the ruthless political struggle at its core, or the legacy we ourselves would inherit from its fallout. What I mean is that the gravity of the situation we faced back then only became clear later on, as Orange and other older students explained the situation more clearly.

I was mostly confined to the school campus, but by all accounts Beiping was full of energy in October 1946. The Communists and Nationalists were busy campaigning among students, trying to win the support of the most talented and able minds of our generation. The Communist Party had just recently unified the New Fourth Army, the Eighth Route Army and several factions of the Liberation Army into a new force called the People's Liberation Army.

Between 1946 and 1948, there were endless student demonstrations out on the streets, including the Anti-American, Anti-Civil War and Anti-Famine Movements and an uprising against American support for Japan. The ebbs and flows of these student rallies posed some pretty problems for the Beiping police. One rumour I remember very vividly was that Beiping's rulers were split into two factions. The first of these supposed factions came under the jurisdiction of Nanjing's central government, which more or less advocated repressing these student movements using force, and its principal backers allegedly included the city's military police and the Nationalist Secret Service. On the other side of this divide was a faction acting independently of central government. In its ranks were authority figures such as Beiping Field Headquarters director Li Zongren, Beiping's mayor, He Siyuan, and Fu Zuoyi, chief of the North China Bandit Suppression headquarters. This group adopted a more enlightened approach which sought to avoid bloody conflict.

Given the one-sided nature of the Civil War, Nationalist government personnel changed very regularly. In May 1948 alone, Li Zongren was elected vice president of the Republic of China, Wu Zhuren left Beiping after being elected to the National Supervisory Committee and He Siyuan was relieved of his duties as mayor of Beiping. Later on, Fu Zuoyi was named Commander of the Bandit Suppression headquarters, keeping watch over Beiping, while Chen Jicheng became deputy head of the same department and head of the Beiping Garrison.

At the same time, the outcome of the Civil War was becoming more and more obvious. The northern and north-eastern areas of China had already been liberated by Communist troops, and while all that was happening thousands and thousands of students from provinces like Liaoning and Jilin descended on Beijing and Tianjin to avoid the conflict raging in their home cities. As a result, the Nationalist government announced that temporary schools and universities would be set up in Beiping and Tianjin – but they didn't keep their word. As the north-eastern students' cries that they wanted to 'study and to live' fell on deaf ears, they sent a representative to negotiate with the Beiping municipal government. Again, they got no response.

Later on, these students were furious to hear that the Beiping National Political Council leadership wanted to conscript them into the army as part of the 'Recruit Exiled Students from the North-east' proposal of 3 July 1948. On 4 July, representatives from around sixteen schools in the north-east got together and decided to hold a mass protest the following day. To express their solidarity, the students' federations of Beiping and North China both sent letters of support and banners to the north-eastern students.

Student representatives proposed that the head of the Beiping National Political Council should make a formal apology in front of the students themselves, but he refused outright. As passions swelled, a mob mentality grew among the crowd, and the students decided to try their luck negotiating again with the council head at his office in the Beiping Legation Quarter. When Chen Jicheng – deputy head of the Bandit Pacification Department and head of the Beiping Garrison – found out about this, he sent a large group of troops to try and prevent the students from entering the quarter.

Fu Zuoyi was against the student protests but wanted to avoid conflict, so he ordered the Beijing military police to confront the students unarmed. Those policemen endured over ten hours of confrontation, taking hits without retaliating, holding their tongues when insulted, staving off their hunger and preserving public order.

However, Chen Jicheng had a different take on the matter, thinking the situation was far more severe. He sent out more than two hundred troops along with four armoured vehicles to encircle the students – who had by then finished their negotiations – and set up machine guns. At that time, the negotiators from both sides were inside, oblivious to the situation escalating outside. When they had reached an agreement, they walked out of the front door, ready to make their announcement.

They were met with a great roar of approval by the awaiting crowd, who rushed towards the front gate. The soldiers overseeing the situation didn't know what had happened inside, and thought that the students were trying to break in. In their panic, they opened fire on the crowd. Everyone dropped to the floor immediately, but when they rose again another round of bullets was fired. In the massacre that day, one bystander and eighteen students were shot dead, and more than forty people were injured.

The 5 July massacre in Beiping sent shock waves throughout China. Students from schools all over the city were furious at what had happened, and held a series of protests demanding that the killers be punished. Students from other cities sent messages of solidarity. On 9 July, more than 10,000 students from thirteen schools around northern China, along with those north-eastern students who had been displaced in Beiping, held a convention in the People's Square of Peking University to mourn those killed and denounce the actions of the authorities.

Thousands of students marched on the official residence of Li Zongren, holding banners that read PETITION FROM NORTHERN AND NORTH-EASTERN STUDENTS AGAINST SUPPRESSING THE MASSES AND IN SUPPORT OF STUDYING. Li met with student representatives on three separate occasions, each time stating, 'I'm just a figurehead, with no real authority here. The most I can do is pass your message on to the central government.'

The day after the massacre, Fu Zuoyi made a speech in which he expressed sympathy for the plight of the north-eastern students. He also agreed to remove those policemen responsible for causing the trouble from their positions, offered compensation to the families of those who had been killed and agreed to solve the problems facing the students.

Fu was dealing with the aftermath of the massacre with kindness and dignity, but at the same time he sent a telegram to the Nationalist Government Executive Branch in Nanjing calling for himself to be 'disciplined' and tendering his own resignation. This forced Chiang Kai-shek to choose between Fu, who controlled the military, and Chen Jicheng, who controlled the police. In the end, Chiang had no choice but to sack and replace Chen, along with the backbone of officials from the Secret Service and Army Secret Services of the Beiping Municipal Government.

Not long after the tension had died down, the Nationalist government launched a spate of counter-attacks, investigating the supposedly manipulated 'student dissidents' who had marched on 9 July. Chen Xuefeng, minister of the Kuomintang Youth League, was given orders to secretly establish the 'Committee to Eliminate Traitors and Purge Dissidents', and almost immediately carried out a series of arrests on 19 August. More than 250 students were summoned, with many of them taken into custody and sent to court so that they could be punished 'according to the law'.

At the same time, the underground section of the Communist Party stepped up their efforts to win student support, calling on students to avoid public student demonstrations and to be vigilant against the Nationalists trying to destroy the city before they left for good.

In those days the whole of China was fighting for change, fighting for political justice. There was also revolution in the classroom as students split into different factions. Some supported the Communists, some supported the Nationalists. Others saw no future for themselves in China, packed their bags and moved to study abroad. Some saw the Revolution as a matter of no concern to them, and took no notice of what was going on outside. Others set their sails to the wind, and followed whichever direction it took them in.

When I look back on it now, it's almost as if our campus was a microcosm of the whole country, host to a range of conflicting sentiments. The 5 July massacre was the last large-scale student uprising during Nationalist rule over mainland China. It lost the Nationalists support from many intellectuals and students, whose sympathies turned towards the Communists.

I was still young back then. On campus, I could smell the heavy scent of gunpowder in the air and sense the panic and confusion among the students, but I didn't feel any of this was of particular concern to me personally. In any case, I formed most of my opinions and feelings under Orange's influence.

It was around that time I noticed a peculiar change had come over my sister. The quiet, reserved young girl I knew suddenly became much more animated and open. For no apparent reason, looks of bashful and mysterious delight would flash across her face, seemingly out of nowhere. When I first noticed, I had absolutely no idea what was going on.

It wasn't long before I found out, though. One afternoon, Orange took me to a quiet part of campus, saying she had something to tell me. 'I think I've fallen in love!' she said. Her face blushed deeply as she spoke.

I looked at her, and asked naively: 'What's *falling in love*?' But my sister had already caught the eye of another group of friends, and went rushing off to see them.

Soon after that, when I returned home for the holidays, I asked big sister Red, 'Did you know that Orange has *fallen in love*?'

To be honest, I was being rather pretentious that day, trying to make things difficult for Red on purpose because I assumed that being stuck at home all the time meant she wouldn't know what 'falling in love' was either.

Red gave me a big hug, and said, 'I know what it means, but I didn't know that Orange was in love, no. If she hasn't told us, then it's not for us to go around asking questions about it. Falling in love is something that happens between two people, not something for everyone else to gossip over, and not something in which family should interfere.'

'So you *do* know what falling in love is?!' I stared at Red in astonishment, and asked again, stupidly, 'Well, have *you* fallen in love?'

Red laughed. 'Come on, let's talk in the vegetable garden. We can pick some of your favourites, and I'll get the chef to cook you up something nice. You can eat to your heart's content; how does that sound?'

It was that holiday when I began to sense that we wouldn't be staying at our Chengde home for much longer. We used to run wild around that garden, where the sun shone brightly and vegetables grew lush and green, but now there were just a few pitiful and lonely-looking rows of cabbages; everywhere else was unkempt and overgrown.

As we picked the last remaining remnants of food to be found in that vegetable garden, big sister Red explained to me that falling in love was a path that a man and a woman walk with each other, and if they choose to follow it till its end, the path leads them to a family rooted in love.

To help me better understand what kind of 'path' that really was, for several days in a row big sister told me some classical Chinese love stories. The ones I remember most were two plays which were later banned during the Cultural Revolution: *Romance of the West Chamber* by Wang Shifu, and *Peony Pavilion* by Tang Xianzu, two beautiful stories about love.

In *Romance of the West Chamber*, Zhang Sheng and Yingying go through all kinds of hardships, but their love endures, and in the end they finally get together. In *Peony Pavilion*, Du Liniang and Liu Mengmei have an even more beautiful story. They never meet in the real world, but later do so in their dreams, and their love plays out in the realms of both the living and the dead.

Lots of Chinese these days believe that Shakespeare is unrivalled for his talent, but these plays are also capable of shaking the earth and moving the gods.

In that holiday, big sister also read me Alexandre Dumas's *La Dame aux Camélias*. The copy we had at home had been translated in 1898 by Wang Shouchang and Lin Shu, printed in carved type in Fuzhou. Only after hearing those stories did I started taking notice of how my body was growing. It was no wonder I enjoyed hearing the stories Orange told me, and unsurprising that I blushed when I spoke to boys.

I don't know what it's like in other families, but I never got any kind of guidance or education on sexuality. Not at home, and not at school. And of course you couldn't find anything written about it in the newspapers — I still blush when I see it in the media today! I don't know how the youth of today have managed to keep any degree of decency and morality. You really have to listen to the stories of our generation before you understand why we worry about them like we do.

(Was Red trying to teach me about sex? I don't know about that! Perhaps, maybe. Red's my big sister, but in many ways she was more like a mother to me in those days.)

I interpreted what she said – about love being a thing between two people, not to be shared with everyone else – to mean that it was a secret. That's why, when I fell in love, I didn't dare mention it to anyone other than my sister Orange. Thinking about it now it makes me laugh! In our day, even if they were in love, a man and a woman would never dream of being alone together before marriage. They would spend time together either with their family or friends, to preserve the purity of love.

They'd be playing with fire by flaunting those rules – even if society didn't punish them, their family would. That's why young people courting and dating was the source of great anxiety for many Chinese families back then. But I was very lucky: I had the wise counsel of Red and the example set by Orange, so I was never that scared during my adolescent years, and I don't think any of my family worried about me either.

When I returned to Beiping after that holiday, Orange said she wanted to take me to meet a special friend of hers, a man she 'greatly admired'.

'There's no need to take any leave. I'll come and find you on Sunday afternoon,' Orange said, mysteriously.

I still felt nervous about the whole thing. 'I don't think that will work. Even if it's the weekend, I still need to request leave. We younger students can't just leave whenever we want.'

'We won't be going anywhere,' Orange laughed. 'You'll know when the time comes,' she added with a smile, gently touching my forehead with her index finger.

I remember waking up strangely early that Sunday. Students would usually take advantage of it being the only day of the week when we could afford a lie-in, but my mind was so preoccupied with meeting Orange's 'friend' that I couldn't sleep. This made me even more nervous that I might make a bad impression on him.

I suffered in silence until after lunch, when Orange showed up, took me by the hand and whisked me away. As we ran, I asked her where she was taking me, but got no reply. My sister just kept bouncing along in front of me. Only when we reached the small grove of trees beside the school playing fields did she slacken her pace. In the shadows of the trees she started looking for something, or someone. I guessed that she was looking for *him*.

Sure enough, out of the shadows emerged a young man. He was of medium height, and although his face seemed somehow familiar, I couldn't quite place it. When she saw him, it was as if little birds were flapping around Orange's chest. I stood waiting at the side, feeling my face getting warm. Even though I knew what dating was, seeing my sister being so intimate with a man still made me feel incredibly awkward.

'Come on, little Green, this is my friend Mr Pan Guoding. He teaches Russian literature at the university.' Orange stood by his side, facing me, as if *he* was the one related to her and I was just some stranger they were meeting for the first time.

But no wonder his face looked familiar. We sometimes held joint events with the university our school was affiliated with, and I must have come across him during one of those.

'Mr Pan, this is sixth sister, Green.'

Mr Pan walked over with great purpose, offering me his hand as he did so. I just stood there, mortified. I was too young to understand these kinds of formalities, and had been brought up in an environment where girls would have no contact with adult men.

Orange noticed my distress, and said, laughing, 'Little Green, we're the children of a new age. Shaking hands is part of our etiquette. We can't be rude to each other, now, can we?'

I extended my right hand with great difficulty, which Mr Pan took and shook ever so lightly. 'It's very nice to meet you; I've heard a lot of good things about you from your sister. She said you're very smart, a deep thinker, and always willing to help others. You have lived up to your name – planting many a green hope in people's hearts.'

Hearing Mr Pan say this made me very embarrassed, and I could feel my cheeks burning. Again it was Orange who came to my rescue, turning to Mr Pan and saying, 'Thank you. I'm sure Little Green will be planting more green hopes in people's hearts soon. But for now, let's go!'

As we went on our way, Orange began talking with Mr Pan in a language I had no way of understanding – it certainly wasn't Chinese they were speaking.

This time, it was Mr Pan who noticed my discomfort, 'Little Green, you don't mind your sister and I speaking to each other in Russian, do you?'

I shook my head in response.

Orange said, very cheekily, 'It's fine. Little Green needs to listen to more Russian to get a sense of the language before she starts learning next term.'

I didn't say anything. In fact, I was glad they were speaking Russian: that way I didn't have to worry about not understanding what they said in Chinese.

When I started school I knew I'd be studying foreign languages, but I didn't know Orange could actually hold a conversation in one. It sounded like she was already very advanced, to my ear at least.

They walked side by side while I followed in silence. That day, Orange was wearing a navy-blue qipao dress, with a white silk scarf wrapped around her neck. Mr Pan was wearing a deep blue tunic, with a dark grey silk scarf. On their feet, they both wore black cloth shoes with white soles. Walking together, they looked a perfect match.

Starting from that Sunday afternoon, Orange would call on me every weekend to go and meet Mr Pan, and we'd walk around campus together. Most of the time they would speak to each other in Russian, and I would follow in embarrassed silence.

One time, Mr Pan brought me a stick of sugared haws, which he presented to me with the words, 'This is a reward for all you've done for us. Thank you for your help.'

'What help?' I replied, not really understanding what he was saying. I hadn't helped them with anything.

Only after many years had passed did I finally realise why those two had brought me along on their dates. Our school rules were very clear in stating that students weren't allowed to have boyfriends, so

Orange brought me along when she met Mr Pan to cover up the fact that they were dating.

In 1950, Mr Pan began working for the Foreign Ministry. He was joined there a year later by Orange, who went there straight after graduating. China back then was really lacking diplomatic talent, and they always encouraged couples to work together, thinking it would make official overseas trips more convenient. But in the end, neither Orange nor her husband ever went on any such trip.

In 1953, relations between China and the Soviet Union began to deteriorate, and many of those who had been working in Sino-Soviet diplomacy became Soviet intelligence analysts and spy officers. Mr Pan had long been a member of the underground Communist movement. After they married, Orange spoke of the great affection they had for each other, sending daily love letters written in Russian. At weekends, they would take part in international events all over the city – meetings, conferences, and also social events like dances. They looked out for me very well, every now and then sending me small gifts like magazines, picture albums and Russian books.

Soon after the Cultural Revolution began in 1966, I received a notice telling me that I must break off all contact with them because they were 'ox-headed devils and serpent gods'!* In the madness of those times, people like Orange and Mr Pan, who worked in diplomatic intelligence, were always likely to be found guilty – even if no one knew what they were guilty of. The state's confidential files were sealed up or burned, their superiors overthrown. The Red Guards were even more ignorant and deranged than the young people of the French Revolution. The country was lawless, families were broken, and no one

---

* 'Ox-headed devils and serpent gods' is a phrase originally used in Buddhism to describe gods and ghosts of the Underworld and which later became a metaphor for ugliness and evil. 'Ox-headed devils and serpent gods' was used during the Cultural Revolution as the collective name of all the innocent victims who were punished for crimes they didn't commit. Anyone who was highly educated, from a rich family, had links to Britain, the United States, the Soviet Union or other 'hostile' countries, had worked for the Kuomintang, or was in any way religious, was classified as one of the 'Ox-headed devils and serpent gods' and was likely to be seized and subject to public criticism from Red Guards. Some were brutally killed.

dared try and prove people like Mr Pan's innocence. The Red Guards could mark you down as a spy based on owning a radio set, they could condemn you as a foreign agent for owning a foreign-language record, and they could even convict you of treason for having a note written in English at your home.

The Red Guards in our unit told me that Orange's husband was in fact a Soviet-trained spy working undercover in China. Within three weeks he was dead, supposedly beaten to death. Orange wasn't even allowed to bury him, as his remains were never found. She's been searching for them to this day. Orange hadn't reached forty by then, but her nerves never recovered from the heartbreak and she hasn't been able to look after herself since.

You want to meet her? I'm afraid that might be difficult. In 1985, our elder brother came back to the mainland to look for his brothers and sisters, but when he found us, Orange refused to see him.

She had three children, two sons and a daughter called Kangmei, which literally means 'Anti-America'. At a young age, the boys were taken by their father's parents back to their ancestral home in the countryside. This was to protect their immediate safety, because of the chaotic scenes in the city, but also to ensure they weren't tainted by their father's supposed betrayal. Kangmei told me that her mother gradually lost touch with the boys as the political movements grew more violent.

Kangmei has always been by her mother's side, though, and it's been hard on the child. She even took her mother with her when she got married, and now there are three generations living under one roof. Kangmei's husband is a good man: although he has to spend a lot of time in the south managing his factory, he always makes sure all three generations are well taken care of. That's right, they have a child together, just the one – a daughter. Under the one-child policy, we urban families are only allowed one!

Even after all these years, I still haven't given up hope of one day helping Orange to open up the door to her heart again, even though it's been slammed shut for so long. You know, for so many of us Chinese, the Cultural Revolution is like a lock which has long since rusted.

I ache to sit down and have a long chat with Orange, about our lives, ourselves, our children.

'Write it in a letter? I'd never thought of that. I always fantasise that one day she'll call me up and say, "Come on, little Green, come over for a chat." But I'm not holding my breath.

I'm over seventy now; soon I'll be eighty. My eyes are blurry and my hands shake; I fear it may be too late.'

So I told Green about my mother-in-law, Mary Wesley, whose first novel wasn't published until she was seventy-one, and who went on to write nine further books. Her writing on women's love lives during the war has inspired me on my journey of giving a voice to so many forgotten women of China.

But I couldn't change Green's mind: 'Your English mother-in-law started writing aged seventy-one? But how many people are there like her in the world? No, you write our story, and I'll get my grandson to read it to me!'

We left our family home in Chengde for good not long before big sister got married. About six months before, I think, during the 1948 Mid-Autumn Festival. At the time, we didn't know she would be getting married so soon. I'd already left to go back to school a little early, as Orange wanted me to accompany her and Mr Pan, without knowing that it would be the last time I'd ever set foot in the house I'd grown up in. Youth is a time of blissful ignorance. It may be beautiful, but sometimes you pay a huge price for that beauty. Some people spend their whole life paying back the debt of youth.

As winter set in that year, someone sent word to Chengde that the Civil War was escalating, and that Hebei Province and Beiping were both under great threat. Father began selling off property right away, keeping just a small row of houses behind the main villa for those family members and servants who remained as caretakers.

My eldest brother had already moved to Hong Kong, and my second brother had moved to study in the US. Father stayed behind with big sister and Rainbow, to take care of what was left of the house. He also hoped that Orange and I would come home quickly to gather up our belongings before we left for good.

But before we'd even had the chance to discuss when we would go back, the PLA surrounded Beiping, and an order was issued forbidding female students from leaving the city. Father used his influence to have a letter delivered, urging us to stay calm, stay in school and not do anything rash. He was making arrangements for what would happen next.

We waited more than six months for that next letter, which arrived handwritten from Hong Kong. In the bluntest way possible, he told us that we were to stop school immediately and reunite with the rest of the family in Hong Kong.

By that time, Orange was head over heels in love, and I looked up to her so much that I would follow whatever she told me to do. For me, Mr Pan was a kind of Prince Charming figure, and I remember making a secret promise to myself that the man I married had to be just like him, only a bigger revolutionary – both physically and spiritually. Why? At that time, I had no idea about the Revolution. Looking back now, I must have meant that I wanted the man I married to be even more intellectual and more capable than Mr Pan, perhaps a bit taller too.

Under Orange's influence, I'd become a fervent supporter of the Communists. It wasn't just us sisters; in those days every female student gave their all to the Revolution. Marrying a revolutionary was the height of fashion.

That's why Father's message went in one ear and out the other, never really registering in our minds. Our young hearts were burning with excitement for the new country, the new age, the new future that lay before us. I was even naive enough to think that after we had helped found the country, Father would be proud of us.

Somehow it never occurred to us that Hong Kong was a British colony and had been a so-called enemy of China for the past fifty years. Looking back on everything that happened, what I regret most is that I never saw my father again.

In the final weeks and months of 1948, our campus was overrun with both Communist and Nationalist agents trying to gather intelligence from the various student activities held there, to win people over to their side, and to start building future networks. Endless rumours came in from all corners, and fighting broke out sporadically on the streets.

The PLA's radio station announced that they were closing in on Beiping, while Nationalist radio maintained that they had all but wiped out the 'Communist bandits'. Some people said that the two sides were in negotiations.

I used to pick things up from Orange and Mr Pan when we went on our walks. I heard them talking about how everyone was so confused and no one knew what was around the corner, and how scared those people were who had once opposed the Communists.

Apparently, there was a Theology student at Yanjing University who heard that the Communists were moving in on Beiping and getting ready to purge anyone of faith. Terrified about what would happen, he killed himself by throwing himself into a lake with a big rock tied to his jacket.

Orange told me to keep studying hard and avoid walking around outside after dark. The fighting between us and the enemy, which had previously been simmering under the surface, was gradually finding its way out into the open. Mr Pan and his friends had already begun taking measures to protect the school, to prevent any last-gasp attack from the Nationalists as they retreated from the city. A group of older students would patrol the campus every night.

I learned from Mr Pan that the peaceful liberation of Beiping was achieved through negotiations between Nationalist army general Fu Zuoyi and the Communists, arranged with the help of his daughter, an underground Party member. That's how the city managed to avoid any great damage.

If I remember it correctly, the PLA entered the city at the beginning of February 1949.* The weather that day was so cold. The school's underground Party mobilised people to gather at Qianmen to welcome the troops, but Mr Pan didn't allow Orange or I to go with them, saying we'd be serving them better by making banners to welcome them into the school.

It wasn't long before a group of PLA troops came to live on campus. With the help of underground Party members, they put up recruitment notices around the school, which led to a huge surge in the number of students enlisting in the army. At the time, it seemed that no one was interested in graduating or getting their diploma; everyone just wanted to serve the country, and repay the debt they felt they owed.

In those days, no one said anything about 'toeing the Party line'. That gradually crept in later on. At the time of liberation, we were full of excitement and truly believed – like the Chinese scholars of old used to say – that the state always comes before the individual. I was seventeen that year, not yet old enough to officially join the Party, but I had already earned a reputation among my peers as a true revolutionary.

In those days, we wanted everything to be new. In fact, it wasn't just our generation who felt that way. 'Overturn the old and welcome the new' – perhaps that's something we Chinese have picked up over the centuries of upheaval in our country, learning how to adapt to the new regime when they take over. If you don't believe me, just take a look at the names of our city streets. How many of them have stayed the same over the past five generations? Even the name of our capital has gone back and forth between Beiping and Beijing several times.

---

* Green's estimate was close: the PLA's Fourth Field Army entered Beiping to take over the city on 31 January 1949, concluding the campaign.

Green was right. Beijing – literally 'northern capital' – was known as Beiping – 'northern peace' – as early as 12 September 1368, before it became known as Beijing when the Ming dynasty made it their capital in 1427. Beiping was used again during the Nationalist Era that began on 20 June 1928. The Japanese invaders renamed it Beijing on 12 October 1937, although the vast majority of Chinese refused to accept this change and the city continued to be known as Beiping in everything but official documents. When the Japanese surrendered in 1945, the Chinese Nationalist Party changed it back to Beiping, only for the Communists to change it back to Beijing when they officially took power on 27 September 1949, also making the city their capital.

A seedling unearthed by revolution

I can still remember to this day that we didn't have a full night's sleep in the month leading up to 1 October 1949. We were all taking part in the preparations for the grand ceremony being held to mark the founding of the People's Republic of China. As Mr Pan put it, an entire country was going to be born out of our dedication and hard work. This was both a feat of great historical significance and a moment of great pride. We saw ourselves as the pacemakers of the new China.

Orange was part of the team responsible for working out evacuation routes for the ceremony, along with some older classmates and a few university students. Mr Pan and some military representatives took this team on a number of scouting missions, where they'd discuss strategy and analyse where people could be evacuated to in case of emergency. I was also fortunate enough to be able to follow them on this 'sightseeing tour' of Beiping's ancient city, where I'd never been before.

Why do I call it the 'ancient' part? Well, in those days, Beijing was completely different to what it is now. Back then, the city was divided up very carefully according to social rank. There was the Forbidden City at Beijing's heart, where the emperor and his cohorts used to live; Wangfu, the princely residence; then the Baqi area reserved for soldiers.

There used to be another gate on the central axis of the city. During the Ming dynasty it was known as Daming Gate, in the Qing dynasty it was known as Daqing Gate, and it was later changed to The Gate of China during the Nationalist period. Before it was torn down in the early 1950s when the Soviets said we needed a big square, it was located where you can find the Monument to the People's Heroes today, near Mao's Mausoleum, right in the middle of Tiananmen Square.

That wasn't the only ancient gate to be torn down, either. The Chang'an Left Gate and Chang'an Right Gate used to flank Tian'an Gate to form a T-shaped square with the Gate of China. They too were destroyed to improve traffic flow and allow more space for large-scale national parades.

Outside the Imperial City, east of Beihai Park and west of Jingshan Park, there is a Daoist temple called Dagao Xuandian. Before they were destroyed in January 1955, it used to have some of the most beautiful ornate pailou archways.

Mr Pan told me that in July 1949, Liu Shaoqi led a team of experts on a secret trip to the USSR, to listen to the Soviets' advice on founding a new country. The two parties reached an agreement that the Soviets would send 220 experts to help China build itself up.

When they arrived, these experts had near-absolute diplomatic immunity. The man responsible for preserving the ancient buildings of Beijing's ancient city, Liang Sicheng, didn't stand a chance against their 'Tear Down and Relocate' plan. And that's how the ancient city, whose foundations had been laid in 1264, was largely torn apart. It was a great pity.

The night before the opening ceremony, Mr Pan and Orange took me and a group of students from the Russian department to assist them with the task of stewarding the event. We arrived at Tiananmen Square to start work at midnight. I followed the two of them, working in shifts to supervise the inventory of people's personal belongings on the square and to make sure no one was carrying explosives.

I saw all those groups directly involved in the ceremony coming into the square, including a twenty-one-gun salute band. The recently painted Tian'an Gate had an enormous banner hanging across it that read OPENING CEREMONY OF THE CENTRAL GOVERNMENT OF THE PEOPLE'S REPUBLIC OF CHINA. Right in the centre hung a huge portrait of Chairman Mao, not the one you'll find there today but a photo taken in the 1940s, of him wearing a cap.

The slogans on either side read 'Long Live the Central People's Government' and 'Long Live the People's Republic of China'. The north side of the Golden Water Bridge doesn't have the viewing stand which it does now, but two temporary stands were erected on the day, one for the conductor of the ceremony, and one for the sole foreign delegation in attendance – a group of Soviet writers, artists and scientists, led by author Alexander Fadeyev, who had arrived the previous day.

Perhaps the hardest-working people there were the sanitation workers, and the team responsible for restoring the square over the past few months. Their job was to ensure the cleanliness of the square and the safety of those temporary viewing stands. They worked in shifts, day and night, for four days straight.

The founding ceremony of the People's Republic of China was held on the afternoon of Saturday, 1 October 1949 in Beijing – changed from Beiping just a few days previously. At the time, the Nationalists still had troops on the mainland, and the western part of the country remained under the rule of Chiang Kai-shek and military warlords. Swathes of southern China were yet to be liberated at that time, and the Nationalists had tens of thousands of secret agents and military police left, which meant there were still a number of skirmishes and other incidents of war going on throughout the country.

But the biggest threat came from the sky. The Nationalists still had several military strongholds in the south-west and the south, and domination of the skies lay completely in their hands. From their base in Sichuan province, the exiled Nationalist government sent a number of planes on missions to bomb places like Beiping and Shanghai.

Nights were the only time when the city wasn't under threat. Mr Pan explained that this was because the Nationalist planes were unsuited to flying long-haul or in darkness, and so if they were sent out to bomb somewhere during the day, they had to return to their base in the south before nightfall. Therefore, if the founding ceremony was held in the morning, it would give the Nationalist fleet enough time to get back before dark. But if it was held later, say at three in the afternoon – the sun sets in Beijing in October around half five – then they wouldn't have time to fly back. I think that must have been why the ceremony took place in the afternoon.

Only later, when the Communist air force grew in size and strength and became more capable of coping with the Nationalist threat, were the National Day holiday celebrations switched to the morning. That's also why the curfews and restriction of movement around the city before the founding ceremony were so strict. We were all expecting to hear sounds of gunfire or bombing at any minute. It was nothing like the way the propaganda films made it out to be, 'the motherland brought together in peaceful celebration' and all that.

There was something almost holy about the sunrise of 1 October 1949. We all held our breath as darkness gave way to light, heralding the start of more than just a new day. The weather was overcast to begin with, and we felt drops on rain on our heads throughout the morning. But the skies cleared in the afternoon and the sun shone down on us, as if God himself wanted to join in the celebrations.

At that time, most people had never actually seen our new national flag with their own eyes; they'd only heard it described on radio broadcasts, or from friends who had probably never seen it for themselves either. That's why, on the day of the ceremony, Tiananmen Square was filled with all these different variations on the official Five-Starred Red Flag. Lots of people brought star-shaped red lanterns too.

I think what left the deepest impression on me that day, looking out over the sea of red flags and red lights, was the group of Hui people – so-called Chinese Muslims – wearing their white hats and carrying green flags with white moons and stars. In those days, there were a lot of Hui people in Beijing.

People were happily waiting in their designated areas, some sitting on the ground. Everything was very orderly. Our lunch that day consisted of water and cold *mantou* steamed buns, with some sweets and fruit specially provided for the festivities. The younger students at our school, under the instruction of the military representative, listened to the broadcast of the ceremony on the radio at school, and then later joined us in Tiananmen for more celebrations. We heard later that at dusk, many students from schools all over the city hadn't been able to enter the square itself, so they had just found a spot nearby where they all sang and danced deep into the night.

Mr Pan told us that he'd heard around thirty thousand people from both the city centre and its outskirts had taken part in the ceremony, including workers, students, cadres, local residents and city garrison teams. When it was all over, the Golden Water Bridge that separates Tiananmen Square and Tian'an Gate was covered with lost shoes.

Did Mao Zedong really say, 'The Chinese people have stood up'? According to all the propaganda you'll come across today, yes. But why don't I remember him saying that? I remember Mao saying, 'Comrades! Today marks the establishment of the Central People's Government of the People's Republic of China!'

Whatever was or wasn't said, that day I had a sense of attachment and belonging that felt unbreakable: this new country was mine. Not only that, but for me, that day was the opening chapter of my own family, for it was then that I first met my future husband.

A poetic sapling in revolution

In the viewing area we were looking after there were many student volunteers, as well as a number of armed PLA troops keeping order. I suppose it was all a bit too much for some: after all, this was a truly historic moment. Just as Chairman Mao finished his speech, one of the younger students collapsed with what looked like a bad case of exhaustion. At once, a soldier standing nearby sprang forward to support her and I too instinctively grabbed her by the arm to help out, even though she was too heavy for me to support her alone. Together, that soldier and I took her to a nearby medical assistance stand.

As the medical staff tended to her, we were asked to wait there and help take her back to school. As we stood there by the medical stand, we got chatting.

He introduced himself first. 'My name's Meng, Meng Dafu.'

'Han Anbi, but my family and friends call me Little Green.'

Later, he arranged for an army jeep to meet us at the emergency exit, to help send the young student back to her dorm. Only when the matron on duty there told us that all was well did Dafu take his leave.

As I went to see him off at the campus gate, we arranged to meet the following Saturday at the Friendship Club. This had originally been set up by the Beijing government for the Soviet experts based in the city, who themselves later began inviting Chinese students who could speak Russian. It quickly became a renowned leftist student union, which Orange and Mr Pan would often attend. Meng Dafu said he went there most weekends as well.

'Do PLA soldiers *really* join in student activities?' I asked him.

'Of course! Why wouldn't they?' He seemed surprised I had asked.

'Oh, no reason.' I didn't know why I'd asked either. I suppose I was just very naive back then, and so curious to learn more.

'Well, thanks for seeing me off. See you next weekend!'

'Thank you ever so much for helping my classmate. See you next weekend!'

As I watched Meng Dafu disappear into the night, I don't know what came over me. It felt like he was walking away from me, but into my heart. I was seventeen back then, and spent most of my time in the girls' school. Apart from accompanying Orange and Mr Pan on their dates, I'd never spent any time alone with a man before. At that age, the force of attraction between a man and a woman is so powerful, sometimes to the point where nothing else in the world seems to matter at all, don't you think?

Those seven days seemed more like seven years. I knew how I felt about Dafu, but I didn't know what to do about it. In those days it had to be the man who courted the woman.

Green broke off to address me directly at this point.

'Certainly, Dafu has always been under the impression that it was he who fell for me and not the other way around. Don't go telling him otherwise; it would come as quite a shock to him, I'm sure!'

The idea that the man has to chase the woman is truly ingrained in Chinese culture – a heavenly principle. In the past, men and women who went against this would be driven out of their family homes, sometimes even sentenced to death. This is recorded in the annals of Chinese history, and is a common motif in classical Chinese literature.

As Red once said, the New Culture Movement of 1917 was in many ways the original Cultural Revolution. Women no longer had to bind their feet; they could cut their hair; they could go to school. They were no longer subject to arranged marriages, or forced to take their husband's surname. All these signs of social progress arose from that period.

However, Green's story illustrates just how slow this tree of women's liberation was to grow. Even Green – an educated woman and in many ways a revolutionary – was still bound to this 'heavenly principle'.

Did I tell Orange? Of course I did, but the day I told her about going to the Friendship Club with Meng Dafu, she was busy printing some leaflets with the woodblock. Without raising her head, she said, 'I can take you after supper on Saturday. I'll wait for you at the dorm entrance at 5.30. Don't be late.'

That was the first time I took part in any of those youth club activities in my own right, as opposed to just being Orange's sister. I dressed myself in a way I had learned from watching Orange, wearing a pale pink qipao big sister Red had given me; yes, it was known as a Chinese traditional dress, but for the Han Chinese the qipao only has a four-hundred-year history. Anyway, my pale qipao was a bit different from today's fashionable qipao, which is designed to be tied in a way which emphasises the female figure, but it still looked much more feminine than my school uniform. I'm not sure which sister it had belonged to previously, though, as it was a little big for me. I also used a reddish-green handkerchief, folded into the shape of a flower and fastened to the top buttonhole of my dress. I didn't own a pair of those fashionable narrow black leather shoes that Orange liked to wear, so I had to make do with the old wide-fitting cloth ones I wore for school.

Orange was stood waiting for me at the gate of the dorm. When she saw me coming, it was like she'd seen a ghost. 'Little Green, is that you? Did you dress yourself?'

'Of course I did!' I couldn't stand it when she patronised me like that.

'Well, you look great. Seems like Little Green hasn't just gone through an ideological revolution, but a fashion one too,' she said, teasingly.

Mr Pan, who was waiting at the school entrance, appeared dumb-struck when he saw us coming, eventually saying, 'You sisters look so similar.'

When we arrived at the club, I caught a glimpse of Dafu's tower-ing figure standing at the entrance, glancing round in every direction. I furtively took Orange by the hand. 'That tall soldier standing over there – that's Meng Dafu.'

But my sister was whispering something into Mr Pan's ear, and paid no attention to what I had said. Dafu caught sight of us, and with huge strides bounded over in our direction. I wasn't the person he wanted to speak to, though.

'Mr Pan, good evening, sir. I'm on duty tonight – a great chance to get to know some of the club's newest student members, I reckon.'

Mr Pan patted Meng Dafu on the shoulder in a very familiar fash-ion. 'Thanks for your hard work, Dafu. Last night you were patrolling the school campus, today you were helping out with the enlistment exams, and now you're on duty here at the student union.'

'It's nothing, really. At the founding ceremony there weren't enough of us, but many hands make light work, I say. We all need to do our bit for the motherland. And your two friends?' Dafu was looking at us now.

Mr Pan made the introductions: 'These two are student comrades, sisters. Elder sister Han Anzhi, who we call Orange, and younger sister Han Anbi, who—'

'We call Little Green, right?' Dafu looked very pleased with himself as he said this.

'You know each other?' Mr Pan and my sister both blurted out the same question at once.

'Ah, so *you're* Meng Dafu! Little Green mentioned you before!' Orange finally cottoned on.

'Yes, we met at the founding ceremony. Miss Green, how's your friend doing?'

'She's … she's fine. The school doctor said it was due to low blood sugar; she just needs to eat more and it won't happen again.'

Mr Pan opened his arms. 'Great! Well, shall the four of us go inside?'

Meng Dafu waved his hands. 'Sorry, it's my job to wait at the entrance and greet the students as they arrive, so I'm afraid I can't go in with you. But you go first, please.' He was looking at me as he said this.

I could feel my face growing warm, as if his gaze was someone burning my cheeks. Luckily, no one else saw.

I walked into the club with Orange and Mr Pan. The place was already buzzing with activity. The men were split up into various groups, all talking obnoxiously loud, with throngs of girls seated to one side, listening in. There were also a few girl students from the older years sitting in the corner, gossiping in a foreign language I didn't understand – it may have been German. Every so often they'd burst into fits of laughter, and I guessed they must have been commenting on those boys.

We walked through to an even bigger hall, where a large group of students was sitting in a circle round a Russian man. He looked much older than the rest of the people there, but he spoke in such a powerful, charismatic and forceful manner that you could tell from the faces of the crowd sitting round him that they were completely captivated by what he said, hanging on his every word. When he saw us come in, he stood up to greet Mr Pan. Orange whispered to me that he was the Russian representative of the Beiping Student Association –Beijing, I mean. Even now I'm still used to calling it Beiping!

Great swathes of people entered the main hall. All of them seemed to know Orange and Mr Pan well, and I was brushed aside by the ever-growing crowd. I didn't recognise a single person there, so I decided to go outside and find Dafu.

There were still lots of people stood talking at the entrance, and many others trying to enter the hall. It seemed I was the only one trying to get out. I hadn't yet freed myself from the oncoming crowd when I heard some call out, 'Miss Green! What are you doing out here?'

It was unmistakably Dafu. I followed the sound of his voice to escape the great stream of people.

'I don't know anyone in there. Orange and Mr Pan are busy talking to their friends and haven't got time for me. Would you mind if I stayed out here with you?' I felt nervous asking him this.

'Oh no, not at all. In fact, you can help me clear the entrance by asking these people to move inside.' Dafu's relaxed tone made me feel much more relaxed.

'Sure. I'll do it now,' I said very matter-of-factly. I like having things to do; it gives you a way of showing off your talents. But it wasn't long before I realised I might have been a little out of my depth – the crowd at the entrance kept getting bigger and more chaotic. It was like a piece of Beijing sticky candy, all glued together. My voice and my energy seemed lost on the crowd, and I was like a lonely bee buzzing around its edges. It was a crisp autumn day, but my dress clung to my body with sweat.

When the rush had finally died down, Dafu came and found me. 'Miss Green, thanks so much for your help. You did a great job: I heard you shouting yourself hoarse back there! You really held your own.' He later told me that it was then that he decided that I would make a good wife.

From then on, Mr Pan and Dafu would often take Orange and me to take part in some Beiping student activities, especially those to do with Sino-Soviet friendship. Both men told me of the importance of following a particular Party rule: 'Don't ask about what you don't know; don't tell others what you know.' That's why I didn't dare ask Meng Dafu about his family background. In any case, there was such energy between us when we were together that I didn't feel any kind of social division.

Those three months were perhaps the happiest of my life. To put it in a way my young granddaughter would, I was 'loved up' for those three months, and so I suppose it's only natural that everything I saw was pleasing on the eye and everything I did gave me great pleasure. Kids these days have a lot more experience than we did at their age; their eyes were opened much earlier than ours. But then again, that just gives them more to worry about.

Why just three months? Well at the end of December 1949, Mr Pan started work at the Foreign Ministry, and Meng Dafu started work at the United Front.* Of course, this meant our work schedules were no longer so compatible, and we had fewer chances to meet. Orange and I felt a deep sense of loss.

On New Year's Day 1950, Mr Pan invited us for a meal in his dormitory. On the way over, we stopped off at a street vendor to buy some stewed pig's head, salted peanuts, wheat cakes and a bottle of *erguotou* liquor. Mr Pan had also bought some sugared haws to give to Orange and me, saying, 'You girls eat your sugared haws, us boys will drink our *erguotou* – perfect!'

That evening, Mr Pan and Orange told us that they were engaged. They planned to marry as soon as Orange graduated, and they asked if Dafu and I would act as their best man and bridesmaid.

Emboldened by the alcohol, Dafu plucked up the courage to ask me if I would like to come and meet his folks this coming Spring Festival.

'Will Orange be going too?' I asked instinctively.

---

* The United Front Work Department is a government agency tasked with managing relations with China's diverse religious believers and ethnic groups, and the peoples of Hong Kong and Taiwan. In so doing, the United Front seeks to ensure that these groups are supportive of and useful to the Communist Party.

Mr Pan and Orange both burst out laughing. I don't know whether it was the effect of the *erguotou* or that he felt embarrassed, but Dafu blushed. 'No, it will just be us two.'

'Little Green, Orange is coming with me to meet my parents. You'll be going with Dafu to meet *his* parents,' Mr Pan explained to me, patiently.

Orange had to spell it out for me, whispering in my ear, 'Dafu is going to propose to you, silly!'

Now my face was twice as red as Dafu's! How did I respond? The way relationships worked back then was nothing like they do now – we didn't shout about our love on the streets. My parents' marriage had been arranged by their parents; even big sister Red and fourth sister Blue didn't have a say in theirs. They were a few years older than me, but the gap was more like a generation. That might have been a new era, but no one really knew how to do things in any 'new' way. That's why I had to turn to Orange for help.

I looked up at her and asked, 'Fifth sister, what do you think?'

Again, the three of them collapsed in laughter.

Wiping the tears from her eyes, Orange said to me, 'Little Green, how can I answer that question for you? Dafu is asking *you!*'

Deeply embarrassed, I finally said to him, 'OK, I'll come and meet your parents this Spring Festival.'

Before the words had left my lips he grabbed me by both hands, lifting them up in the air. 'That's great!'

Spring Festival 1950 fell in mid-February. A week before the holiday, Dafu told me that there was a military train leaving soon from Beijing to Jinan, from where we could easily reach his home town on the outskirts of Liaocheng. The train guard was happy for us to hitch a ride – he was from the same town as Dafu and they had both served in the Eastern Liberation Army, which later became the Third Field Army of the PLA.

Dafu was worried I wouldn't be able to handle the stuffy conditions on board the train. I tried to calm his nerves: 'So many revolutionaries laid down their lives to build a new China, sacrificing everything they had. Why should the idea of taking a train worry me?'

Dafu went to speak, then held back. Looking at me, he finally said, 'It's really not what you imagine. No, let me think of a different way.'

I couldn't stand it when people looked down on me like that. 'What better way? I don't fear hardship!'

When I look back now at how childish I was, it makes me laugh! It's terrible, really.

What kind of hardships did people face? Compartments on those old military trains had just one small window, with no other source of light or ventilation. Dozens of soldiers would be cramped inside, where they'd eat, drink, sleep and use the toilet. In winter they'd huddle together for warmth; in summer they'd strip off completely to stay cool.

To prevent surprise attacks from Nationalists, the trains would only stop in the dead of night to pick up supplies, even if it meant the journey would take several days. Soldiers were allowed just half an hour to stretch their legs and empty the toilet buckets.

Only later, when I saw the train with my own eyes, did I realise why Dafu had been so reluctant. Not only would I have been in great discomfort, but my presence, as a young female, would also have made things even more awkward for those soldiers, who hadn't exactly lived blessed lives.

The guard was truly a *tie gemen'r*, a true friend willing to go out of his way to make space for us in one of the tanks that was being transported on the train. The soldier accompanying the guard proudly told us that those tanks had all been captured; some of them had even been made in America. The US had indeed given a number of tanks to the Nationalists, to help them in their war with the Communists. Around the time of the PRC's founding ceremony, those vehicles and weapons captured from the Nationalists were added to the arsenal defending the capital. Now they're part of the Eastern Field Army, a section of the Special Mechanised Forces.

I later checked historical records to get a better idea of the context of what Green had described to me. In January 1947, at the height of the Civil War, the Communist Eastern Liberation Army captured a large part of the Nationalists' mechanical weaponry in a battle at Lunan, Hebei. This included around 470 military vehicles, 217 guns (including forty-eight 105 mm howitzers), other heavyweight weapons and twenty-four tanks. Of these, six were lightweight US-made M3A3s.

These weapons, along with the experts who had been captured by or defected to the Communists, became an integral part of the Eastern Field Army special forces, providing much-needed quality and technological expertise.

So that's how I ended up taking a tank to meet Dafu's family! Who knows, I may even have been the first Chinese woman to ride in a tank. I took with me some flatbread I had prepared, and a military-style flask Dafu had given me. The space inside was tiny, pitch-black and had a strong smell that I couldn't quite place. Dafu and a few other soldiers were outside, sitting on the tank's tracks. We hadn't yet married by that point, and men and women weren't allowed to be alone together. Even couples who were already engaged had to make do with the odd clandestine glance into their sweethearts' eyes.

Even under the cover of darkness, we didn't dare touch each other in any way. My urban upbringing and the customs of Dafu's village were actually very similar in this regard.

Trains back then were painfully slow — perhaps because of the heavy loads on top — and I was sat shaking around in that tank for what seemed like days on end. To help me pass the time, Dafu would describe to me the scenery outside. But we were travelling in the heart of winter, and in the vast emptiness of snow and wind there really wasn't that much to portray. Dafu was worried about me getting lonely, and to ensure all the guards and soldiers stayed awake he would engage them all in conversation one by one, so that they wouldn't fall asleep and I wouldn't get bored.

Dafu told them how he had been taken from his home and conscripted by the Nationalist army at the end of 1945. During his first battle he was captured by the Eighth Route Army and taken in as a prisoner of war. All of them were given two choices – take three silver coins and find their own way home, or join the Communist forces. Dafu didn't even know what part of the country they were in, and feared that even if he did leave to try and find his way home he would only be picked up again by some army or other. Strong young men like him couldn't escape such a fate in that decade of constant fighting and unrest. He figured he might as well stay with the Eighth Route Army.

Because of his physical presence, the commander of the company who found Dafu presented him as a 'gift' to headquarters, to serve as an assistant to the army chief, saying that they needed big men like him to carry heavy equipment. For three years, Dafu served in the Eighth Route Army in the Civil War, where he fell in love with *da-you* poetry while attending the company's literacy classes.* The Communists set these up to help those soldiers who had no educational background learn basic literacy and political thought. This way, they could learn and fight at the same time.

Later, Dafu tried his hand at writing a few war reports and some catchy slogans for the troops, which went down well with his superiors. After the Eighth Route Army was integrated with the New Fourth Army and the North-eastern Field Army to form the People's Liberation Army, he was transferred to work in the Propaganda Department. When Beiping was peacefully liberated, the Communists were in desperate need of capable people to work on school campuses, so he then began working as a military representative there.

When he had finished telling his story, Dafu began enthusiastically encouraging others to tell theirs: 'Come on, who else can tell us about how they came to join the PLA?'

'What?'

---

* *Da-you* is a traditional form of Chinese poetry, similar to the Western limerick.

'Us?'

'What d'you want us to say?'

'What is there to say?'

'Same as you. Doesn't matter who you're with, it's still just carrying guns and eating!'

'Story of our life!'

When I heard the racket they made, all of them talking over each other, I thought they couldn't have had one day's schooling between them.

Later, I asked Dafu, 'How is it that all those PLA troops were so uneducated?'

'Never mind school,' he replied, 'most of them had never even had a hot meal before. During the war, young men were being driven out of their villages and conscripted into whichever army happened to come across them first. They weren't concerned with any grand political theories; they'd be happy with anyone who offered them food to eat and a pillow to rest their heads. It was only later, when they'd gained more experience, that these people claimed to have joined up because they believed in the Revolution.'

The truth is that although Dafu didn't receive as good an education as I did, he had this unique ability to open my eyes to see the whole picture. I saw the world as I was taught to see it; but with Dafu, his mind seemed to transcend my own superficial understanding, especially when it came to looking back at history.

But those were all things I found out later on. That day, as I sat in the tank, I just felt bad that Dafu's attempts to inspire others had fallen on deaf ears. You know that my parents' love was built on poetry? Our nicknames came from the lyrics of some of their favourite poems, and big sister Red would often help us younger sisters to write poems and *fu*. So when I found out that Dafu also liked writing poems, my admiration grew for him no end. But in those early days back in the city, there was never any chance for us to be alone together, and I didn't dare ask him to recite poetry to me in front of anyone else. Now, though, as he was talking to the other soldiers about his love of *da-you*, I took the opportunity to ask him to share a few with everyone.

Hearing my proposition, the others joined in with cries of 'Come on! Let's have it then!'

I don't know how many soldiers were sitting on the tank, but it sounded like more than just a few. Most of the voices I could hear had strong northern accents.

Hearing what I said, he let out a very uncharacteristic sigh, and his voice seemed somewhat nervous. 'What I'm talking about isn't so much what cultured people would call a "poem", it's more like a *da-you*, or just a jingle really.'

'Jingles? I can do those!' The voice had a slight southern twang to it.

'You can? Come on then, let's hear one!' The icy atmosphere had been warmed by the crowd's curiosity.

'All right then. Have a listen:

Grandma's feeling good, looks younger than she should,
Auntie's feeling good, as happy as a bell,
Wifey's feeling good, she's such a little trooper,
Sister's feeling good, no reasons left to whine.'

I guessed he didn't have much education; his vocabulary was very limited, but the other soldiers seemed very interested in it: 'What about your dad, brothers, uncles? Is everyone in your family a girl?' The voice that asked this hadn't yet broken, but it was full of tenderness.

'There was a lot of fighting where I come from. My dad, granddad and uncle were all conscripted. None of them came back alive.'

All those warm feelings once again drained from the group with the answer that the southern voice gave.

As I listened, my heart sank, a feeling I'd never experienced before. Before then, war for me had just been just a backdrop for heroic deeds and epic stories. It had never made me think of those lives lost and the grief of their families. I had never felt so close to the suffering of war.

'Come on, let's use this sadness as a source of strength. How about it?' Dafu's voice, so downbeat just moments earlier, was now urging everyone on, trying to lift the pain of their war wounds:

Riding a tank in the freezing cold,
Like a huge river our stories unfold,
Come on, PLA, let's win this damn war,
Let young and old be reunited once more!

Dafu's fighting talk didn't quite achieve the intended result of lifting their spirits. To back him up, from inside the tank I asked him, 'Can I try one too?'

'Of course, of course! Comrade Green's got one for us boys!' Dafu later praised me for following the idea that 'the wife should sing to the husband's tune'.

I recited my made-up *da-you*:

Snow falls thick as the vast, open ocean,
Deep like the bonds of perpetual devotion.
Providence schemed to bring us together,
To warm each other's hearts in this cold weather.

When I'd finished, I waited for the voices of approval from outside the tank. That was, after all, the first time I'd ever even heard the word *da-you*, let alone tried reciting one. After hearing a few of their offerings, I felt pretty self-confident and maybe even a little smug, knowing as I did that poems weren't just a random set of sentences; there was a whole set of rules and forms of versification. But when I had finished my *da-you*, which I felt was much better than theirs, there wasn't a single sound. What was going on? Where was everyone? I felt most puzzled.

Finally, I heard Dafu's voice, his tone sounding more than a little forced: 'Comrade Green, that was a great *da-you*!'

Afterwards, he very cautiously told me that the reason why no one spoke that day was because those illiterate soldiers didn't understand what my *da-you* was about.

'Well, did *you* understand?'

'I ... I understood *most* of it. I didn't understand the part about "perpetual devotion", and I didn't know what "providence" was.'

Dafu felt those soldiers might struggle with making up their own *da-you* poems. Instead, he told us about their history. '*Da-you* poetry,' he explained, 'was first told in the Tang dynasty. It was created by a peasant actually, a man called Zhang Dayou. Zhang had never learned how to read or write, but he loved catchy little sentences. He came up with something which people would later call "Snow Song":

> Fog on the river,
> Well dark and hollow,
> Yellow dog body white,
> White dog body swollen.

'Those few sentences managed to conjure up both the image and the feeling of a snowy landscape without ever even using the word "snow". Zhang had made up a whole new form of poetry without even meaning to, and he became an overnight sensation. They even named a special type of poem after him, the *da-you*. People realised that the more you practised this type of catchy poem, the better they got. Better, and dirtier too!'

Dafu then told us the story of a woman from the countryside in Guangdong. Every day for many years, she would deliver food to her husband in jail, gaining some degree of fame in the area for her loyalty and perseverance. This was around the time the famous poet Su Shi was exiled to Guangdong for insulting the emperor. One day, Su came across the countrywoman, and seeing how filthy she looked, he reeled off a couple of lines of cruel poetry:

> With straw-like hair and muddied breast,
> She goes to feed the jailor's guest.

Never did he expect that this quiet and unassuming woman, seemingly lost in her own world, would shoot back at him and finish off the poem herself:

> A poet who once was so blessed,
> Your failures now surpass the rest.

Not only did that *da-you* get back at Su Shi for the disrespect he had shown her, but also rubbed salt into the wounds that still stung from the shame of being exiled.

I suppose those soldiers couldn't have understood that story either, because when Dafu had finished there was, once again, complete silence.

When our 'tank train' finally arrived in Jinan, we still had to wait until nightfall before it could enter the station. We bid farewell to our travel companions under the faint glow of the station lights, and only then did I realise they were nothing but teenagers – youthful faces that belied the horrors they had lived through.

With his special military pass in hand, Dafu went looking for our transport onto Liaocheng. It didn't take us long to find a group of horse-drawn carriages in the warehouse outside the station. They had just delivered military supplies to the city and were now ready to go back to where they came from. Clusters of people gathered round them, lost souls either looking to return home or else escape some episode from their past.

I'd been holed up in the tank for two sleepless days and nights, and as soon as we got into the carriage I fell into a deep, drowsy sleep, not even registering how the carriage looked inside.

'Little Green, wake up! We need to get off.' Dafu's words brought me back to consciousness. He told me later that I was only half-conscious when I got down from the carriage; it was as if I were sleep-walking. I think I was so out of it that moment that I would probably have followed anyone, even if they were selling me into slavery.

Only when I found out we'd be making the rest of the journey by foot did I finally wake up.

That day we walked for what seemed like forever. It must have been at least six hours, step after painful step. The midwinter frost chilled our bones, and there wasn't any scenery to take comfort in. Dafu said that every day was a picture once spring bloomed, but the earth was yet to wake from its winter slumber. To raise my spirits, he told me a few *da-you* poems the soldiers used to share, some of them very vulgar. I didn't object: after all, he was a PLA officer, the matinee idols of the day.

Would you like to hear some of them? Somehow quite a few have stuck in my head. They cover topics as ambitious as the universe and the human race; they sound a bit ridiculous now, mind you:

As soldiers we will not fear death,
Our cause we won't misplace,
Let's all get rid of Chiang Kai-shek,
And free the human race!

Spread out the road from north to south,
Lay tracks from east to west,
Let boats sail far across the seas,
And planes fly round the rest.

A seed was planted in my mind,
And in my heart I see:
The Pacific Ocean covered red,
Long live the CCP!

I couldn't understand what this had to do with the Pacific. Dafu explained, very earnestly, that if we liberated all the countries in the world, starting with those in the Pacific, our descendants would also have the chance to play a part in this great revolution of ours. It's no wonder my husband later went on to work for the United Front!

Slowly but surely the gaps between us disappeared, bridged by the growing bonds of our affection. As we laughed our way down that icy road, no longer did I feel like a timid little girl. No longer did I feel burdened by our different class backgrounds.

But we were living in an age of unbending class divisions. In other people's eyes, we came from different worlds – he was the son of the proletariat, I was the daughter of the bourgeoisie. Everyone said that it wouldn't work out between us. Well, we proved them wrong in the end.

My whole family looked down on Dafu, even going so far as to suggest he was only interested in *da-you* poetry because of me. This kind of cultural and class arrogance drove me up the wall – why couldn't they respect him? The truth was that Dafu approached *da-you* poetry as if it were an academic pursuit. In his later years, he would collect all kinds of poems and research the history and legends associated with this very Chinese art form. But it wasn't just a hobby. Dafu's love of *da-you* poetry meant that in all our years of marriage there was never a dull moment between us. They made us happy in the bitter times, and thoughtful in the happy times. Our marriage may have been a consequence of the founding of the PRC, but our love was a road paved by *da-you* poetry, a long journey which began that day we went to visit his family.

After several hours of walking we stumbled upon a pathway, a low bank of earth set between two fields. Looking up, the landscape stretched out before us as far as the eye could see. I turned to Dafu and asked how much further there was to go. Still staring into the distance, he said:

> The heavens are high,
> The earth is low.
> Joy lies therein,
> If your heart makes it so.

What he meant was that our feelings are controlled by the heart and the mind. The only way to stay happy is to have a positive outlook on life.

Struck with admiration for his artistic talent, I did my best to follow up with my own verse:

> The universe is boundless,
> Its history has no end.
> But we, like words in poems,
> Endeavour to transcend.

I was trying to say that no matter how intimidating the world seems, or how meaningless your life feels, we must all strive to leave our mark in the short time we have here.

Hearing me respond in the same poetic form, Dafu stopped in his tracks. He stood there, quite still, for what seemed like an eternity, looking right into my eyes without saying a word. Later he told me that all he wanted to do was take me into his arms and kiss me!

In the midst of those political storms we would later run into, we'd often think back to that gruelling journey we made to Dafu's family home, and the *da-you* poems we told on the way. It gave us the strength to carry on. Just as Dafu said, it's all about how you choose to look at life. That was an important lesson to learn before we arrived in Dafu's village to celebrate Spring Festival 1950 with his family. As I said, I didn't mind the supposed cultural gap between us, but the living conditions I found there were quite a challenge.

Night had fallen by the time our heavy legs carried us into his village. A man at the entrance recognised Dafu, and it wasn't long before faces started popping out from behind every door and lots of men came out to follow us. By the time we reached Dafu's home, news had already reached his family, and they were there waiting for us outside the front door of their home. His parents, younger brother, two younger sisters and grandma were all there.

His second brother Dagui had gone deaf a few years back from a falling bomb. No one in the village could even say which army was responsible for the bombing. Those poor peasant villages had lost so many lives to the endless political fighting that it hardly made any difference. His first sister Chunhua was sixteen, his second, Guihua, thirteen. One by one, Dafu introduced us and told me what I should call them. I found it all a little strange at first, partly because everyone in the village treated us as if we were already married.

I also found it difficult getting used to the way their family addressed one another. The *Yeye* and *Nainai* for his grandpa and grandma were what I was used to, but they called their father *Di'e*, their mother *Niang*, and a husband and wife 'duixiang'. *Duixiang* was what I was used to calling two people who were dating, but in Shandong Province it seemed that even old married couples were still called that.

Lastly, I couldn't get my head around their body language. All of them, young and old, would compete with each other to hold my hand;

some of the older women would stroke my face, while the naughty little ones would pull my hair.

Once we had paid visits to all Dafu's close friends, his relatives and neighbours gathered together and went into the family home. It was very dark inside, with just a single small oil lamp flickering on a platform built into the wall. I couldn't see what was what, or who was who – I could hear Dafu's voice, but there were lots of people between us. It seemed like the whole village had followed us in there!

People in Dafu's village slept on a *kang*. Most households only had one room in the house, and it acted as both a living room and a bedroom. During the day, the whole family would sit on the *kang* to eat, chat and receive guests. By the evening, they would roll out the bedding stored at the foot of the *kang* and the whole family would sleep there, their feet stretched out towards the far side of the wall. On one end of the *kang* would be a stove, used for cooking food and boiling water in the day and warming the bed by night. In the other half of the room, many families also kept a shrine with an image of the Guanyin Goddess, memorial tablets for ancestors and incense burners. An outer room would be used as a space to store all kinds of family goods, from grain, to farming tools, to water containers. In summer they'd store firewood and assorted pieces of furniture. Dafu said that the outer room would also be used as a place to cool off in the summer, sometimes even to greet guests.

That night, I slept between Dafu's two sisters and his grandma. Dafu's parents slept in the middle, acting as a boundary between the men and women, with Dafu and Dagui sleeping on the other side. I heard Dafu and his father talking until very late. The *kang* was quite hard, but nice and warm, and the mattress gave off the sweet smell of winter sun. My mind was restless, thinking of all the exciting things I had come across on my journey there. It took me a while, but then I finally drifted off. I don't think I've ever slept so well.

When I awoke the next day, I saw that I was the only one still lying there on the *kang*. I got up in a hurry, making a pathetic attempt at rolling up my bedding and placing it on top of the pile the others had made. Through one open window – paper, not glass, of course – I saw lots of chickens, ducks and geese pottering about in the yard, and a black-and-white mongrel dog. Getting off the *kang*, I saw on a table opposite a number of memorial tablets with the surname Meng, presumably those of Dafu's ancestors.

Entering the outer room, I saw piles of goods so big it looked like a grocery store. Near the entrance, Dafu's grandmother was stripping off kernels from a corn cob. When the old lady heard me coming, she turned to face me with a big smile, saying, 'You must be tired, little one. There's some breakfast left for you on the stove; go and grab it. You can eat here and keep me company.'

'Good morning, Grandma!' I greeted her while looking around for my breakfast. On a pile of wood there was a huge iron pot, at the bottom of which was a bowl of poached eggs being kept warm by the water. The three eggs were dazzlingly white and surrounded by osmanthus flowers. I picked up the bowl but couldn't find a spoon, and had to make do with a pair of wooden chopsticks I found in the container on the side. I grabbed a stool and went to sit beside Grandma. The old lady didn't say a word, but kept smiling and glancing over in my direction.

Just as I finished my last mouthful, someone walked into the courtyard. They were covered from head to toe in soot.

'Morning, Little Green. How did you sleep?' If it wasn't for his voice, I don't think I would have recognised Dafu.

'Morning. Sorry, I overslept and only just got up. What, er, what happened?' I could barely stop myself from laughing out loud.

Dafu didn't notice my expression. 'You're a city girl, used to waking up to the sound of bells. Us country folk wake up when the cock crows. Have you finished your breakfast? Would you mind doing a little job with me? The rest of the family have gone out to buy New Year gifts and will join everyone else to watch second grandpa kill a pig. For now, though, let's go and help uncle Meng Xiang next door clean out his *kang*.' The men in that village were almost all named Meng, their ancestry being intertwined.

I went with Dafu to his uncle's house, where we worked through the morning cleaning out the old man's *kang* flue. Before leaving, we prepared firewood and boiled some water for him. We returned home covered in soot and dust, but thankfully Guihua had prepared a basin of water to wash ourselves with.

Dafu let me go first, and when I had finished I went to throw the water out into the yard. Dafu stopped me: 'Let me wash first, then we can pour it out.'

I looked at him in shock: 'This water's as black as ink!'

'Water is as precious as oil here,' Dafu said as he began to wash himself. When he put his face into the basin of ink, it really did come out clean. As he wiped his face with the towel I gave him, he teased me, 'Look, I can change faces like Sun Wukong!'*

I laughed, both out loud and in my heart. This was a man who could turn bitterness into the joyful seasoning of life – a true revolutionary.

Dafu's village was very poor, but when it came to celebrating Spring Festival they had lots of customs. I can never completely remember how things work, even after all these years.

In the time leading up to Spring Festival, people from Shandong like to prepare a huge amount of *mantou*, because people from those parts eat a lot of wheat products. Some of those buns are very different to the ones we usually eat, like *zaoshan*, which are filled with dates. Apart from *mantou* there are also steamed bean rolls, New Year cakes, and lots of other bread-type foods whose names I can't remember. In some places, it's traditional to make all of these on the day before New Year's Eve. They would also prepare fried dough balls, all kinds of meat and fish, and other foods traditionally eaten during the New Year celebrations.

Every day of the festival was carefully planned out, right down to each mouthful you ate and each movement you made. It was said that these were rules passed down from their ancestors and therefore couldn't be broken. For example, at midday on New Year's Eve, you would stick the traditional Spring Festival calligraphy on your door, then visit the graves of your ancestors in the afternoon

---

* Sun Wukong, also known as the Monkey King, is a mythological figure best known as a main character in the Ming dynasty novel *Journey to the West*.

to pay your respects, praying for the spirits to carry them back home for Spring Festival. After that, the whole family would make dumplings together.

On New Year's Day, activities start from midnight, when the head of the family leads everyone in offering sacrifices to the heavens, the earth, the gods and the spirits of the family dead, before beginning the first meal of the Spring Festival – dumplings. When boiling the dumplings, you also have to set off firecrackers. Dafu's grandma said that this was to drive away evil spirits and the bad luck they might bring you.

In some areas, stalks of sesame plants must be used when lighting the fire to boil the dumplings, symbolising how the new year is like the sesame flower, which grows taller every day, just as your days will get better and better. Plenty of dumplings should be cooked, enough so that there are some left over. When the dumplings are ready, first you fill a bowl to give thanks to the gods, then another bowl specifically for the kitchen god, then yet another bowl, this one for your ancestors. A few extra bowls would be filled but the food left untouched, to symbolise a growing family.

Some of the dumplings you eat at Spring Festival have money, dates or chestnuts in them. Eating a dumpling with dates inside signifies that you'll be very successful in your work in the coming year; if you eat a chestnut it means you will have great physical strength; peanuts symbolise a long life; while money means you'll make a fortune that year. No matter who ends up eating what, everyone offers their heartfelt congratulations to those lucky enough to come across one of these 'treats'. Parents are happiest when their child gets the money dumpling, because they think it means he has a bright future ahead of him. You also need to encourage all the children present with a little pocket money too.

On the morning of New Year's Day, everyone gets up early for another meal of steamed buns, date bread and sticky cakes, as well as lots of different kinds of dough balls and starch noodles. All the vegetables are steamed together to make a dish called 'full larder', symbolising how the family will have sufficient food for the coming year. Dafu also told me that in lots of places in Shandong, people make sure they only eat vegetable-filled dumplings, to symbolise a peaceful year ahead.

As soon as breakfast is over, it's time for *bainian*, where people visit family and friends to wish each other a happy start to the new year. Men and married women take part, but always separately. First there is the *jinbai*, greeting relatives within the fifth degree of kinship, followed by the *yuanbai*, greeting friends and relatives more than five times removed.

The first time I went to Dafu's home, all the younger generation had to kowtow to their elders during the *bainian*. It's not like nowadays, where most youngsters get away with a little bow. Businessmen always greeted each other with the traditional phrase, 'May you have a prosperous New Year!' When the younger generations greet the older generations, the elders are expected to give them some so-called 'lucky money', normally in a red envelope.

The day after New Year, women who have married outside the village return home to pay respects to their family. If they bring children, the relatives also have to give the children 'lucky money'.

On the third day, there is the bizarre custom of 'scooping the crescent moon'. Mothers bring their children into the courtyard, where they kneel on a prayer mat facing the new moon. With a spoon in one hand, they first pretend to take a few bites from the moon, then act as if they were taking a few scoops out of their own chest, all the while chanting:

Today we scoop the crescent moon,
Holes in our teeth will all be gone soon.

It's said that this 'scooping' will prevent children from having toothache over the next year.

For the fourth and fifth days, the locals have a saying: 'Pinch the fourth and break the fifth'. On the fourth day you make dumplings, placing inside them all the unhappy feelings you have had over the past year. On the morning of the fifth, you boil the dumplings until they've slightly broken, as if breaking all the unhappiness before the start of the new year. Not only that, but at dawn on the fifth day you put out all the rubbish you've collected from the house in a pile on the street. You then set off 'double-bang' firecrackers on top of the pile, an act known as 'seeing off the poor earth' that symbolises breaking free from poverty.

I can't think of everything Shandong people eat at New Year. There's too much to remember and it seems to change every year anyway, depending on the zodiac. Dafu has a good way of putting it, though – at New Year, every day is different, from the first day to the fifteenth, but it's all based around one thing – dumplings! Different types of dumplings, and different ways to eat them.

For an out-of-towner like me, the hardest part wasn't so much knowing what to do when I was with Dafu and his family, but not knowing what *not* to do! It seemed they had more taboos than there are blades of grass on the earth, or clouds in the sky. His grandma would always be nagging me about one thing or another.

Most of them were things you couldn't do on New Year's Day – carry water, sweep the floor, hit or insult other people. Some people didn't do any needlework or make dumplings, eat meat or grind garlic. At night you couldn't put on any oil lamps, as it was said that the light would attract a swarm of rats into your home. If you broke anything on New Year's Day, you had to say out loud the magic words: 'May you have peace year on year', to expel the bad luck.

If you're boiling dumplings and one breaks, you shouldn't say it 'broke' but rather that it 'fought', to represent how you'll fight to make money in the coming year. You can't say *dasuan* [garlic] either, in case your tongue slips and you end up saying *san*, as in 'to break'.

There are so many rules! That's probably why my children dread going back to their home town for Spring Festival.

Dafu said that although people who had lived for generations in the fields might not read or write so well, they had other life skills. Men learned the ways of the earth from their fathers; women learned from their mothers how to run a house, from one generation to the next.

In times of suffering – be it natural or man-made – these peasants take comfort in their belief in the earth, the sky, feng shui and the spirits. That's why, at the beginning of every lunar year, people offer tributes to the spirits, showing how honest and sincere they are, begging them to bring health and prosperity to their families. Although they remain living in poverty year after year, sometimes even having their families ripped apart and left destitute by the chaos of war, they attribute their suffering to their own errors. They never blame the spirits.

That's just the way we Chinese live. When it came to our generation, the spirits were the Communist Party – we believed in them unconditionally. But young people nowadays, they have no faith. Don't get me wrong, they *want* to have something to believe in; they scour the earth in search of something to believe in. But they always come up short because faith does not live inside their hearts. It's like the old saying goes: 'If you believe it, it will come true. If you don't, it won't.'

I didn't respond to Green, as my thoughts were elsewhere. I was thinking about what the Chinese believe in, and how we have survived the past hundred years when the idols of our belief have changed so often. It's a question I have been mulling over ever since I first became a radio presenter and journalist in the 1980s, but one which I have yet to find an answer to.

As I listened, Green's story was like a river flowing, watering my memories of my mother's life; although she is a similar age to Green, she has never shared her thoughts with me, her own daughter.

Meng Dafu had no university education; his intelligence came from his life experience. The people in his village are also like that. When they come to the city they are completely vulnerable, but they are still able to survive on the fringes of society. We city folk can bring a bellyful of scholarly education to the countryside, but it doesn't mean we'll be able to get by, because our intellect and understanding of the world is too rigid. We have no space to adapt.

I think that we deserve to be called a loving husband and wife – Dafu has always been the hero of my heart. It may be true that we Chinese don't often praise our own families, but I'm Green, and I use words of kindness to plant green hopes and happiness for my family to live off. Dafu is like this too; he has always taken the most pleasure from helping others. Just like during that Spring Festival in 1950: every day we were there it seemed that Dafu was always helping out one old person or another, even on New Year's Day. When we left on the third day, seven or eight elderly locals came out to thank him. I won't forget that scene for the rest of my life.

All Dafu's family are extremely kind people. His sister told me that their village had a lot of old people who lived alone because their sons had all been conscripted into the army, while the daughters had been married off and couldn't come home to look after their parents. Dafu's deaf younger brother Dagui would go from door to door with a group of young children, helping the elderly folk with their daily needs. As for their own family's household tasks, that was all the responsibility of the parents, the sisters and the grandma. For country folk like them, war wasn't a case of bringing justice to the world or punishing evil; it was simply about losing one's family and one's home.

To this day I find it strange that I wasn't the least bit put off by the poverty I encountered there. Even when I was using a toilet surrounded by pigs, chopping firewood on the mountainside till my hands bled, carrying yokes of water for so long that my shoulders swelled up in pain, I never thought about leaving Dafu. I felt very moved, very proud seeing my beloved walking around every household in the village helping those less fortunate than him. The radiance of his character completely concealed our differences in education. What Mr Pan said all those years ago — about planting 'green hopes in people's hearts' — I've kind of taken on as my motto.

When I got back to Beiping, I carried on with my studies. Father had already paid the fees for Orange and me up until we graduated from university. Despite the great political changes happening around us, our school still stuck to traditional teaching methods and the same payment agreements. Dafu could only come and take me out at weekends, and when he did we found out where the most vulnerable old people lived and went to help them out in any way we could.

The difference between winter and summer in Beijing is like the difference between ice and fire — winter temperatures can go as low as minus 20; summers regularly reach over 40 degrees Celsius. In winter we would help the old people dry their clothes, move furniture, sweep their chimneys. It was almost impossible back then to find coal that didn't produce a lot of smoke, and most families had to burn coal chunks the size of a child's fist. The chimneys all had very narrow openings with many curves and turns, which prevented the cold wind blowing in, but meant that they easily got blocked by ash from the smoke. In those days, gas poisoning killed many people, and there were numerous examples of people choking or getting dizzy from the coal gas.

In summer, we'd bathe them, help them wash their mattresses and make their beds. In those days we didn't use bedcovers, and washing sheets was a nightmare. Quilts were made up of two parts: the underside and the cover. The underside was bigger, so you needed to take the two sides apart and refill the cotton padding before stitching them back together in what was known as 'cottoning up'.

I learned about quilts from Dafu's sister Chunhua. She used to say that making a quality quilt is one of a woman's main skills. A bed with a good quilt leaves a good impression. The covers should have even stitching, and the cotton inside must have the same thickness throughout, with equal spacing and careful stitching.

When the weather was good in spring and autumn, we would take a few elderly people out for walks in the local parks and green areas. There was a lot of greenery in Beijing in those days; you'd even find fields of crops being tended to by the farmers. It was like how Dafu described his home town – a painting for every season. Spring and autumn brought particularly stunning colours. Sometimes we'd borrow bicycles and ride out to the Summer Palace, Fragrant Hills or other scenic spots to go rowing or hiking.

We couldn't meet very often, though, as Dafu's place of work was located a long way from my school. The United Front was a secret government department from the 1950s to the 1980s, tasked with catching underground spies from the Kuomintang, although from the 1980s onwards they started helping ordinary Chinese to search for their missing families in Taiwan and overseas. Dafu was always very busy with work in the middle of nowhere at that point, and I was busy with school. I was involved in a lot of student union activities on top of my studies, and I remember having to spend hours and hours taking extra Russian classes. In those days, our idea of what 'international' meant was firmly rooted in Soviet socialism; America's influence back then was tiny.

We did learn a bit about the UK, though. Our textbooks mentioned the history of how 'the sun never sets on the British Empire', all the colonies Britain once controlled, the supremacy they had over the seas, and how Magna Carta had influenced basic human law worldwide. We read about their industry as well, that sort of thing.

In those days we saw America as a country without any real historical influence. For Chinese educated in the 1950s, our understanding of the world was seen through the window of the Soviets – their language, their history, their definition of current affairs. There was also Soviet literature, especially the poetry of Alexander Pushkin, Maxim Gorky's *The Mother*, Nikolai Ostrovsky's *How the Steel Was Tempered*, Tolstoy's *War and Peace*, Boris Pasternak's *Doctor Zhivago* and so on: these were all standards of 'understanding the world'. And their music too, of course, especially Tchaikovsky. In those days we had no doubt that the Soviets would lead us to victory against the Americans and the Brits!

Did Dafu and I write letters to each other often? No, not really. Firstly, because the country's postal service hadn't yet stabilised after the war. Secondly, because of the nature of Dafu's work, all the mail he sent and received was opened and read beforehand. We didn't want others reading about our love, or laughing at the poems we wrote for each other. Instead, before we parted ways each time we met, we would give each other the love letters we'd written the week before. This caused a bit of confusion sometimes, as these letters would always be a week behind current events.

Did we write poetry? There was very little we didn't write! Dafu liked his *da-you* poems, of course, and I used to tease him, saying he couldn't sit still to write anything longer or more complex than that. He said he didn't have the time to write properly. He had tried before he went to bed, but as soon as he'd pick up the pen and paper he'd fall asleep. But *da-you* poems could be written on the move, and they were easy to remember too. He could scribble them down just before we met up.

As for me, I liked translating Russian for him, or finding quotes from foreign literature. I loved reading the poetry of Pushkin.

During the period following liberation, people's hearts were full of excitement. Their blood boiled with passion stirred by government propaganda – take pride in your ethnicity; help rebuild the motherland; liberate the human race; let the people be masters of their own fate; men and women are equal; beat the landlords and split up their land; hail joint public–private enterprises! This passion was so raw that movie audiences would stand and cheer when they saw a revolutionary soldier kill an enemy.

That's why you had to be careful if you went on a date to the cinema. You'd have to be on guard for any outbreak of revolutionary passion from the crowd, otherwise you'd be left seated while everyone else would be jumping up and down in a frenzy. At best you'd be laughed at, at worst someone might start questioning your political allegiance.

You saw dating in some of the old movies themselves, from the early 1950s. From the late 1950s onwards, portrayals of dating and love in general became less widespread. But even in films about revolution, you still saw people expressing their eternal love. Dafu and I rarely went to the cinema together, but I do remember seeing *The Story of Liubao Village* with him at least three times.

People say we Chinese don't understand fashions and trends, but I disagree entirely. We're so scared of falling behind others that it's not just the latest luxury Western fashions we follow, it's everything from political trends to cultural values – even what to eat for good health. But these fashions we adopt and then change with each generation, and with that change comes great loss. Even the films we used to watch back then, the opera we listened to, how much of that have young people today heard of? For example, do you know anything about the plot of *The Story of Liubao Village*? It was the very model for dating for my generation!

The Story of Liubao Village was made in 1957, but it's set during the War of Resistance Against Japan. The New Fourth Army were stationed in a village called Liubao, where there was a beautiful young woman called Ermeizi. A wounded soldier, Li Jin, is sent to recuperate and rest at her house, where the pair gradually develop strong feelings for one another. When the unit leader finds out he scolds Li Jin, because according to army rules soldiers weren't allowed to be in any kind of relationship.

Li Jin is talked round by the political instructor into obeying orders, and for the time being agrees to cut off contact with Ermeizi. Not long afterwards, the unit is called up to the front line, and Li Jin and Ermeizi reluctantly part ways. A few years later, Li Jin's unit once again comes through Liubao, where Li Jin – who is now a company commandeer – goes looking for Ermeizi. Ermeizi has joined a guerrilla force and become a Party member. She has been waiting for Li Jin all along, and they are finally reunited in the place they promised they would meet again years ago. Their love finds a way in the end.

There is a part in the film where Ermeizi makes her little brother send word to Li Jin to meet her by the side of a small bridge. Li Jin is so happy that he doesn't know what to do, rushing to a nearby tree and doing a somersault off one of its branches. You may laugh, but every time we watched that bit, Dafu would reach over quietly and squeeze my hand. The way that film was made is so clever: we don't even need to see them together to understand how much they love each other. It's not like today, where you see people gnawing each other's faces for hours without ever really believing there's any true affection between them.

The family tree weathers the political storms

I graduated from university in 1952. At the time, the country was calling on people to have lots of children, to increase the population of the motherland. That's why we married the following year, and went on to have five children – three sons and two daughters – in quick succession.

We didn't go back to Dafu's home for the wedding, because we only had two days of marriage leave and wouldn't have had time to go all the way back to Shandong. By then, I didn't even have a home to go back to. Orange had taken Mr Pan back to Chengde once, where our old home was now being used as a convalescence home for some of our country's leaders. In the exact spot where all those years ago my father had tied colourful ribbons around the trees for my mother just before they married now stood a huge sign: MILITARY LAND: NON-MILITARY PERSONNEL PROHIBITED.

You know, despite being revolutionaries back then, our generation were all very diligent when it came to marriage. Most people worked for the state, so after they married their work unit would arrange for them to be housed in a room in a collective dormitory. In those days it was all free of charge, I suppose because there were a lot fewer people than there are now.

In the room we were allocated, there were two single beds, which we moved together. Portraits of Chairman Mao and General Zhu De hung on the walls, while above the doorway we had some big red calligraphy cut-outs for good luck. The room was very simple; we only got furniture later on through handouts from our work unit or colleagues who were moving out of their homes. Only when Dafu reached the rank of junior officer did we move into an apartment, a two-bedroom one-living room apartment. It was still very simple, and we were allocated just a few basic household items and kitchen utensils.

Apart from what we ate, what we wore and a few everyday items, everything was free. The apartment, nursery, school, work after graduation and healthcare for the whole family were all provided for by the man's work unit. That's why, in those days, the state encouraged couples to work together in the same unit: they could better allocate social security benefits. Your work unit was like your family, or perhaps even more important than family, because it was the best and perhaps only way to ensure that all your relatives were well looked after.

Orange and Mr Pan couldn't come to our wedding, saying they had foreign affairs business to attend to. Only later did we find out that this had something to do with the UN intervention in the Korean Civil War in 1950. The new China feared a pincer attack from the US in the north and Chiang Kai-shek in the south. They desperately needed Soviet assistance, but the Sino-Soviet relationship was already badly bruised by then. Orange and Mr Pan were working day and night to handle the sudden change in diplomatic relations. From that year on, I rarely had contact with any of my sisters. They all were involved in state intelligence work, which prevented us having much contact.

When I gave birth to my first son, Tiger, we brought the sixteen-year-old Guihua to Beijing from her home town to help us look after the baby. Later, we arranged for her to go to school, and Dafu's mother came to Beijing in her place. By that time, we had already had our second son, Wolf. Later, after Dafu's grandma passed away, we asked his grandpa to come and take her place, but the old man said that he couldn't leave the deaf Dagui behind alone.

Desperate to help out, Dafu used his influence to secure Dagui a mailroom job in Beijing. And so it came to be that the whole family was reunited in Beijing. The two daughters and one son we had later were all looked after as infants by the old man. The country had run into a lot of trouble by then, and even though Dafu had achieved a high rank, we were still in that tiny apartment. In fact, things were so crowded that we used the living room as an extra bedroom. It was a full house, but a happy one too.

The Cultural Revolution? That was a painful time, not least because the United Front where Dafu worked was torn apart and left for dead. But Dafu himself was on the rise. His poor background served him well, as did the fact that he hadn't yet become powerful enough to be considered a target. That's why our house wasn't searched; no one came to confiscate our possessions or denounce us as counter-revolutionaries or anything like that. Compared with so many other families, we did all right. But just like everyone else we lived in a constant state of anxiety, unable to tell which way the political winds would blow next. That's what made following others such a dangerous game – no one could tell who would be the next to fall.

It's still hard for me to talk about these things. I'd rather focus on the good times, the ones worth storing up inside. When the time is right, we can speak again about everything else. All I'll say is that it was very hard for families to walk into the present day. To live in peace is better than having any lofty ambitions, wouldn't you agree?

Our family wasn't just us, though; it was the whole of Dafu's village. If any of the villagers had reason to come to Beijing, they would always come and stay with us. On some summer days, you'd find three or four people sleeping on makeshift beds out in our courtyard. Dafu's parents always said that if you go back far enough, we all come from the same root.

We began to notice how every time the villagers came to stay with us, there would be something ever so slightly different about them. When our children were small, the most the villagers could bring us was a few sweet potatoes or a few pears, and in return we would give them some of our rations of food or clothing to take home. Later, they started bringing us local speciality goods, and we would give them little radios, children's books, clothes, toys and things like that. Dafu also started giving them ideas about how to develop the local agriculture industry, and contacts for fertiliser suppliers.

Later still, they started bringing all sorts of fruits and different kinds of grains for us. By then, apart from squeezing money into their pockets, there wasn't much we could give them because they didn't lack anything in their lives, aside from perhaps some big electrical products which we had. Later, Dafu helped connect them with market channels to sell their local products in a number of cities. The gap in living standards between us grew smaller with each passing day. These past two years, we've even been discussing whether to move back to Dafu's home town to enjoy our retirement. The air is good, and the food is all grown locally. My biggest regret is that Dafu's parents didn't live to see the good days we have now; they had died by the time Reform and Opening Up came around.

We couldn't do anything to help Chunhua, though. Her husband's family wouldn't agree to leave their countryside home. Her father-in-law said, 'For generations all we've dreamed of is owning our own plot of land. Now the country's given us one, it'd be a disgrace to just waste it. Why the need for all this change? Change is what has messed things up in this country!'

The sad thing is, that of all Chunhua's grandchildren, not one of them now looks after that plot of land – they've all run off to make a living in the city.

When I got home to London, I found an email from Green waiting for me in my inbox. It had in it over ten of Dafu's *da-you* poems, and six of Green's poems. Meng Dafu's *da-you* had the simple and unassuming style of the countryside, while Green's poems had a classical and European feel. More than anything, this made me think that since 1949, Chinese people had been brought together from all different levels of education, awareness, class and knowledge. They had all been brought together by the politics of their time.

Green – she really can plant beautiful green hopes of life in people's hearts. Or in my heart, at least.

PART III

A Bird's Love during the Cultural Revolution

|||||||||||||||||||||||||||||||||||||||||||||||||||||||||||||||||||||||||||||||||

Green's Daughter

CRANE

· born 1958 ·

Before we parted ways, I asked Green one last question: if I was to interview just one of her children, which one would she recommend?

She had to think about this for some time, gathering her thoughts in silence.

'My five children had very similar upbringings: all of them were born in the 1950s or 1960s, all grew up in the same city and all went to the same schools. But in terms of personality, they couldn't be more different. And they have completely contrasting views on life and the direction this country has gone in.

'My husband Dafu used to say:

Our house is like a zoo,
All kinds of beasts on view.
There's tigers, wolves, cranes and monkeys,
You may even find a little ducky.
To top it all off, in that crazy old house,
The mother's a cat, and the father's a mouse.

'Dafu worked as an undercover "mouse" for the United Front, whereas I was a "cat" searching out those traitors who had supposedly betrayed our country. The cat was in charge at home as well. Oh yes, despite his illustrious career, Dafu wasn't the most practical man around the house. When he went to the market, he'd pay but forget to pick up the vegetables; changing light bulbs, he'd always try and screw them the wrong way; he once put a bowl covered with a metal lid into the microwave and it went off like a bomb! In his own words, he still "hadn't got the hang of city life".

'The names of our five children all end with the character *guo*, meaning "country". But their nicknames, chosen by their grandparents, all come from animals. It's a bit of fun, really. But perhaps, as the elders used to say, your name reveals your true character – which is another way of saying your name has a huge influence on your feng shui later in life. It's been that way with my children, anyhow.

'My eldest son, Meng Jianguo, has the nickname Tiger. His is a very calm, steady character, and the way he acts is actually very similar to my husband and me. His children say he's old-fashioned, and they're terrified of those flashes of his tiger-like rage. He's lucky: he had a son and daughter just before the one-child policy was introduced.

'His wife once told me about a time she had been debating the current state of China with her two children. The young ones were complaining, asking why, compared to how the Western world had developed, the last two generations of our country had been so politically ignorant and economically backward. Tiger, who had been sitting reading the paper nearby, suddenly jumped out of his seat in a furious rage. Banging the table with every other word, he roared, "If you two could only understand the indulgent nonsense of Western democracy, and not the live-or-die simplicity of Chinese politics, then you should have a think about what Chinese people have been through over the last hundred years. You fools! The last thing we need is for the lives of our countrymen, and the price they paid, to be defined by your muddled, idiotic minds. I'd like to see you try living through what we lived through! No, you read a few pages of Western commentary making jokes out of our misery, criticising China's present without the faintest idea that our great country is rooted in thousands of years of history. Impudence! Arrogance! Ignorance!"

'The two children were scared witless. Needless to say, they never dared talk about national affairs in front of their father again. What were his views? Probably something similar to what you'd find in the *People's Daily*.

'Our second son is called Meng Weiguo. When he was very small we used to call him Little Buddy, but we started calling him Wolf when we decided that all our children were to have animal nicknames.

Wolf is probably best described as elusive and stubborn. He's very competitive, mind you, always trying to compete with his elder brother in one way or another. But by almost any standard you can think of, Tiger is far more accomplished, with his successful career and loving family. Wolf has always been, well, a lone wolf, travelling extensively without ever settling down in one place.

'I suppose that's why he thinks he was born ahead of his time – people nowadays, they respect tigers but look down on wolves. Of all our five children, he's the most impulsive, and the one his father and I still worry about most. I'm afraid Wolf's story would be a little too dark, not such an objective representation of the overall experience of his generation.

'Our third child, and first daughter, is Meng Aiguo. We call her Crane. When she was little she never cried or made a fuss over things. She would just sit there quietly, watching her brothers play or observing the adults going about their daily tasks. My husband and I used to worry that she might have some kind of learning difficulty, but my mother-in-law was adamant that we were wrong. "Children who don't speak," she said, "always grow up to be the deepest thinkers."

'Some people say she's a woman who stands aloof from the world, but as parents we've come to realise it's actually the complete opposite. Crane knows exactly what she wants, and exactly how to get it. She has this uncanny ability to understand what's going on around her, and is often able to point out some small mistake people may otherwise have overlooked. I'd say Crane is probably the best candidate for your search.

'Then there's our third son – Meng Baoguo, or Monkey. You could see the monkey in him from the moment he started walking. He would always be jumping around the house, and when he spoke you could never get a word in edgeways. Later, he became obsessed with computers. Whenever any kind of new computer technology came to China, he'd be one of the first to get his hands on it. But he seemed to lose touch with everyday life, and he lacks what I would call human feelings. God knows where he got those genes from. No, you won't get hold of Monkey, he won't waste time talking about something other than computers.

'Finally, there's Meng Liguo. She didn't have an animal nickname to begin with either. We used to call her Little Ya. But then she started speaking very young, and she was constantly giggling and babbling on like a little duck, so we called her Duck, or Ducky. Her elder brothers and sisters would tease her by saying that she was an ugly duckling, and my father-in-law would say she was "a little duck with a big mouth", because she never stopped talking. When she later heard the fairy tale "The Ugly Duckling", every time the others made fun of her she would pout and say, "You wait and see. One day I'll turn into a beautiful swan, and you'll all be nothing but my stupid duck brothers and sisters."

'Talk to Ducky? I fear you might be spending the next ten years going through the notes you'd make with her. There'd be more pages than there are leaves in a forest!'

'So, Xinran, if you're looking for someone who'll talk about every little detail, and I mean *every* little detail, then Duck's your best option. But if you want to understand the true feelings of that generation, then I'd go with Crane – she can give you the deepest and most profound reflection. She doesn't talk to the family all that much, but she's the only one of our children who's stayed on good terms with all her siblings. They trust Crane completely, and open up to her about their problems – even Wolf.

'Go and speak to Crane; I'll help put you in touch. You won't be disappointed, believe me.'

A bird driven out of the nest by Mao's Order

My very first thought about Meng Aiguo was how much I loved her nickname. Apart from swans, cranes are the bird I'm most fond of. When we met I wasn't disappointed; she really was as Green had described – gentle, insightful, thoughtful.

We first met in Beijing, soon after I had returned from interviewing her mother in Qingdao.

I was pleasantly surprised when Crane asked if we could meet at the pavilion in Beijing's Taoran Park, as my grandmother had often taken me there as a child. Located in the city's Xicheng District, the park was one of the first public spaces built after the founding of the People's Republic of China in 1949. The lush trees, waterfront pavilions and shaded pathways make it one of the most pleasant and scenic places in the city – its name, Taoran, means 'carefree'.

The pavilion has a much longer history than the park itself. Built in 1695, the thirty-fourth year of the Qing dynasty Emperor Kangxi's rule, it is one of China's Four Great Pavilions. The story goes that the court official who had the pavilion built loved the Tang poet Bai Juyi and took its name from his poem 'A Drink with My Friend Mengde':

Wait till the chrysanthemums are yellow,
And the home-made wine is ripe.
I'll drink with you and be carefree.

My grandmother had told me that, for as long as she could remember, Taoran's pavilion had been famous and attracted an endless stream of visitors. Many of these were southerners living in Beijing, who would meet up there at weekends to reminisce about their home towns.

Since I moved to the UK in 1997, every time I go back to China my schedule is completely packed, and it's hard to find the time to return to my home town or indulge in any kind of nostalgia for my childhood. A few years ago, though, I found myself near the park with my husband Toby. I tried to persuade him to go in, but he was put off by the great crowds of people at the gate and the blaring music of the 'dancing aunties' in the square outside, and I only caught a faraway glimpse of the pavilion, the image of which was lodged deep in my childhood memories.

I couldn't help but feel that it was fate, therefore, as well as Crane, that had brought me back to this place. Fate, or perhaps divine intervention.

For two days straight, we met at the park's gate before taking a stroll along those shaded pathways, past those waterfront pavilions reflected on the lake. As the sunlight filtered through the stained-glass canopy of leaves, we shared the flavours of Crane's life and love: sweet, sour, bitter, spicy – it seemed to have them all.

On the first day, Crane turned to me and said, ever so gently: 'My mother tells me you two spoke a great deal. And did I hear you also interviewed my aunt? Now it seems to be my turn. My mother said you want to know everything, and that I should speak about whatever I want. So tell me, Xinran, what is it that you want to *hear*?'

Crane's question, with the emphasis on 'hear', shocked me somewhat. She didn't ask what I wanted to know, as almost all interviewees do, but rather what I wanted to *hear*. The talk that followed left me in no doubt that she really was like her namesake, perched patiently on the bank of a river, waiting in silence for the ripple of a fish.

'We're both nearing sixty. We've both heard countless tales of our ancestors, and we've both witnessed much of what our parents have lived through. The books of our lives would be pages and pages thick, and if you were to add to that the stories of our own children they would be boundless. So what is it that you want to hear? Give me a topic, and I'll do my best to help you understand the Chinese stories you seek.'

The moment she said these words, it was as if a path had suddenly appeared under our feet. I knew then how important Crane would be to this book. I told her very frankly that the book I wanted to write would be about the love lives of Chinese people over the past hundred years. The four or five generations who have lived through these times have very different stories to tell when it comes to love, their experiences having been shaped by the chaos and turmoil of war, the changing political situation, technological breakthroughs, and many other reasons. I wanted to hear about her experience alongside other members of her family to better my understanding of Chinese families, women's history in this period, and human nature in general.

'Stories of our love lives?' Crane blushed for a brief moment, but she quickly regained her usual composure. 'There's a saying doing the rounds online that those of us who grew up in the 1950s are the children of the revolution, void of love and passion. You've heard that too, I presume?'

'Yes, I've heard that. I've even interviewed people who think they fall into that category. But it's not a view I subscribe to myself. Love is a human instinct – it can be suppressed, but never destroyed.' I was perhaps a little too forceful in my response, but only because it's something I believe in with all my heart.

Crane smiled ever so slightly. 'Indeed. Love is part of the natural order of the world. You can see it in the birds, the fish, the insects, even the flowers. How could something as fleeting as war suppress human instinct? We just had to develop different ways of dealing with and adapting to the situation at hand.

'I hear we're the same age, both born in 1958. It wasn't until 1975, when I was seventeen, that I had any kind of romantic feelings towards a man. What about you?'

But before I could reply, Crane was already off, telling the story of her life so purposefully it was as if she was speaking to herself.

Hindsight is a precious thing, isn't it? So much of what we know about our lives is learned afterwards. At the time, in the moment we're actually there, we can't comprehend our own experience. That's particularly true of our generation of Chinese. From the moment we were born to the moment we became parents ourselves, the stories of our lives were defined by a political narrative written by the generation before us.

These days, my mother goes around telling everyone she meets that our family have always been happy together, because she's the kind of person who prefers good news to bad. But the way I remember it, war placed a great strain on our family when I was growing up. My parents would come and go in hurried panic without ever having a moment's peace between them. They wouldn't even have time to spend with us at weekends or during the Spring Festival. We were all brought up by my father's parents and his little sister. During the day, we'd each go to kindergarten or school, the campuses always being within the compounds of the United Front. Actually, in those days, aside from studying Chairman Mao's Little Red Book and the history of the Communist Party, we didn't have any normal classes.

Placed under the care of our grandparents, my siblings and I never really played with other children. The outside world was plagued by political movements, famines, the Cultural Revolution and the Sino-Soviet split, but it was as if they had nothing to do with us. Besides, there was no way of us finding out more about them, even if we had wanted to. Newspapers were only for adults to read, and very few households had radios. We did have one, actually, but it was always in our parents' bedroom, and we didn't understand the policy slogans that we heard sporadically drifting through the house. Adults would never dream of discussing their political views in front of the children; at least that's what it was like in our family.

It wasn't until 1975, when I was sent down to the countryside, that I realised the world I had grown up in was completely different to that of most other children. Among my group of rusticated youths, many hadn't met their own parents since they were small. Some had been sent to be reformed in labour camps, some had been locked up in prison; some had even been beaten to death by Red Guards.

My two elder brothers? They weren't sent down to the countryside themselves. When they reached eighteen they both joined a special division of the army. Up until the 1990s, the military held a very privileged position in Chinese society. Those who held power would always send their children into the army, telling others that this was to toughen them up. But everyone knew the real reason was that military school was the only place you could receive a formal education back then, not to mention getting a leg up in your career.

When you look at the political figures who hold power in China today, practically all of them went through military school. What other country has such a high proportion of leaders with a military background? Perhaps just Israel and a handful of African countries.

'Compared with most other children, we grew up in very privileged surroundings, thanks to the protection of our parents. If you have time, you should go and listen to my cousin Kangmei's story – she's the daughter of my aunt Orange. It's as if they grew up in a different world, full of misery. Their lives were as wretched as those of the characters in *Les Misérables*.'

Crane hung her head as she said this, clearly still burdened by her inability to stop her family's suffering.

I knew the misery she was talking about, though, for I had also grown up in that world – the Chinese *Les Misérables*. In my book *The Good Women of China*, I had opened up those old wounds to allow my readers to understand how countless people like me suffered through the hell of the Cultural Revolution. But no one knows how long it will take for those wounds to heal once more. I don't even know myself. I just know that to this day, there are still nights that I wake up from the pain.

Crane raised her head, and continued cautiously.

The China of today has once again become polarised, but privilege no longer belongs to the military; it now belongs to money and power. Society has changed, though, and even those in high positions who have 'untouchable privileges' cannot protect their children any more.

When I graduated from high school in 1975, I was too weak to be accepted into the Special Division of the army. The Cultural Revolution was still going on, so university wasn't an option either.

Everyone knows that from 1966 to 1977, Chinese universities were 'remodelled' into bases for revolutionary training. The simplest of peasants and most enthusiastic of workers acted as teachers, preaching the failings of the class system and how we had to struggle against it. The only students to receive recognition and praise were chosen from the worker, peasant and soldier classes. Many of our current leaders are those very same students who made their way to the top by flashing the so-called 'diplomas' they earned at those universities as proof of their right to rule. When students graduated from middle school or high school, they had to 'broaden their horizons' by working with the peasants. Sending urban youths down to the countryside was already a national policy by then, and we became known as the rusticated youths.

Our national policies weren't passed by any constitution; they were either concepts proposed in Party meetings or just ideas that flashed across the mind of one of our leaders. Our national and constitutional laws were derived from the concept of family law; we just gave them different names.

The policy of sending urban intellectuals down to the country-side during the Cultural Revolution was Chairman Mao's idea. The thinking behind it was that China is a great agricultural nation, so young Chinese middle-school and high-school graduates should go to the countryside to learn all about peasant life and be agriculturally re-educated. Urban families were only allowed to have one child stay behind – even the privileged few were not exempt from this. I had younger siblings in my family, so I had no choice but to go.

I was sent to a place called Bashang, a temporary site about 300 kilometres north of Beijing, near the area where Hebei Province meets the Inner Mongolian plateau. It wasn't part of the very beautiful Bashang Plateau, though, with its clean air, beds of sweet-smelling grass, groups of sheep wandering around like clouds, and horses galloping through the valleys. No, our group of rusticated youths was put up in a hastily arranged camp, built by Han Chinese in an impoverished mountainous region.

I went back to the area around the camp just a few years ago, and still encountered that old familiar face of poverty. I thought it must be one of those places destined for eternal poverty that had been left untouched by the reforms that had transformed large parts of our country. But then, just recently, I found out that they've actually been developing and modernising the area. I had quite mixed feelings when I heard this – happiness that the peasants there will finally have the chance to make something better out of their lives; sadness that urbanisation will probably destroy the natural landscape and bring to an end thousands of years of local customs.

There's no going back on modernisation. It's a one-way street, from the village to the city. I believe that sooner or later we Chinese will come to regret this; if we lose the local customs and cultural traditions that this country was founded upon, then won't we just become a 'human factory' like the US or Hong Kong? But maybe that's just my own prejudice talking. To quote my father: 'Don't stand at the foot of a mountain and go criticising those at the top!'

When I first moved to the countryside, I was like a lonely little bird flying across a vast, boundless ocean. Not only had I lost sight of the mainland, but there wasn't anywhere for me to land safely and rest awhile. I'm not ashamed to say nowadays that I couldn't have survived that period without help from others: I couldn't cook using a firewood stove, I couldn't make sweet potato cakes, I couldn't bake cornmeal pancakes, I couldn't do anything with the local 'naked oats', I couldn't carry a shoulder pole properly, I couldn't wash my clothes in the creek. I couldn't make a quilt, couldn't use farming tools, I didn't understand when to plant this and when to pick that. I couldn't even walk on the rocky mountain paths.

These chores were the most basic survival skills for local people, the kind of tasks which their children could handle by the age of seven or eight. But I couldn't do anything: I didn't understand anything! In hindsight, the only thing which kept me from going under was my willingness to learn. But getting used to that impoverished way of living wasn't easy. The rest of my group? There were a few children there belonging to high officials, but they could all more or less manage a few household tasks.

At that time, China was incredibly poor – televisions, washing machines, bicycles, even watches were controlled goods you couldn't buy. Even if you had the money to pay for them, there simply weren't places that sold those kinds of everyday household items. What's more, luxury was considered a capitalist notion back then, and no one dared even think about it.

Even rich families needed help from the older generations in looking after the children, otherwise they'd be left to look after themselves. Children born into families who were part of the Five Black Categories quickly became experts in dealing with the hardships of life.* Not only could these children handle everything that needed doing around the house, but they were very serious in their approach to farming work. Growing up with humiliation had taught them how to endure deprivation; some even saw it as a happy twist of fate that had given them this chance to flee the class struggle of the cities and the persecution of the Red Guards. But when this fate befell me it was awful, truly terrifying. It actually made me think of a children's story my grandmother had once told me: 'A little baby bird was doted upon by her mother. When her wings slowly started to grow feathers, the mother felt uncertain. She knew her baby wanted to start learning how to fly, but she worried that she might falter and fall from the sky. The baby bird saw all the other little ones her age practising their flying, and she thought they were stupid. "Birds can fly without practice, silly!" she said. "It's in our nature. When I need to I'll be able to fly, no problem." When autumn arrived, it was time for all the birds to migrate south. On the day they set off, the baby bird perched on the edge of the nest, flapped her wings, and flew off together with her mother. At first, the weather was perfect for flying, and the baby bird felt very pleased with herself. "Flying is so easy," she thought.

'But soon the sky grew dark and started to rumble. The baby bird saw some of her friends going in and out of the clouds as if they were playing hide-and-seek. She really wanted to join in, but her mother told her that she couldn't yet fly well enough, and that it was too dangerous. "Stick with me," she said. But the baby bird was stubborn. "I'm a bird," she cried, "and I can fly!" As she said this, she darted into a huge storm cloud. But the very moment she did so, the baby bird was

---

* During the Cultural Revolution (1966–76), the Five Black Categories were groups considered enemies of the Revolution. They were: landlords, rich farmers, counter-revolutionaries, bad-influencers and Rightists.

struck by a bolt of lightning, and she started falling to the ground. She didn't know what was happening, nor did she realise her wings had been badly burned. "Why am I falling? Why won't my wings work?" she panicked. When her mother finally caught sight of her again, the baby bird had already fallen down onto the side of a small hill. She was still alive, struggling to get back up, but approaching her slowly was a hungry fox …'

Was I that little baby bird? Was it too late for me to learn how to fly? Was I already inside that dark cloud? Was I destined to end up as that fox's next meal? For weeks on end, I dreamed of nothing but that little bird.

Flying in pairs during the Cultural Revolution

I got lucky. In our group of rusticated youths, there was a kind and gentle young man called Tang Hai. People said he was an orphan. He loved writing and practising his calligraphy, and always carried a pen and some ink with him, whereas I loved drawing and always carried a pen and lots of paper with me. Our commune secretary was a man who loved reading, and when he heard about our artistic talents, he went to the cadre who controlled our production unit and said that our commune was in desperate need of talented writers, a boy–girl pair working together to take charge of the monthly blackboard bulletins, a job worth seven days of work points every month.*

Not only did the cadre agree to this, but he also took Tang Hai and me out of the fields altogether. We were given new jobs calculating the work points accumulated by the rusticated youths in our production

---

* People's communes were established in rural China to manage agricultural production in accordance with the policies set by the central government in Beijing. Within each commune were several production brigades, and within every brigade were several production teams, made up of a group of farmers. Farmers earned work points based on their daily contribution to the commune. At the end of each year, they would be paid based on their annual accumulation of daily work points.

unit and collecting data for the weekly work reports we sent to the production brigade. That's how we became clerks for the three administrative levels of rural society – the commune, the production brigade and the production team. Looking back on it now, I think the cadre wasn't only thinking about our literary talents, but also how much we struggled with manual labour.

Of the three main aspects of our work, updating the commune blackboard bulletin was the hardest. It's just like the ones you see on the wall outside every commune office, built from cement and painted black. Those blackboard bulletins not only acted as news centres for the peasants, but were also 'propaganda fronts' for the Party. The local peasants, most of whom were illiterate, would gather there once a month on market days, and the commune would send someone to read out Party messages to them. Later, they would take back these smatterings of 'principles' to spread throughout their villages, or they would go out in earnest to implement them themselves.

Folk in the countryside believed in Mao Zedong much more than we did. They would worship him like a god and turn to him for comfort, when in fact it was only their own ignorance that caused them grief. While they may have had a deep knowledge of the cycle of the seasons, agricultural work, farm animals and things like that, they completely lacked any understanding of politics or propaganda. This meant that Tang Hai and I needed to convey Mao's words and his philosophy using simpler language, which we did in the form of 'book reviews' to help them understand Mao's 'great and holy' calls.

If the villagers misunderstood what we taught them, or communicated a directive wrongly, it was likely that we'd be punished. At the very least we'd have a few work points taken away; at worst we could be sent to jail for being counter-revolutionary.

Different people often interpret the same thing differently, depending on how they've been brought up, how they've been educated and so on. For those peasants, who had grown up without ever having enough food or warm clothes, let alone any type of formal education, the only way they reacted to the chaos and poverty that surrounded them was to panic, and follow blindly those in power.

So while we rusticated youths were left confused and disorientated by the frenzied Red rage of the Cultural Revolution, those peasants were at even more of a disadvantage. They couldn't even understand political slogans.

One member of our group, who'd been in the countryside the longest, told us that towards the end of 1970, Chairman Mao had released an article calling for the whole country to fight against *xiān yàn lùn* (a priori philosophy). But because that sounds a lot like *xiān yàn* (brightly coloured), all of the villagers went home immediately and hid all their brightly coloured possessions in the cellar. Some even burned or smashed up heirlooms that had been passed down through generations of their family. Those peasants feared Mao so much that they thought natural disasters were a result of someone offending him.

Our production team secretary – who only recently passed away – was extremely revolutionary. To win the praise of his seniors, every time Chairman Mao gave a new directive he would get us rusticated youths to write it out on red slips of paper, under the heading 'Highest Directive'. We'd then hand these out to the peasants coming to the market. Again and again the secretary would stress to the peasants that this was the 'highest directive'. Only later did we find out that they were pasting those slips of red paper to the ceiling of their homes, because that was the highest point they could reach!

Tang Hai arrived in the countryside before me. He once told me about a time when, under the instruction of the commune, the whole village was taking part in a struggle session against a teacher and his wife who had been demoted to work in the countryside.* One of the villagers stood up, pointed at the teacher and shouted, 'You've gone against Chairman Mao! You've opposed the Party! You think all your books and your wife are your own private property! You won't let me look at them!'

Everyone listening was baffled; they couldn't work out why he wanted to see the teacher's wife. Then a young villager stood up and

---

* A struggle session was a form of public humiliation and torture used by the Chinese government, particularly during the Cultural Revolution.

spoke with rage: 'How can this kind of thing be happening in socialist China? How could you keep your wife as your own private property? She should definitely be public property!'

I knew that Crane wasn't lying, or even exaggerating any of these stories. I knew these types of events were typical of that part of Chinese history. It's estimated that 80 per cent of China's urban population took part in destroying sites of cultural heritage, or committed inhumane acts against their fellow humans. As for those uneducated peasants, fear led them to blindly follow and never question the actions of their 'superiors' or the consequences of these actions. I once heard a funny story that goes some way to demonstrating this point.

During the Criticise Lin, Criticise Confucius period,* in a village somewhere in the Chinese countryside, a male tenor and female soprano were standing on a stage, leading the crowd in front of them in shouting slogans.

'Down with Lin Biao!' they cried, to which the crowd responded, 'Down with Lin Biao!'

'Down with Confucius!' they raged, to which the crowd responded, 'Down with Confucius!'

'Criticise Confucian teaching!' they screamed, to which the crowd responded, 'Criticise Confucian teaching!'

At that moment, a man rushed onto the stage, and shouted to one of the leaders sitting on the stage, 'Director Li, someone's looking for you,' to which the crowd responded, 'Director Li, someone's looking for you!'

Crane took no notice of my daydreaming, and carried on with her story.

---

* A propaganda campaign started by Mao Zedong and his wife Jiang Qing against former vice president of China Lin Biao and the ancient Chinese philosopher Confucius.

If publishing newspapers is a politically risky line of work, then you could say that gathering production reports is a strain on the conscience. You know Yuan Longping – the so-called 'Father of Hybrid Rice'? Well, after decades of scientific research, in 2000 he found a way to breed a type of rice which allows farmers to produce 700 kilos of rice from only 100 *mu* of land.* Yet, back in 1976, we were asked to report yields of over 1000 kilos per *mu*!

The cadres said that our superiors didn't understand agriculture and only looked at the figures. He thought that the more rice we reported, the happier they'd be, and in return they'd allocate us more fertiliser, which would guarantee a better harvest for next year. But the peasants said that false production numbers would lead to higher taxes, and if that happened, it would leave them with much less grain. Sometimes, after a hard year's toil on the land, there wouldn't even be enough grain left after taxes for people to provide for their families.

Tang Hai and I had no choice but to do the collecting and reporting, all the while torn between duty and morality. He was much braver than I, though, and he would often stand up to the production brigade cadre on these matters. He was smart too, often playing little word games with our superiors on the reports, tricking them into giving the peasants just that little bit more grain. He would then get me to praise the person in charge of distributing fertiliser, in an effort to secure more of it for the villagers.

Don't think I'm belittling our work on the commune blackboard bulletin. It may be like the local papers of today – always running cover stories of 'outstanding results' in something or other – but Tang Hai and I used that blackboard to great effect, doing a lot of good deeds on behalf of the villagers. But we were just a drop of water in the swirling tide of the times. We were part of the wave, and therefore you could

---

* A *mu* is a Chinese unit of land measurement that varies depending on location, but is commonly 0.165 acres, or 666.5 square metres.

even say part of the problem, too. The false prophesies, fake results, outrageous slogans and vulgar personal attacks you found on those blackboards were the 'masterpieces' we created under threat of persecution.

What pained Tang Hai and me the most was handing out work points to our fellow rusticated youths. Work points were essentially grain rations. Generally speaking, a local man would earn ten work points from a day's manual labour in the fields if he worked from six in the morning to six in the afternoon. When distributions were made at the end of the year, you could turn that into 8 *fen*, equivalent to 1.5 *maos*' worth of grain.* Women could only make around six work points a day. The price of rice back then was around 3.5 *mao* for one kilo, which shows you that in those days a man could toil in the fields for a whole day and struggle to buy half a kilo of rice by the end of it. It's no wonder any expenditure – from buying clothing, to seeing a doctor, to paying for a wedding or funeral – was seen as a huge event for the locals back then.

As for us rusticated youth, we had to struggle every day to make enough money for food. We'd only get 1 *mao* for every ten work points, but lacking both the strength and experience of the locals, we could only make between six and eight points a day. Because I was young, small in stature and lacking in any kind of manual labour capability, on my first shift I only made two points, which meant I'd struggled for a whole day in the fields for only 2 *fen*. Although Tang Hai and I tried to think of ways to help the weaker members of our group gain a few measly work points, cultivating the land wasn't the same as writing characters. How much was grown reflected how much you planted – there was no hiding from the facts.

Sometimes we gave girls with period pains a few extra points on the sly, which only amounted to a couple of *fen*. We would watch our friends toiling out there in the fields, drenched in sweat from head to toe, bodies aching all over, all the while knowing that our table could only offer them a few tiny mouthfuls of grain. My heart used to sink at the bitterness of it all.

---

* Ten *fen* were equal to 1 *mao*, which in 2013 was roughly equivalent to 1 penny in the UK.

Aside from the three main aspects of our work as clerks, we were also responsible for writing couplets for weddings, eulogies for funerals and all sorts for festive occasions for the whole commune. The peasants had a huge number of local customs and festivals, and so those couplets and *jifu* (a kind of prayer paper) became almost a daily part of our work. It was tiring, but it did give me the chance to better understand a lot of the local customs, and how their lives depended on the changing of the seasons. At the same time, it allowed me to get closer to Tang Hai.

I was in awe of the way Tang Hai had such a good understanding of local customs and how seasonal medicines worked. I suppose you could say that was the source of the well of my attraction to him, a well that is yet to run dry.

He told me that apart from the many Han Chinese festivals celebrated in the Bashang region, there were also several local customs. For example, there was the Full Warehouse Festival on the twenty-fifth day of the first lunar month where all families would eat millet rice and mixed-grain soup because of the old saying passed down by their ancestors: 'When the warehouse is full, serve up the millet rice and soup.' And of course you had to let off firecrackers to represent the collapse of the warehouses: this symbolised a bumper harvest so great that there was no room to store it all.

Tang Hai also said that because the local soil quality wasn't good, food was so scarce that people would regularly have to go hungry. Only on special occasions could they allow themselves to eat a meal as 'lavish' as millet rice and naked oat noodle soup. A couple of years ago, I heard that they eat dumplings and noodle soup at the same festival these days. Life has obviously improved a lot for them there, but it's still far removed from the city, where people can eat those sorts of things to their hearts' content.

According to Tang Hai, these modern dietary changes aren't necessarily a good thing for the people there. In that dry climate, often devastated by storms, the health benefits of eating wheat and rice aren't enough. Without fibre from vegetables, people will easily fall ill. He believes that leading people to understand the importance of eating right – and improving their overall health – should be at the forefront of local government work up and down the country. I think he's living in a fantasy world myself – what local government gives a damn about what normal people have to eat?

While celebrating the holiday of Li-Chun, which marks the beginning of spring, Tang Hai told me that the locals called this holiday the Spring Cow Festival, although it is known in some places as *Bianchun*. In ancient times, feudal officials would organise Spring Cow festivities, the most important being the opening ceremony, where they would beat a cow. The Spring Cow would be made with a wooden frame, and only after the winter solstice could mud be dug up from the ground to mould the cow's body. That cow is made in a very detailed, particular way. The body measures 36.5 Chinese *cun* (1 *cun* = 3.3 cm), to symbolise the 365 days of the year.* The tail is 12 Chinese *cun*, to symbolise the twelve months. The four hooves symbolise the four seasons. The whole body needs to be a representation of the four seasons, eight major festival seasons, 365 days and the twelve two-hour periods. The four seasons are a fundamental part of farming culture. The eight major festival seasons dictate how farmers cultivate the land: they are the beginning of spring, the spring equinox, the beginning of summer, the summer solstice, the beginning of autumn, the autumn equinox, the beginning of winter, and the winter equinox. The twelve two-hour periods in the day came from the way people in ancient China would tell the time according to the sunrise, separating the twelve hours of night from the twelve hours of day – essentially what we today call the twenty-four hours of the day. The day before the beginning of spring, people make sacrifices to their ancestors, then whip the Spring Cow with a coloured willow branch which symbolises spring. The whip must be 24 Chinese *cun* long to symbolise the twenty-four solar terms.

---

* The *cun* is a traditional Chinese unit of length, measured as the width of a person's thumb at the knuckle.

Later in the day, people 'lead' the Spring Cow down to the local memorial hall or the activity centre, and make an offering of wine. All the family, young and old, will help lead the 'cow' and tow the 'plough', singing songs about planting seeds and praying for a bumper year. When we were there, the Red Guards were busy 'destroying the Four Olds' and no one dared hit the Spring Cow that year, but some of the older folk still tied red cloth to the bridles of their livestock or hung it from the front of their tractors. Some also asked Tang Hai to write them a couplet worshipping the Spring Cow, to pray for prosperity. Apparently, when some of the rusticated youths saw all those pieces of red cloth flapping in the spring breeze, they thought it must have been a new directive from Chairman Mao. They looked at each other in bewilderment, wondering how none of them had heard about it.

The Tomb-Sweeping Festival, which in Bashang was around 5 April, didn't seem to have been interrupted by the Cultural Revolution. It was actually the first time I'd heard of it; my parents had never taken us to make sacrifices to our ancestors before. The first time in my life that I made a sacrifice to the dead was actually when I went with Tang Hai to honour his late mother. I told Tang Hai that my family history starts with my grandparents. Who came before that, or what they did, I have no idea; it was something my father never talked about. Sometimes my grandparents would let slip a few sentences here and there, but they would always be cut off by my mother: 'Please! Don't talk so much about the past in front of them, they'll only get curious and start stirring up trouble.'

In response to my story, Hai said, 'Our present is rooted in our past – ignoring one's family history is a great sadness, and disrespectful to your ancestors, just as not understanding your country's history is an insult to your race.'

I wasn't so convinced. 'You could say that, but there's nothing written about it in books, no information I can find. And if the older generations won't tell me, how will I ever find out?'

This really struck a nerve with Tang Hai. He fixed his eyes on mine with a penetrating gaze. 'History lives with us and within us; ancient customs breathe in our everyday lives. We should make an effort to understand what is happening around us by looking, asking questions, finding proof, using our brains to analyse what's right and what's wrong. In this way, we can find all the evidence we need to record history for future generations. Isn't that also how our elders record their own present, which then becomes our history?'

I was lost for words at that moment, and to this day I still don't think I've found a comeback for what he said. He may be right, but I still believe that there are many people in China just like me who believe they have no other means of discovering history other than through books – they don't believe they are part of history themselves, or that they are writing the next chapter of the history books for future generations.

Tang Hai never stopped trying, though. He's spent his whole life asking questions, recording history, verifying facts. The material he's made over the years covers all aspects of society.

Soon after southern China had celebrated the Dragon Boat Festival,* our region held what's known as the Auntie Festival, on the sixth day of the sixth lunar month. The locals welcomed back all the daughters who had married outside the village, to be reunited with their families. Tang Hai took the opportunity to go and interview some of the women who had come home for the festival, to find out more about the eating habits of their adopted home towns and what kinds of folk medicines their husbands' families used.

He once said to me, with a sigh, 'Women are the seamstresses that hold together the heavens and the earth – family, life, local customs and art are the carefully woven works of women. And yet those daughters who come home for the Auntie Festival "celebrate" by helping their mothers with the needlework. I never met a single daughter who didn't have to work when she came home, or one woman who could actually have a break during Spring Festival.'

The one festival Tang Hai avoided talking to me about fell on the seventh day of the seventh month, when the Magpie Bridge would

---

* The Duanwu Festival, also known in south China as the Dragon Boat Festival, is a traditional Chinese holiday.

form over the River of Heaven, allowing the herd-boy and the weaver-girl to meet for just one day.* He didn't mention it, but I found out about it easily enough. In the run-up to the seventh day, the Night of Sevens, there would be endless talk among the villagers and rusticated youths alike about which couples were real-life 'herd-boys and weaver-girls', which couples had broken up or were just about to, and which disreputable women had been seen buying fruit at the market that day. The strange thing was that, around the time of the Night of Sevens, young men and women would actually go to great lengths to avoid each other. I know I was scared of working together with Tang Hai on that day. Only later did it hit me how in those days, it was only when people started avoiding their sweethearts that they came to understand their true feelings.

Tang Hai told me that no matter where you went in China, people cared a great deal about the so-called Three Great Ghost Festivals – the Qing Ming Festival (and the Cold Food Festival that went with it), the Ghost Festival and the Winter Clothes Festival. They weren't just about showing filial piety to your ancestors, but also gave families the chance to reunite and teach children their various customs to ensure that folklore survived through the generations. For example, for the Qing Ming festival in spring, you would sweep your ancestors' tombs, take hikes and eat spring fish, river shrimp, shellfish and lots of other cold dishes.†

The Ghost Festival at the start of summer is where you burn fake money in honour of your ancestors. It carries particular significance in

---

* The Night of Sevens, also known as Chinese Valentine's Day, is a Chinese festival held on the seventh day of the seventh lunar month, which originated from the romantic legend of the herd-boy and the weaver-maid, who were lovers banished to opposite sides of the River of Heaven. Once a year, on the Night of Sevens, a flock of magpies would form a bridge to reunite the lovers for one day.

† The Cold Food (or Hanshi) Festival is a traditional Chinese holiday, which began after the death of Jin nobleman Jie Zhitui in the seventh century BC. The nobleman had chosen to live as a hermit in the mountains, which angered the Zhou, and to drive him out they set fire to the forest, resulting in his death. On the anniversary of his death, the lord ordered all fires in every home to be put out for the day. What began as a local custom was turned by the seventh-century Tang into an East Asian occasion for the commemoration and veneration of ancestors, in which the lighting of fire was avoided, even for preparing food.

China for being the festival of repentance and atonement. Anyone who has done wrong over the past twelve months can on that day, through a series of rites and rituals, confess their crimes and beg the heavens and the earth for forgiveness. The Winter Clothing Festival takes place at the start of winter, allowing people to donate winter clothes to those who might need them. On the day, people offer sacrifices to the graves of their ancestors and burn coloured paper, cut into the shape of clothing, to symbolise the giving of warmth to the deceased. This day also serves as a reminder to families to make the necessary arrangements for the upcoming winter.

Before being 'enlightened' by Tang Hai's teachings, I had very little idea about any of those traditional customs. On one of my rare visits home during my time as a rusticated youth, I asked my mother whether she knew that the fifteenth day of the seventh month was the Ghost Festival? She said that all those kinds of festivals had all but died by the time she was my age. She knew them as you know a familiar-sounding word whose meaning you don't exactly know.

The day before our first Mid-Autumn Festival at our village in Bashang, Tang Hai managed to get his hands on a small basket of exotic fruits and a duck's egg. To this day I have no idea where he got them from, but I have my suspicions. Anyway, he said, 'As part of the Festival, you should pray to the moon and eat moon cakes. We can't afford the latter, so I've written the characters for my two favourite types of moon cakes for us. And you, you can draw us a huge moon, so that we can show our admiration for the moon.'

Under the moonlight, he recited a passage from the diary his mother had left behind after her death: 'Mid-autumn is a time to recover, to build strength for the coming winter. Autumn is not just a season for farmers to harvest the crops, it is also the best chance to rest during the whole year. To rest your heart, clear your head and nurture your soul.'

Through Tang Hai's teachings, I started to feel the origins of our culture in those local customs, bound as they were to the cycles of nature. I also discovered how Chinese culture is inherently linked to nature and the human spirit alike. For example, on the Double Ninth

Festival on the ninth day of the ninth month, we pay tribute to the older generations of the family, which teaches the younger generations to respect their elders and appreciate the value of life. Then there's the Laba Rice Porridge Festival, on the eight day of the final lunar month, when we make porridge using eight different kinds of grain to teach children the importance of prudence. We offer tributes to the gods, from those in the heavens to those with us in the kitchen.

On the twenty-third day of the final lunar month, people sweep their kitchens and offer tributes to the kitchen god Zaoshen in the hope that he will pass on this tribute to the Jade Emperor, so that he in turn will ensure the whole family will be clothed and fed over the coming year.

Some Chinese people say we don't have faith. But in fact, when I lived in the countryside, faith was present in almost everything I did. And that faith was always very pragmatic, directly related to people's lives.

The twenty-third day of the final month of the year is what you might call a minor New Year. Tang Hai and I became extremely busy around that time because there were copious amounts of couplets to compose, a huge pile of *gongfu* prayer messages, and then of course the endless '*fu*' characters that needed writing. In those times, the traditional depictions of the Door God were considered feudalist, capitalist and revisionist. You couldn't buy or sell them anywhere.

So with all the characters and the couplets we wrote, we became the only supplier for New Year art in all the villages that were part of our commune.

The work was exhausting, but it also left me astounded at how those peasants could fear the political gods so much and yet still be unable to shake the traditions passed down to them through the generations. Even if it meant their families would be torn apart, their lives ruined, they would never change their unwavering loyalty to a higher power.

Speaking of writing couplets, there's something else you might enjoy hearing about. Thinking about it now, I don't know whether to laugh or cry.

One of the old villagers was making preparations for his son's wedding, to be held on the first day of the fifth month. He asked us to write out a special couplet for him:

Two hands that were meant to be
A couple, and a family.

But when one of the more revolutionary members of our group saw this, he warned the old villager: 'That suggests they won't be paying any attention to collective production after they marry, only looking out for their own family. I don't know, it seems pretty capitalist to me.'

The old man heard this and requested that we make some changes. For the old man's peace of mind, Tang Hai tried again:

Two hands toiling endlessly,
For production, and for glory.

The next morning, the cadre in charge of propaganda at the commune happened to be in our village on business. When he saw the couplet, he said to us: 'The revolution is growing every day, comrades! It's about much more than production theory alone. This just won't do – change it!'

And so we did:

Two hands joined in harmony,
Revolution, and conformity.

That afternoon, the director of the county revolutionary committee came to inspect our village. When he came across our couplet, he said, 'Class struggle comes before any type of union. To talk about harmony and union at this stage is confusing the matter of class struggle. Worse, it's counter-revolutionary!'

This scared the life out of the old villager. He rushed over to see us. 'Write something, anything, that won't cause us any more trouble,

I'm begging you! This is supposed to be a happy occasion. Don't go making the cadres angry!' Tang Hai thought all this had gone too far, and he told the old villager he just didn't know how to change it any more. Luckily, the revolutionary I mentioned earlier was on hand to volunteer his services. He made the final changes to the couplet:

Two hands joined together,
Furiously struggling against one another.

Looking back, wasn't that just an age of insanity?

In the end, it seemed that the young couple were fated to offend the political gods. Soon after they married, they heard about the latest popular revolutionary trend of the time: covering the walls of your room with portraits of Chairman Mao alongside lines and lines of his quotations. One day, a fellow villager asked them, 'Do you do it in the presence of Chairman Mao every night, right under his eyes?!'

'It's fine,' they replied. 'When we turn the lights off at night he can't see a thing.'

Not much later, the couple were taken away by the county police. The leaders of the commune notified the whole village: 'Someone has taken them away. Our almighty leader can see through the thickest fog. He can even see what we're doing in the darkness!'

How did we rusticated youths cope when all around us those peasants were just blindly following the leaders? We had to tread carefully in that age when we had no choice but to fend for ourselves – no one would come to our rescue if we got into trouble. But our education didn't go completely to waste. When the opportunity arose, we would work out a plan to fool those uneducated revolutionary leaders.

In our group of rusticated youths, there were a few students from the Central Conservatory of Music. When we first arrived there, none of them dared sing or play their instruments for fear it would land them in trouble. Later, the commune organised a 'Mao Zedong Thought Propaganda Team' as a gesture of goodwill towards us urban youths. They even organised a concert to show that the lower and middle peasants stood with us in solidarity.

Those music students were smart. When they stood up on the stage, they told the expectant crowd that they would perform a violin arrangement of Beethoven's 'Honour the Red Sun in the Sky'. The hall exploded in applause and cries of approval. They didn't know who Beethoven was, but since he wanted to honour the red sun, the symbol of our great leader, he must have been a true proletarian revolutionary! With applause still ringing around the hall, the music students played a grandiose version of Beethoven's 'Romance in F major', then performed 'The Toreador Song' from *Carmen*, which they introduced to the crowd as 'Lower and Middle Peasants Farming Around the World in B Flat'.

In years of ignorance, knowledge attracts. In years of chaos, thinking is a currency. In the shadows of recklessness, morals shine bright. Every day brought a new political movement, a new challenge, and we couldn't talk openly about such things. We used discussions about 'art' and 'literature' as a pretence to talk about the morality of the times, or lack thereof. Actually, you could even say those talks were our form of dating. People in our commune would tease Tang Hai and me, saying the two of us were the left and right hands of calligraphy – him on the left, me on the right. Well, that's how the left hand fell in love with the right.

As she said this, a gentle smile stretched across Crane's face. So gentle, I thought to myself, that if a butterfly were to land on her smiling cheek, it would not look out of place.

Building a nest

It wasn't until the first time we touched hands, though, that the love between us was made clear.

That's right, not held hands, not shook hands – touched hands. On the day of the harvest, everyone had to go out to the fields to gather in the corn. Children and the elderly broke off the corn kernels while we 'able-bodied' youngsters cut off the corn stalks at their root, which we piled up and transported back to the production brigade yard ready for distribution. Those stalks were prized possessions for each family in the village. They'd be used as scaffolding for houses, fencing for animals, even as a kind of mattress for the peasants when it got really cold. That said, it was exhausting work cutting them down – for me, at least.

Towards the end of that day, I slipped and accidentally cut the back of my left hand. '*Aiya!*', I cried out instinctively. No one around took any notice, but out of nowhere Tang Hai came bounding over to me. Without saying a word, he took out a cloth from inside his vest and wrapped up the wounded hand. As he did this, our hands touched. Both of us blushed, and my heart beat so fast I thought it would leap out of my mouth.

Later, Tang Hai would use my 'injury' as an excuse to hold and caress my hand. The wound itself healed very quickly, but he would still come and wrap it for me. Of course, I let him keep doing it without saying a word. We understood in our hearts what it really meant, but at the same time there was a nagging worry; we couldn't use this excuse forever – what should we do next? That was when the two of us knew we were in love. Romance for us was walking together in the wilderness on the edge of the village. It's a pity there weren't any forests around there fit for furtive lovers. The most intimate thing we did was hold hands, and even that was in secrecy.

The first time we hugged? That was on the road back to the village one night after watching a film at the commune. At that time, there were hardly any forms of entertainment in China. In the years I spent in the countryside I only watched three films, all of them about war – *Tunnel Warfare* (1965), *Landmine Warfare* (1962) and *Fighting North and South* (1952). During the Cultural Revolution, there can't have been more than ten films made in the whole country. Beijing was more privileged than other cities, though: they had the Eight Model Works, which were performed throughout the period.* Most Beijingers of the day could sing along to all those old tunes.

When our commune showed a movie, people in the surrounding villages celebrated as if it was New Year. They'd dress up in their best clothes – always black, blue or grey, of course. The whole family would be there, young and old, trailing folding stools from home, setting off early to make sure they got a good position. But for most young people, the film itself wasn't important; what *was* important was what else went on during and after the film. This was a chance – the only chance, really – for them to meet up with their sweethearts. We rusticated youths would go to the cinema in groups of two or three, boys and girls separately, but return as couples under the blessed cover of darkness. For our generation back then, dating was kind of an open secret, don't you think?

That day, we watched *Fighting North and South* for what must have been the seventh or eighth time. I remember wearing a special kind of military overcoat that was fashionable in those days, which my mother had managed to send to me via a mutual friend. It was a perfect autumn day – crisp, clear and not at all cold – but we wanted to show off: a youthful impulse people have at that age. On the way over we saw Tang Hai and a group of his friends on the road in front of us. My friend understood the situation perfectly, and she quickened her pace on purpose so that we could walk ahead of the group of boys. The road was full of people, bustling with activity, like on market days. It wasn't long before we heard a man's voice cry out from behind us:

'Hey, who's that wearing the overcoat? She's quite something.'

'Isn't it Meng Aiguo?'

'Yeah, I think it is!'

My heart was filled with joy. Although none of the voices belonged to Tang Hai, he had clearly seen me and heard what the others had said. He might even have felt proud.

---

* The Eight Model Works, or Eight Model Plays, were the most famous of the few works of performing arts permitted during the Cultural Revolution. They included five operas, two ballets and a symphony, all with revolutionary themes.

The local people had a rule: 'When the sky turns dark, the film will start.' That day, just after the film began, I felt someone tugging at the back of my coat. When I turned my head, I saw Tang Hai quietly signalling for me to follow him. I asked a friend to keep my seat, and made my way back through the crowd. When I emerged the other side, I was dumbstruck. The space at the back was completely occupied by couples – I don't think there was a single person there on their own!

'I'm behind you.' Tang Hai's mouth was pressed against the collar of my coat, and I nearly jumped out of my own skin. I was about to cry out when he covered my mouth. 'Shh, shh,' he whispered as he reached out and hugged me. I didn't struggle. Later, Tang Hai said the first time we embraced it felt as if I had been waiting for that moment for a long time. And he was right: I had. Even though I couldn't express them clearly myself, it's impossible to hide feelings of true love. Don't you think so?

No, we didn't kiss that day, and I'm pretty sure those couples around us were the same. We just hugged, held hands, that sort of thing. Kissing in public was still seen as indecent behaviour. For us 'good girls', it wasn't just the threat of punishment which held us back; we had all been brought up to believe that kissing was something you did after you got married.

However, it turned out that I wasn't one of those 'good girls' after all. It wasn't that much later that Tang Hai and I shared our first secret kiss – all the education and social stigma in the world couldn't have held back our passionate impulses!

Crane looked at me without showing any hint of regret over this 'violation' of a strict social taboo. For it was indeed how she described – in pre-1990s China, people ended up in prison for kissing in public. Young people of today might find it hard to believe, but this was the reality for a long time.

In the 1970s, love was a 'restricted product', sex even more so. I remember a book called *A Young Girl's Heart*, which got banned for being 'pornographic'. The only copies available were handwritten and passed from person to person by young men and women who ran and took part in an underground literature movement. That was perhaps the only sexual education manual out there for young people at that time.

When did Tang Hai propose? He never actually did. In those days, it was more a question of when the heads of both families could meet. When that happened, it basically meant you were engaged. Don't talk to me about roses and diamond rings — we didn't even say 'I love you'. Dating was just a case of two people quietly walking towards a common understanding, slowly growing in each other's hearts. None of our generation saw love as something you should talk openly about — the idea made people cringe.

Did that period of re-education have any positive effect on our lives? We all went in with grand visions for the future, thinking that we could achieve anything we put our minds to. But then again, most of us rusticated youths just ended up in the fields, learning how to plant crops while picking up bad habits from the peasants. By the time we had gone through this 'proletarian re-education', the morals we had learned from our civilised education had been all but washed away by sweat and dirt. Our survival instincts compelled us to return to a most primitive form of existence. You're hungry, so you steal some food. You're cold, so you take someone else's blanket. No one taught us about the differences between men and women, or the physical changes you go through at that age. Lots of rusticated youths got their 'sex education' by watching animals on heat.

Looking back now, I realise we were some of the lucky ones — many other girls who were sent down to the countryside ended up with a very different fate. Back then, no one knew where our future was headed, and we were terrified that we'd have to spend the rest of our lives in those backwater towns and villages. Boys would think of ways to become soldiers or factory workers, anything to get them back to the city. No job was too low. Girls would exploit themselves, exchanging their virginity for the chance of a better future. Some wasted no time in marrying the children of local cadres, to position themselves closer to power because they could no longer bear to suffer the poverty of their countryside homes or the hardship of working out in the fields. Others sacrificed their bodies, giving themselves up to commune cadres in the hope that this would help them find a road that led back to the city.

There was only a two-and-a-half-year gap between the day I was sent down to the countryside in 1975 and the day I joined the first batch of students to take the restored *gaokao* university entrance exams in 1977. I was surrounded by people who had paid a great price during that period, some of whom are still suffering the consequences to this day.

Because we were a 'left-and-right-hand' partnership, Tang Hai and I were able to stay calm. We thought to ourselves that even if we had to raise our children out there and live like those peasants for the rest of our lives, we weren't scared. We had pens and paper, and all the poetry, literature, painting and calligraphy we could create together, not to mention each other's love. In short, we created for ourselves an alternative reality to block out the real-life hardships.

To give ourselves a more substantial and meaningful life, my father recommended that this 'left and right hand' come up with some kind of joint project, one that brought to life the local environment and customs we had come to know so well. This could serve as a means of helping those locals preserve their heritage, recording folk customs that had been passed down through generations of Chinese families without making it into school textbooks. In other words, the essence of Chinese culture.

My mother said that she too learned a lot of folk customs from the poverty she encountered in my father's home town. This local culture may not be the kind of thing that appears in poems or paintings, but what it has done is inspire countless poets and painters.

So as the 'left and right hand', we started thinking about what we could do. We finally decided to put together a record of all the folk medicines Tang Hai's mother had made, editing them before they faded from memory altogether. If there was an opportunity to get them published, then we could share them with society. If not, then at least they could act as a model for our own family. While the 'left hand' concentrated on that, I went out collecting, recording and in some cases even putting into practice different aspects of local dietary culture. This way I could protect my own health while also digging into and recording local customs – 'the intangible cultural heritage' of a place. The most important thing was to immerse ourselves in agricultural life as a means of continuing the adult education that had been denied to us previously.

How long did this go on for? We've been working on it non-stop since the beginning. Editing and sharing these accounts, these records, has become a huge part of our life together. Even when we were forced to spend years living apart, we didn't stop. In many ways, those records were our love letters.

I'm still trying to go through and sort out all the recordings I made of my investigations into folk culture. I think it'll take ten years, or thereabouts. In trying to mine Chinese history and folklore, I've come to realise that I'm walking on a road which has no end. But the further I walk, the more energy I have.

When my father finally found a way to bring me back from the countryside to work in the city, Tang Hai was forced to stay on. His father was a translator of German from Shijiazhuang, and because of those overseas connections his whole family was classed as one of the Five Black Categories. In 1957, not long after Tang Hai was born, his father was locked up and sent away to a *laogai* for re-education through labour.* His mother worked tirelessly as a doctor in traditional Chinese medicine to support Tang Hai up until he joined junior school. When the Cultural Revolution broke out in 1966, Red Guards forced her to divorce her husband. Even her family advised

---

* A *laogai* was a political labour camp.

her that she had no future with that man. As the Cultural Revolution intensified after the Spring Festival of 1967, just two weeks after she had signed the divorce papers the ringleader of one of the Red Guard factions came to see her. He told her that raising a child alone in uncertain times like those was tough. Her son was still very young: living without a father, he'd surely be a target for bullies. No, it would be better to marry him and provide a stable family for the boy. That Red Guard ringleader had had a wife who died in childbirth; this had led him to focus all his energy and emotion into the revolutionary cause, dealing with his own pain and loneliness by making others suffer with him.

Tang Hai's mother was like a tiny boat drifting aimlessly in an endless sea. Now that this great ship had turned up, what could she do other than think of it as a huge stroke of luck? And that's how she ended up in a confused blur, marrying a Red Guard. However, within a few short weeks, the political winds changed quite suddenly, and Tang Hai's stepfather's faction of Red Guards was overthrown. As the ringleader, he was the first to fall, and even his new wife was sent to a *laogai*.

Because he was sick, Tang Hai didn't go with his mother, and he moved in temporarily with a neighbour. Not long afterwards, someone arrived with news of his mother's death, and two volumes of notes she had left behind for him. To this day, no one has been able to tell Tang Hai how his mother died.

None of his father's family came forward to adopt him, but thanks to the kindness his mother had shown in providing neighbourhood families with folk medicines, there was no shortage of families willing to look after the not yet ten-year-old Tang Hai. First, he lived with an old auntie who lived on his street, a revolutionary through and through who was even part of the revolutionary committee. When she passed away, he lived in the revolutionary committee's night-duty office, setting up a small bed in a corner; he lived there right up until he graduated from high school in 1974. That's when all those neighbours who had helped him out over the years pinned a big red flower on his chest and sent him on to his new countryside home – Bashang.

I don't know if his father is still alive. We've tried hard looking for him: we still are, in fact. There hasn't been any news yet, but perhaps the internet will help us find him.

My own father used his influence to get me back to Beijing in 1977. He also set me up with a job in the military logistics unit elder brother managed, working in a non-combat role looking after the families of military personnel.

I was back by my parents' side, back in the home which seemed at once both familiar and strange. I wasn't the same person I was before; I had flown a long way since then. I'd found my beloved. Leaving Tang Hai made me feel once again like that little bird who couldn't find the shore. I begged my father over and over again to find a way to bring Tang Hai back. He tried, but then his subordinates discovered that Tang Hai didn't have a file. This was most unusual: only peasants didn't have files back then. More importantly, it also meant that no one could prove he had ever had a city residence permit.

It's incredible to think that up until our residency laws changed in 2003, you basically didn't exist in this country if you didn't have a city permit. The great swathes of people who came from the countryside to the city had no official rights in their new home; they could even be arrested for coming. That's why my father urged me to 'face reality', and to look for a new partner in the city.

The single most definitive characteristic of us Chinese – or perhaps just those of us who are Han Chinese – is that apart from being able to suffer in silence, we tend to submit to trends. If someone could find a way to analyse Chinese family trees over the past hundred years in a way that tracks people's marriages and careers, I think you'd see very clearly how relationships have followed political trends. In the 1950s people married for political reasons; in the 1960s it was class; in the 1970s everyone wanted to marry a PLA officer; in the 1980s it was university students. By the 1990s people had begun to trust their own instincts in who they married, and since 2000 it's been every man and woman for themselves.

As for women and the evolution of their taste in men, it was workers in the 1950s, soldiers in the 1960s, scholars in the 1970s, poets
in the 1980s and wealthy men in the 1990s. Now it seems to be all
about high-ranking officials ...

I feel very grateful that Tang Hai and I managed to avoid being
caught up in those political landslides. With the belief that we loved
each other, and our shared love of recording folk culture, we stayed
true to our own ideals in the face of political trends.

Tang Hai once wrote me a letter describing how he felt as if he
had just one chance left in life; he felt that his youth was fading and
he now found himself clinging on to its tail. He wanted to go to
university, change the fate the political gods had allocated him and
eventually reach the same political, social and educational level as me.
Then, and only then, would we get married. I replied to him saying it
was our destiny to be each other's left and right hand, and we would
spend the rest of our lives gathering twigs and leaves to build a nest
for our love.

Of course, I kept our correspondence. That's our only family
property, and the only thing we have to pass onto our children.

Later on, Crane picked out a few photocopies of these letters to give to
me, so that I could better understand their love.

> Comrade Crane: Health in body and mind does not depend on medi-
> cine, but on the state of your heart. Be careful what you say to others,
> in solitude hold on to the truth of your heart.

Tang Hai's letter was written in pencil on an old work points record
sheet, about half a side of A4. The writing was barely legible.

> Comrade Tang Hai: The heart is like a blue sky, and your senses are
> like the winds and the rain. A blue sky is never disheartened by a

storm, even though it knows the destruction it will bring. Nor will a blue sky get angry at the sun, moon and stars for not shining through the darkness.

Crane's message was written on a university library book lending slip, each character written in the most elegant of fonts:

My sky is but a beautiful white crane.

In the freezing cold field, a frog prince is keeping itself warm just by thinking. His mother once said that the three key elements of life are energy, circulation and balance.

One's mind can supplement the energy one gets from food. A positive mood satisfies any hunger, and turns bitterness sweet. So when I think of you, I feel content, and even the rockiest earth can nourish me.

Exercise can help circulate qi between the organs. That's the circulation I was talking about, but without water to replenish it, flow can lead to disaster. That's why, in this freezing weather, I always drink hot water, so that I have the energy to communicate with you.

Balance comes from choosing the right food to eat. If your health isn't balanced, some organs will feel it is unfair. If this isn't settled in time, there will be a war between organs. Rebuilding peace after the war will be very hard, because it always takes longer to recover than it does to fall ill, just as it is easier to fall down a mountain than it is to climb up it. Now I eat everything, broadening my tastes to take in all kinds of different nutrients, so that I might make a peaceful sky out of my body, for my beautiful and kind white crane to fly free.

Tang Hai's letter was written on a slip of red paper, the kind usually used for couplets. It was very long, very narrow, and very red. Crane had also attached a note to it:

Tang Hai's calligraphy was all out of shape, as if his hand had been shaking from the cold as he wrote. But between the lines I could still feel the emotion.

By that time, we weren't using any form of address for one another. There was no need; the sky we lived in was ours and ours alone. At the same time, we didn't want any cadres at the post office to be able to use them against us as evidence of our 'reactionary guilt'.

The bluest skies over an endless sea:

There is a saint in the West who often used poetry to comfort mankind. He once wrote: You will stand firm and without fear. You will forget your suffering, recalling it only as water that has long since passed by. Your days on this earth shall be brighter than the midday sun. Even in darkness, you shall be as the morning.

Crane had copied this passage down on the edge of a newspaper clipping, dated October 1982. The article next to it was headed 'Decision Concerning the Entire Party' and had been issued at the Second Plenary session of the 12th Central Committee of the CCP. This was the announcement that denounced the Cultural Revolution while exposing and criticising those involved in acts of vandalism and violence, cutting short their political lives in the Party. For reasons unknown, Western media has always maintained that the CCP has never recognised the catastrophic mistakes made during the Cultural Revolution.

Spring Crane:

Fire burns life to the ground,
but fears the tenderness of water.
Water brings devastation,
but gets swallowed up by the soil.
Soil can build up high,
but be swept away by the uncaring wind.
Wind can wreak havoc,
but be blocked off by the mountain.
Mountain paths are treacherous,
but people still walk upon them.

People have an indomitable spirit,
but are ruined by love and power.
Love and power can compete with time,
but time will make them scatter and disappear.
Time exists all around us,
but is owned or forgotten by the heart.

That was taken from a well-known essay paper. From the age of about three, all Chinese children start getting to know the series of small squares we use to practice calligraphy, as they set out on that painful journey towards learning the 18,000 characters we have left. Their education helps them, then, to retell the story of 5,000 years of civilisation and history through those little squares.

There was a note from Crane attached:

By this time, all of the rusticated youths who were sent down with us to live and work in the countryside had gone back to the city. Only Tang Hai was left.

It was at that time that Tang Hai told me about his plans to apply to military school. He wanted to study telecoms engineering, a compulsory step for anyone who wanted to work in industry. I immediately volunteered to help him find some more relevant information. But the Cultural Revolution had only just ended, and most public libraries were still being renovated after having been vandalised by the Red Guards. On top of that, telecoms engineering was a new field of study, and it was hard to find the right books even in a bookshop.

I was told that the only place I could find these types of books would be a university library, but these weren't open to everyone. To help Tang Hai more effectively, in 1980 I applied for an Open University correspondence course in computer science, back then an unknown field of study in China. For all I know, we might have been the first group of Chinese students to study it.

Computers back then couldn't have been more different to what they are now. They used to be huge machines, whereas now they've been reduced to microchips the size of your fingernail. My computer studies weren't in fact at all useful to my career, but what they gave me was a student ID, which allowed me to use the university library to look for books and resources for Tang Hai.

In 1983, the year I graduated from the Open University, Tang Hai tested in the top four in the province and was accepted into the Electronic Engineering Institute of the PLA. Spring Festival 1984 was the first time Tang Hai came to see me in Beijing, but he didn't meet my parents and he didn't come to my home; instead, he made do with cramming into a friend's house.

I was a worker in those days, while Tang Hai was surrounded by all those talented female students. My mother used to worry and say things like 'Tang Hai's grown into an eligible young man. I'm sure he's not short of marriage options.' I didn't give anything away by responding to her concerns, but my mind was restless. To ensure I didn't fall behind in that ever-developing society, I applied for another correspondence course, this time in psychology. What made me choose that subject? Maybe I was worried about losing Tang Hai and wanted to build up some kind of 'immunisation' against any future lovesickness.

'Don't laugh: it had a lot to do with how worried I was feeling at that time.

'Did Tang Hai continue sending me folk prescriptions during his studies? Yes, once a week, without fail. He used to say that he was a poor student, but those home remedies managed to save him a lot of money and make him a lot of friends.

'Would you like an example? Well, not long after he started school, my little sister Ducky got married. Tang Hai sent them some 'sex secrets' as a gift. Ducky told me later that this was the most practical gift she'd ever received in her life! Later, when we were married, Tang Hai made a copy specially for me. If you're interested, I can send it to you.'

It took Crane no time at all to send those folk sex secrets to me:

There are three 'void' periods when one should refrain from having sex.

These three voids refer to the annual void, the monthly void, and the daily void. The premise of it all is that to maintain good health during the year, one must follow the twenty-four solar terms and be aware of all seasonal changes to nature.

Don't have sex on the days of the annual 'void'

There are two annual voids: firstly, the winter solstice. There is an old saying, 'yang is born at the winter solstice,' meaning that's the day when fire and energy, the symbols of yang, start to build up inside you. If you don't take advantage of this build-up of yang, then you will miss out on this good energy. It is also called 'The Void of the Year', meaning that the winter solstice is the day when people go through the most significant weakness.

The second annual void is the summer solstice. The saying goes that 'yin is born at the summer solstice,' which is around 22 June in the Gregorian calendar. On this day, yin, symbolised by earth, darkness and cold, begins to rise inside you. But yin and water levels are still very low, and the human body is vulnerable to the 'voids'.

Fluctuations of yin and yang are particularly prominent at the summer and winter solstices. Qi is also more active than usual, and the body is in a relatively weak state. Therefore, it is best not to have sex during or on the days surrounding the summer and winter solstices. On the one hand, you might lose your vital energy, on the other there is an imbalance between your energy and your blood. If you get pregnant then, the child is likely to bear you ill will.

Don't have sex on the day of your monthly 'void'

The monthly void occurs on the first few days of the first lunar quarter, the final few days of the last lunar quarter and the days when the new crescent moon is so thin that you lose sight of it. In Chinese medicine, the moon represents yin. On the few days mentioned above, there is excessive *yin qi* in nature, and it is best to avoid having sex then as well. If you get pregnant on those days, it's likely to have a grave impact on the child's future physical and mental health. Therefore, beautiful things are best left for nights when the moon is full and the flowers blooming. Be at one with the world, and with nature.

Don't have sex on the day of your daily 'void'

The daily void occurs when the sky turns black and storms gather, during a lunar or solar eclipse, for example. It's best not to have sex on days like those. On days when a solar or lunar eclipse occurs, there is a powerful change in the qi, and the external forces of nature this leads to can easily damage your body.

The Five Sexual Taboos

Do not have sex after consuming alcohol. Alcohol raises your body temperature, especially in men, and this damp heat leads to birth problems. Heat can also lead to a reduction in the potency and efficacy of the sperm.

Nowadays, lots of people start making preparations a few months before they conceive. They stop smoking, stop drinking. This is very good, and responsibility for the future of the child should be promoted.

Do not have sex when you feel angry. When you are irritated or angry, blood surges through your veins and your qi is affected. Next, you will find your energy and blood levels drop significantly, as your body moves to suppress its own qi. If you get pregnant on one of those days, the child will grow skin ulcers.

Do not have sex when you feel scared. Some young people today feel inhibited by their surroundings, or worry about being caught in the act. As for adults, many have been scarred by the infidelities of past partners, to the point where they feel terrified in the bedroom. This causes great harm to the body, such as impotence, sweating, heart palpitations, and so on. Children conceived during these times are likely to be miscarried, because the parents have low qi at the point of conception.

Do not have sex when you are ill. Intercourse in itself causes a great loss of *yang qi,* and when you are ill, you need the *yang qi* to help you fight the disease. If you do have sex at this time, you will be using up your *yang qi* inappropriately, and you will suffer twice as much.

Do not have sex in public. There's an old Daoist saying, 'don't frolic under the stars,' meaning it's best not to conceive a child when having sex outdoors. This is because elements found in the dew on the ground will damage your body and affect the quality of the pregnancy.

Tang Hai said that while those old taboos about pregnancy and conception looked as though they were matters of the gods, they were actually all emphasising the fact that people need deference in their hearts. The real purpose is to illustrate that only when a person respects and fears nature in equal measure can they truly protect themselves. After all, you are creating a human life.

Tang Hai and I got married after he graduated from the military academy, where he had become an instructor. That was at the end of July 1987. Beijing was particularly hot that year. Chinese homes didn't have air conditioning yet, but we didn't have it as bad as the poor southerners, who had to contend with the mosquitoes and the 30-degree heat at night. At least we could get a good night's sleep. No, Beijing was practically a cool summer resort compared with those southern cities.

Don't think that we were surrounded by culture and entertainment just because it was the capital. We weren't. The vast majority of people didn't have a TV, and families who owned a radio were considered pretty well off.

My parents owned a 9-inch black-and-white television set, though. This meant that our yard became something of a meeting point for people in our neighbourhood to come and cool off. They would arrive carrying their own folding stools – my parents' home still only had the simple furniture allocated to them by their work unit – and sit in our yard watching TV.

That day, I think we watched a rerun of the sci-fi movie 20,000 *Leagues Under the Sea*. Foreign films were still very rare in those days, so we ended up watching 20,000 *Leagues* over and over again.

All of a sudden, Tang Hai appeared in the yard, his military uniform drenched in sweat. Before I had even had the chance to greet him, he dropped his travel bag to the floor, grabbed me by the hand and led me inside.

In those days, you know, we still believed that men and women shouldn't touch hands under any circumstances. Tang Hai's actions made me feel embarrassed, but he had moved so quickly that neither my parents nor anyone else there had had time to do anything about it. He led me out to the small alley next to the house, where we were alone.

'I ... I've graduated. They've asked me to stay on as an instructor. You realise this means we can get married?' Tang Hai was gasping for breath as he spoke.

'I ... We ... You and me? We can get married?' In that moment I wasn't so much a crane as a stupid old goose! But the man in front of me had suddenly transformed from being a frail old scholar to a soaring eagle.

When did we get married? You won't believe it, but we got married the very next day. There was nothing we needed to prepare, no one we needed to notify, no one we needed to invite. After all, we'd been preparing for this day for ten years. During that time we had started our journeys apart, separated by the class divisions of the age, but had found each other in a sky forged from our own beliefs, where we could finally fly free, two birds united in love.

It wasn't until Spring Festival the following year that my brothers and sisters had the chance to congratulate us and give us gifts.

We married in 1987, a time when the most popular wedding gifts were the 'three wheels and one speaker': a bicycle, a watch, a sewing machine and a radio. These were also considered the basic items for a marital home. However, apart from love, we had nothing to our names. This is what young people today call a naked marriage.

About six months into our marriage I transferred to Tang Hai's military academy, to work as a librarian. Because of the one-child policy we were only able to have a single child, a daughter who we named Tang Li, or Lili as we call her. Lili studied English at university, and went to the States to do a master's in translation. Now she works for a foreign company. She never met her paternal grandfather, who was himself a translator, but she's definitely inherited some of those family genes. The forces of nature never fail to amaze me.

There's an old Chinese saying that the front waves of the Yangtze are driven out by those behind. It means that the old is constantly being replaced by the new, and the new generation always exceeds the achievements of the one it replaces. But I've never found this to be true, not in my lifetime at least. The history of our family is perhaps captured better by what old Mrs Jiu Jin said in the story by Lu Xun: 'The youth of today; it wasn't like this in my day!'*

You've heard many stories from three generations of my mother's family. My grandparents rooted their love in ancient poetry. My

---

* This quote is taken from the short story 'A Storm in a Teacup' (1920), which was originally published in the journal *New Youth* and was later included in his first collection of short stories, *A Call to Arms* (1920).

parents understood each other through classic Western literature and *da-you* poetry. The China I was born into didn't have literature and romance; it didn't even have movies, books or theatre. It had slogans.

How will our generation be defined in Chinese history? Tang Hai and I often stay up late into the night talking about the differences between our generation and the ones that have come before and after, especially those of us who drowned in the great political tide that swept its way across our country. How will we be defined? As the generation when everything was uprooted, perhaps.

We were born into a world of incessant war and suffocating politics: the Korean War, the Three-Antis and Five-Antis, the Great Leap Forward. Our childhood years were defined by unprecedented disasters, both natural and man-made. People walked around like living corpses, their heads supported by nothing but a few jutting tendons. At school we didn't have expert teachers, and we didn't become lifelong friends with any of our classmates either. Every other page in our textbooks spoke of class struggle. We were snatched away in the prime of our youth and cast into a darkness that taught us only to accept fear as an unavoidable truth.

When we were finally allowed after a long absence to return home, it was only to discover that the dreams this country had been built upon and the people who created these dreams no longer existed. Nobody was left to help us grow and develop as people. Our dreams quickly faded, to be replaced by the cold realisation that we no longer had a foothold in the world, not at home and not outside of it either. In this way, anguish and indecision brewed inside us – the bittersweet life experience of our generation.

Reform and Opening Up in the 1980s offered us a lifeline, a way out. It became the norm to come across high-school students in their twenties, university students in their thirties, night-school students in their forties.

All our lives we'd been sat on a rollercoaster of different policies, lurching many times between elation and despair. But from this we learned to have courage, the courage to think, to speak, to do, to win, to love, to hate; even the courage to fail. Those without one *fen* in their pockets dared to cast themselves out into the great sea of Chinese businesses. Those who couldn't speak a word of any foreign tongue went out to explore the world and find their futures there. Those without any relevant experience dared to become the leaders of vast corporations. Some were brave enough to buy large tracts of land in Europe and the States, despite having never set foot in those countries. Those skeletal figures who suffered in silence for so long have now become the backbone of our nation.

The way Crane spoke that day, stressing each syllable with such power, made me feel that these words didn't belong to this fifty-something Chinese woman alone. They were the deafening cries of a generation whose voice was finally reverberating on the monument of Chinese history after more than half a century of suppression.

I asked Crane whether her brothers and sisters identified with her own views, as I'm always amazed by the gap that exists between many Chinese siblings because of the country's fast and dramatic changes. It's like my husband Toby once said: 'Generations in China seem to last only two or three years.'

'It's possible. We might be one generation, but in that short space of time China went through changes that no one could have predicted or planned for. I suppose it's like my mother and her siblings. The China my aunt Red knew was very different to the one her younger brothers and sisters knew, and the age gap between her and my mother was more like a generational gap. There are only two years between my mother and my aunt Orange, but fate took them in different directions, into different worlds. Then there's my big uncle in Hong Kong and little uncle in the States. When they sit and talk about the motherland, with their Western-influenced views, I find it hard to fathom that these two voices come from the same family, let alone my own family.'

A bird singing

My father once said that our home was more like a zoo because of our nicknames – Tiger, Wolf, Crane, Monkey and Duck. But I'd say we're more like a great global counsel, where all different political factions have sent a representative.

Elder brother Tiger's political leanings are closest to those of my parents, in that he's very conservative. They are the beneficiaries of the Communist Party's victory in 1949. They excel at explaining away the mistakes the Party made in the past, even those which caused such profound suffering. They're not fools; they knew some policies were wrong, but they make excuses to justify their beliefs, or else they try and forget the negatives altogether. My elder brother believes that China is a great country, with a huge population and complicated national affairs, within which many contradictions and problems coexist. It's just like Lao Zi said: 'Govern a great country as you would cook a small fish. The ruler must not constantly meddle, lest he ruin the balance of the nation.' Cooking fine cuisine requires both time and skill, neither of which can be neglected. For him, enlightened leaders will always pay more attention to the latter – skill. Successful generals must also be good soldiers. Governing a great country is no different; it requires a keen awareness of what the country needs, when it needs it, and how these needs change over time. Just as you wouldn't begrudge a person for making the odd mistake in life, you should also be willing to forgive mistakes made by the country and the Party, because the country and the Party are made up of people.

Elder brother believes that no matter how grand their ideals, how unlimited their talent, how broad and refined their interests, men, above all else, have to be responsible. And not just that: they have to be willing to pay the price for this responsibility. In our role as their children, we should bring happiness and peace to our parents. When you start a family, you just want to allow your family to live in security and comfort. In your career, you should ensure your work unit achieves success.

I think lots of people from the past two generations in China recognise this kind of value system, because they grew up in a warped political reality where life was always up and down. They followed the Party as one follows the seasons, with the same reluctant sense of inevitability. Apparently, during the Cultural Revolution, when my elder brother was in his twenties, he was so revolutionary it scared people: women who weren't Party members could forget about getting involved with him. Later on, he started dating a woman from one of the Party branches. Every time the two of them met, the first thing they did was read the selected works of Chairman Mao, before discussing the revolutionary experience. When the two of them married, even their vows were an adaptation of the popular revolutionary song 'Sailing the Seas Depends on the Helmsman':

Sailing the seas depends on the helmsman,
Life and growth depend on the sun.
This marriage shall honour the Party,
A legacy never undone.

His wife, my sister-in-law, once said to me in secret: 'Back when we were young, there was a huge group of us who took part in the revolution as if we were possessed by it. By day, Mao's Little Red Book would never leave our side; we would say grace to him before we even touched our chopsticks. At night before the lights went out, we'd all lie prostrate in front of Mao's portrait, begging his forgiveness or imploring him to strike down someone who had wronged us. If Chairman Mao had something to say, we'd jump out of bed and take to the streets, singing praise for whatever it was he said. Your brother would jump around very earnestly, but he was always out of step with the others!

Later, a foreign diplomat – I can't remember where from – presented Chairman Mao with a case of mangoes, which Mao then presented as a gift to some workers in Beijing. Deeply moved by this gesture, workers up and down the country marched through the city streets for no reason other than to parade mangoes. Your brother was even one of those chosen to hold the fruit during one of the processions. Later, I asked why that foreigner had given us so many mangoes. Wouldn't they all go bad soon? Your brother looked at me and replied, in all seriousness, 'The great helmsman's mangoes never go bad!' That might have been true, but it probably had something to do with the fact that hundreds of wax imitation mangoes had been made and shared among the workers of various cities.

Yes, he was certainly one of those people who worshipped Chairman Mao as a god. It was as if there were three of us in our relationship. On the night of our wedding, your brother got into bed and turned the light out straight away, saying it would be disrespectful to undress in front of Mao's portrait!'

But big brother Tiger's loyalty to the Party wasn't completely unwavering. Or at least, in the interests of the family, he used his position of power to help out his brothers and sisters. Second brother Wolf and I both found work thanks to him, and little sister Ducky and her husband got away with a huge fine after he helped them 'alter' their housing registration after they were found to have married too young.*

Second brother Wolf was easily the most rebellious among us. My mother used to say the wolf's character is a combination of angels and demons. Although he too joined the special division of the army, he was never one to act according to the rules in the way that elder brother did. Wolf's political commissar used to serve under our father. He took great care of Wolf, but Wolf threw it right back in his face, refusing to accept his seniority. No, whenever he noticed the smallest hint of injustice, he would want to rush over and fight against it.

The commissar was left with no choice but to report the situation to my father, who was furious with Wolf. In fact, Father was so mad that he sent Wolf away to work on the construction of the Chengdu to Kunming railway. My mother, who rarely argued with Father, was

---

* After 1981, the Chinese family planning policy of 'late' marriage and 'late' childbirth carried an age requirement for marriage of twenty-five for men and twenty-three for women. Violations usually resulted in fines.

really angry with him. She couldn't bear to see her son go through such hardship.

I still remember Father calling Mother out into the yard, shouting about how their second son was an upstart who needed teaching a lesson sooner rather than later: 'Would you rather he learns it now, or wait until he goes to jail?' Mother didn't say anything more on the matter.

Wolf ended up working on the railway for three years. In his own words, those years spent cutting through mountains, digging craters and repairing tracks were what turned him into a real wolf. Father was at heart a very kind and protective man, and he thought that in three years – over a thousand days – any kind of wild wolf would be tamed, so he sent Wolf to Shanghai to study technology.

Do you know, he nearly ended up being sentenced to death along with Hu Lijiao's son Hu Xiaoyang?* When the Cultural Revolution ended in 1977, China opened its doors to the West. The fast-food culture of McDonald's and sexual freedom flooded into China's major cities such as Beijing, Shanghai and Guangzhou. But most Chinese couldn't accept this kind of sexual freedom, which flew in the face of more than five thousand years of Chinese tradition. They thought China had lost control and been poisoned by Western culture. In response, the Chinese government arrested and sentenced a group of gangs to death who were associated with the new sexual freedoms. This group included Tiger and Hu Xiaoyang, who was the son of the former chairman of the Shanghai Municipal People's Congress Hu Lijiao and the grandson of former PLA Commander-in-Chief Zhu De.

Father was both furious and terrified. He immediately called Wolf back to Beijing, and made him work as a staff officer under his big brother. This shattered Wolf's self-esteem. When they were very young, he had always looked up to his elder brother, but that admiration slowly turned into envy as they began competing over anything

---

* Hu Xiaoyang was the son of Hu Lijiao, a former chairman of the Shanghai Municipal People's Congress. In February 1986, he was sentenced to death for being part of a gang accused of sexually assaulting more than fifty women.

and everything, and he became obsessed with outdoing Tiger to prove his intelligence. Now he found himself being disciplined, held back even, by his big brother. Wouldn't that have been a crushing blow?

It all became too much for him to take, and Wolf took off in anger, leaving behind a letter for my father. No one told us younger ones about it then; we only found out much later on. Father has never told anyone what was written in that letter.

Wolf cast off his military uniform and set out for Inner Mongolia, trading horses on the great grasslands. When he had spent the money he'd saved from the army, he made his way down to Shanxi Province, transporting coal. In those days coal dealers didn't make the kind of money they do now; Wolf and his team worked day and night, driving back and forth between the coal mines and the railways.

A year later, Wolf came home and told us he'd had dealings with a corrupt coal dealer and become involved with the mafia before his sense of justice had kicked back in. That's when he followed his instincts, and the smell of money, down to Zhejiang Province. Six months later I got a call from him saying that people in Zhejiang really knew how to do business, and that the networks were huge. The only problem was that to access those networks you needed to speak the Zhejiang dialect. Without it, he felt like a wolf amid a group of humans, being hunted down like a beast.

I once asked Wolf what he'd done that was bad enough for him to have been sent back from Shanghai so soon after he had arrived there. He told me that in the three years he'd spent working on the railways in the remote Qinling mountains, he'd never read a newspaper or heard a radio report. Every passing day was just another battle with the mountain. The Engineering Corps was full of young guys in the prime of their youth, who were always joking around and making vulgar comments about women.

Wolf wasn't used to that kind of talk to begin with; that is, until he came across a painting of a young woman and a great physical change came over him. So when he arrived in bustling Shanghai, which still reeked of debauchery despite the Cultural Revolution only just having ended, he was hooked. City life was like a drug to him. It wasn't long before he joined a nightclub gang, a group of young men and women whose parents were top Shanghai officials. 'Nightclub', of course, was basically another way of saying a place where people went to act like a bunch of hooligans.

Wolf flung himself into his new life, and was always bringing home some new different lamb between his teeth. Mother was horrified, and urged him not to become a hooligan. 'Bigamy is a crime!' she yelled at him. Wolf listened to her and placed a reassuring hand on her shoulder. 'Poor old Mum, you worry too much! It's Reform and Opening Up, the age of progress. Relationships between a man and a woman aren't hooligan behaviour any more. I won't marry a revolutionary, but I won't marry a counter-revolutionary either. If they don't love me, then we can't be together. If they do love me, but my family don't approve, then we can't be together either. Get married? Family isn't like business, where goods change hands or people change jobs and everything's fine. If I have a child but achieve nothing else in my lifetime, that would be a disgrace to my son and his children.'

Of all the lambs Wolf brought home, mother particularly liked a young Mongolian woman. Mother said that she liked her from the moment she walked through the door with Wolf, because she was very orderly in her work, and had a kind personality as well. It was just that voice of hers, that booming voice from the hillside, that put people off somewhat. We used to say that as soon as she opened her mouth she nearly shook the roof off!

But later on, that Mongolian girl took off with a band of travelling gypsies, never again to return to Wolf's side. Now? Wolf trades stock down in Shenzhen. None of us know if he's with anyone. Elder brother said once, 'When Wolf comes home, he's part of the family. If he doesn't come home, he's an outsider, none of our business.'

How does Wolf look upon our generation? He often ridicules us, saying that those of us who simply follow the Party line have been 'duped', fooled into taking the lowest pension while looking after both the elderly generation and the Little Emperors of the 1980s and 1990s, with their inability to let go. We've worked so hard, with great suffering, without ever achieving the *Xiao Kang* (slightly better-off society). And now they say *we're* the ones who have held back the 'Chinese Dream'. *We're* the guilty ones, apparently …

He felt that our generation discovered itself in an age of twisted fate, which instilled in us a burning desire to be the masters of our own destiny. Because the generation above us went through war and peace and we lived through chaos and ignorance, our children are now living in a world of three 'nos' – no responsibility, no sense of value, and no feeling. They have no understanding of history, no care for their family, and they are blissfully ignorant of the realities of this world.

I doubt this level of social upheaval, over just three generations, has a precedent in human history. So to fight back against this fate, it's very hard for the Chinese, because we have no examples to follow. Chinese leaders say that we cross the river by feeling for stones. But do we have the time to find out how deep and how wide that river is? And do we know which stones will ultimately help us cross it? Which stones are big enough to handle our next step forward? Perhaps it was the unrest and upheaval that Wolf lived through that made him forever question the world around him.

Crane finished telling Wolf's story with this question to herself. Her description made me feel as if I had seen for myself the image of a middle-aged man swimming against wave after wave of questions.

Without waiting for me to react, she began telling me the story of her younger brother, Monkey.

Little brother Monkey was the fourth child. More than any of us, he has lived a carefree life. Very much his own man, he boasts of being a 'nothingist' – no faith, no class, no desire. He used to say, 'Faith is the origin of war. Class is a pretence for exploitation. Desire is the source of evil.' In everyone's eyes he was just '100 per cent monkey', as my mother put it: restless, talkative, fun.

In fact, not only was Monkey the most well read of us children – everything from astronomy to geography, history to science – but he was also by far the most practical. He could fix tables, chairs, windows and doors, replace bicycle tyres, tune channels on the TV and set up the antenna, clean the dishes in a flash, and much more. I've no idea where he learned it all.

The year Monkey graduated from high school was the year the *gaokao* was reinstated after the Cultural Revolution, but he failed three years in a row. It wasn't that he was stupid; it was just that he could never agree with the 'standard' answers. Mother said that challenging the established theories of scholars with your own made-up ideas was like fighting with eggs against stones.

Monkey's response was that if we only think what the 'standard answers' tell us to think, then that's basically just 'single-cell repro-duction', while only 'hybrid theory' can contribute to the evolutionary development of civilisation.

At that time, I was helping Tang Hai collect information for his studies, and Monkey would often help me copy down some useful chapters to send to him. There were no scanners in those days, or any of the other digital scanning services you see today. Copying it down by hand and sending it to Tang Hai was the only way for him to read it.

One day, while copying down page after page of notes, Monkey spoke up: 'Maybe the development of telecommunications will lead all humanity into "nothingism"?'

Later, Monkey really did follow a 'nothingist' line of work. He plunged head first into a career in computers, before moving to internet-based work. Now he works in cloud computing. My mother says he's only a 'nothingist' because he's unemployed, unmarried and uninterested in anything but computers. But Tang Hai has always maintained that when it comes to understanding communications development, Monkey has always been way ahead of him.

How does Monkey get by? He actually has a higher income than the rest of us. Much of society views him as an unemployed drifter, although he prefers the word 'freelancer'. He's been hired to set up urban traffic control systems, work in university computer labs, train company executives and create special effects for movies: there are more examples, so many in fact that I can't remember them all myself. In any case, he's a busy monkey, jumping from tree to tree in the forest of his career. A place where there really is no faith, no class and no desire.

How does Monkey view our generation? He doesn't want to think about it! Monkey would say that Chinese people have got far too used to others 'cleaning' and 'adapting' their own history. They like to passively accept the history they are given, rather than explore historical truth for themselves. Only a tiny fraction of the recorded history of the past century is truth, a drop in the ocean. What's left is the famed beauty of our antiques, the supposed brilliance of the Communist Party, the tragic stories from the Loess Plateau and the Great Northern Wilderness found in our popular literary movements, and the howling wolves and braying sheep of the infamous Misty Poets.

Of the history books we will leave to the next generation, how many will be able to look back and reflect on those insane political struggles and lives lost?

How many chapters will speak of those filthy apartments in the Cultural Revolution, where children would squat at the foot of walls stained black from soot and smoke just for being born into families who were part of the Five Black Categories?

How many paragraphs will tell of those veterans who were wounded protecting our country and yet still need to borrow money to see a doctor?

How many pages will describe the couple selling breakfast on the freezing winter streets whose lives afford them just a few minutes to themselves every day?

How many lines will reveal the stories of those children and elderly left behind after the great migration to the cities?

Rebuilding faith, doing away with class divisions and struggling to avoid the temptation of desire cannot save China, because the Chinese have yet to truly understand what faith, class and desire truly are.

Monkey is still single to this day, and I've never heard of him having a girlfriend, or indeed a boyfriend. Back when he was renting an apartment, he used to come home often. But since he bought a two-bedroom flat a few years back, he seldom does any more. I suppose he's what people nowadays call an *otaku* – a man addicted to computers and computer games. Elder brother always says that computers are his life, his wife, and his world.

Whichever way you look at it, Monkey really does live in the 'three nothings'.

As she said this, it made me think that in many ways the internet is really just a space for Chinese both to develop desire and to release it. But I refrained from saying this out loud, not wanting to disrupt the flow of Crane's narrative, as she had already begun talking about her little sister.

Little sister Ducky is the news centre of our family. Every inch of her body is capable of spreading news, any time, anywhere. My grandfather used to say she was a little duck with a big mouth. My grandmother used to say her mouth did more work than the rest of her body put together!

When she started speaking, the whole family faced endless questions about why something is like this, why something is like that. We had to have an encyclopaedia to hand at all times, as my parents wouldn't allow us to spread ignorance by giving her a wrong answer. The moment she learned to walk was the moment our family and all our neighbours lost any shred of privacy.

On her first day at nursery school, Ducky's teacher learned all the eccentric habits of each member of the family.

'Grandpa's feet smell, so Grandma has to put flowers in his bath water' – this was in fact saffron to help with his circulation.

'Grandma doesn't eat seed houses, she only likes seed babies' – she likes the kernels, not the shells.

'Daddy likes playing hide-and-seek so much that he doesn't come home till after dark' – he's busy at work.

'Mummy keeps books in her trousers' – Mother was horrified when she heard that one; all she'd done was hide a few volumes of poetry in her wardrobe. Thankfully no one took the then three-year-old Ducky's words too seriously. Still, Mother felt she had to burn those beloved poems of hers, because in those days possessing anything feudalist, capitalist or revisionist was considered a grave offence.

'Elder brother and auntie can only have a little nephew or little niece, not a little brother or little sister' – the one-child policy, of course.

'Second brother likes lighting fires when he comes home. The whole family start sweating' – this one was actually quite accurate.

'Big sister likes talking to fish, but doesn't like fish bones' – I once got one stuck in my throat, and from then I was always scared.

'Third brother's like the Monkey King Sun Wukong, he likes tearing things open' – we were always comparing our Monkey to the character in *Journey to the West*.

My mother later told me that she and my father lived in constant fear in the run-up to Ducky starting primary school. They were terrified that she would run her mouth off, as she often did, and blurt out something which might be considered reactionary, bringing political ruin on the family.

Sure enough, before Ducky had even finished her first month, Mother was called in to see the recently transferred director of the Revolutionary Committee.

In a most serious tone, the director asked her, 'What on earth does "red is only beautiful with a bit of green" mean? Why should revolutionary red need green in order to be considered beautiful? Don't tell me red isn't beautiful!'

Mother was struck dumb. She had no idea what the director was on about!

'But that's what your daughter Meng Liguo – *Ducky?* – has said. Children don't joke, so was this or was this not some kind of reactionary thinking you've been instilling in her at home? Making her think that revolutionary red isn't beautiful!'

Poor Mother, she honestly couldn't say where Ducky might have learned this from.

'May I ask when Ducky said this?' She was shaking as she asked, and sweating despite the freezing temperatures outside.

The director reached into her desk and pulled out a piece of paper. She glanced at it and said, 'You'll see written in this report here that today our revolutionary students were studying "Introducing the Family". Just here, student Meng Liguo writes that her mother Han Anbi goes by the name of Green, and that "red is only beautiful with a bit of green".'

Hearing this, Mother let out a huge sigh of relief. 'Director, we've got a big family. Before she started school, Meng Liguo's illiterate grandmother must have taught her this as a means of showing her how to introduce all our relatives – she can't write the characters, so instead she comes up with cute little phrases like that. I'll give you another example. Grandmother always says that Meng Liguo's father is called Meng Dafu – *fu* as in wealth – because she believed the Communist Party would make us all rich!'

The moment she heard Father's name, the director's expression changed. Suddenly, she was all charm and welcome.

'*Aiya!* So you're Commissioner Meng's wife? Why didn't you say so earlier?'

Again, Mother was left speechless. 'I, I—'

'This is just great! My husband works in Commissioner Meng's department. We can look out for each other.'

Mother smiled, saying, 'We have two other children here too. Meng Liguo's elder sister Meng Aiguo and her elder brother Meng Baoguo.'

'Hear, hear! What great revolutionary names. They'll surely lead the children on to the golden path of revolution!'

The two women both understood in their hearts that 'looking out for each other' meant a kind of unwritten political contract: 'Party A shall ensure that her husband supports Party B's husband. In return, Party B shall be responsible for supporting the children of Party A in their time at school.'

Now, every time we make jokes about 'red is only beautiful with a bit of green', my mother says, 'Thank heavens for that little mutual understanding I had with the director, otherwise Ducky would have sent us all to jail!' Ducky, feeling wronged, will grumble, 'Not this again! I've said it so many times: you're "children of the revolution, void of love and passion".'

Perhaps it really is as the old saying goes, 'life has a path of its own', for as soon as she entered university, Ducky fell head over heels for a young man in the business administration department. He was the kind of person who could go days without speaking, practically a mute. They dated for four years, moving together to work in Zhuhai after graduation. On the day of their wedding, their close friends asked how they had made it together so far, given how different they were.

The groom, my new brother-in-law, blushed and looked at his bride, who said, 'This time why don't *you* say something? It can be a kind of memento of our wedding.'

After a short pause, the groom spoke, taking his time over every word. 'She loves talking, I love hearing her talk, so we fell into "talking love".'

Father was the one to respond. 'Very well said!'

If society is like the sea, then Ducky is a girl who knows to work around the waves. While others struggle to stay afloat, drowning among the competition, she knows exactly when to dip her toes in the water without ever endangering herself. At the very most she'll wade as far as her waist. In that way she's become an expert at enjoying the lapping of the waves while staying away from the dangerous tide.

How can I explain it better? When they went to Zhuhai, the company they worked for was affiliated with the government. That meant they could run development projects while also bringing in a stable income from government subsidies. Ducky was trading stocks well before Wolf, but she never chased a greedy profit, always taking just what she needed, always having a plan and sticking to it. Later, they jumped on the bandwagon of people going to Yunnan to set up a second home. In fact, if you count my parents' home in Beijing, it was their third.

While most businessmen and -women prefer the hustle and bustle of a main road, Ducky and her husband set up a shop on a lonely old street along the bank of a river. It was really just a bamboo house owned by a local old man, but they put some tables on the terrace and offered tea, coffee and simple meals. This ended up attracting a lot of foreigners, who enjoyed its quiet elegance, and it became something of a meeting point for travelling Europeans and Americans. Ducky and her husband used the money they made to help the old people renovate the bamboo building, adding in an indoor toilet, a kitchen and a hot water system.

Yunnan later became a travellers' hotspot, and they helped the old man find someone to manage the shop, a Dutch photographer who spoke Chinese. Ducky told me that the Dutchman stayed in Yunnan for nine years. He'd travelled all over the world, but had never before come across such mysterious landscapes or rich culture.

For the past two years, Ducky and her husband have been dealing in antiques. One day they picked up two old jars and brought them home. Father saw them and said, 'Back in my village, every home had those in their outside room – preserving pickles, keeping bread dry, fermenting wine – those jars were used for everything. People nowadays are just too much, using things they have no idea about just to make money.'

Last year, they set up an online shop, and begged our parents to give up a room in their home for them to use as a warehouse. Soon after that, things got so busy that even my eighty-year-old parents were running around helping send items in the post. Even though the post office was in the compound, elder brother was still angry with Ducky for her unfilial behaviour. Ducky hit back, saying, 'Honouring your parents isn't about worshipping them as if they were bodhisattvas. It's about helping them understand and appreciate the things their children are interested in. And if they can stretch their legs in the meantime, all the better. The legs are the first thing to age, right?'

And it seems that everything Ducky said was true — my parents' health really did start getting better after that.

Children? Ducky's daughter Yoyo was raised by my parents, with her parents always travelling around, shooting from one place to another, coming in and out of her life like the tide, not attending to her in the least. When Yoyo came back from studying in Australia, they bought her a two-bedroom apartment, to give her some 'freedom'. She only really sees her parents at Spring Festival at my parents' place. Right now they're out at the Qinghai–Tibet Plateau somewhere, trying to find themselves in nature or something.

How does Ducky see things? She sees too many things, to be honest, and they're always changing. She says that's because she's a risk-taker, and by most standards she's made a success out of all her little projects. But she's never quite been able to follow through with any of them.

We were born in an age where many hands made great strength. We had lots of brothers and sisters, and every household was like a mirrored prism — every time something happened in China, however small, you could see all the different types of reaction reflected in that small space. Nowadays, the doors to our country have been opened wide, and we have entered into a kaleidoscopic world. A cultural tide of five continents is upon us, and falling in love is no longer limited by age or gender. Many members of our generation, now in our fifties and sixties, feel like tigers bursting out of their cages. The rich among us go and buy vineyards in Europe to satisfy our romantic tastes. The rest of us dance along to the music blared out in the public squares, reminiscing about our youthful loves.

Finally, Crane said, 'I always thought that being in love was the source of all life, that it couldn't be restrained by faith, politics, culture, folklore, material goods. Then again, when I look at the experience of our generation in China, I think I may have been proven wrong.'

I was looking at Crane as she spoke these words, my heart saying: *There isn't a country on earth in which love has managed to conquer all those things. There is and always will be a gap between truth and reality. That's why people always aspire to achieve it, and struggle for it.*

Later, through repeated inquiries, I finally found out about the childhood experiences of Kangmei – Orange's daughter. Hers had been a childhood far more miserable than mine. After her father was beaten to death by Red Guards, her mother Orange's passion and even her sanity seemed to have gone with her late husband. For the sake of her children, she chose not to die, but she lived in the constant shadow of death.

Kangmei, aged just twelve, began to take care of her mother, who barely left the house and was showing signs of dementia. She never dared mention to her the physical and emotional abuse she was suffering at school; sometimes her lunch coupons would be stolen, and although she was starving, Kangmei would always bring back the rice she had begged for on the street to give to her mother.

One day, when she was fifteen, Kangmei was abducted off the street by a middle-aged Red Guard. He dragged her to an abandoned factory and raped her. Kangmei couldn't face going on like this, and she climbed up to the top of her building to throw herself off. But as she stood there, she was persuaded not to by a worker, who talked her down and took her home. When he saw the bleak conditions Kangmei and her mother were living in, the worker began to support them quietly, helping them recover from the Cultural Revolution.

In 1979, Kangmei's father was included in the first group of diplomats to be posthumously rehabilitated by the state. In the same week she moved into the new house awarded to her as compensation for her father's misfortune, the then 23-year-old Kangmei married that worker who had saved her years earlier, a Mr Wu. A year later, they had a daughter.

Their daughter was given the name Wuhen, meaning 'no scars', in the hope that she would never have to suffer as her mother and grandmother had. The scars that marked Orange's heart have not healed to this day.

As I was writing the passage above, I found myself recalling something my grandfather once said: 'The colours of clothes are always washed away with the stains.' China's Cultural Revolution scoured the country of those stains identified by the Communist Party – feudalism, capitalism, revisionism – but at the same time they caused the colour of China's love to fade.

PART IV

Diverse 'Lovers'

The 3D Generation

LILI

· *daughter of Crane, granddaughter of Green, born 1988* ·

YOYO

· *daughter of Duck, granddaughter of Green, born 1984* ·

WUHEN

· *daughter of Kangmei, granddaughter of Orange, born 1980* ·

After I'd heard Red, Green and Crane tell me the stories of three generations of women in their family, I knew I couldn't stop there. My interest and curiosity meant I had to speak to the next generation as well – a generation who were carrying China into a 3D age by breaking free from the shackles of tradition, taking the giant leap into Westernisation and pushing the boundaries of what an individual could achieve in society. Theirs was a world so far removed from their parents' and grandparents' worlds that it was hardly recognisable.

But when I told Red and Green about my idea, they both said it wouldn't be possible. Although I put the question to them at different times and in different places, their answers were the same:

'Xinran, you won't be able to pin them down! If you want to speak to one of them, that might just be possible. But if you're looking to interview all five, then you'll be spending the next three or four years just chasing after them. After that, you'd need another ten years to listen to their stories the way you listened to ours. By the time you'd finished writing it all up, they'd probably be grandparents themselves!'

'The tempo of their lives has been sped up by computers – even their dating partners seem to change in a flash. The way they communicate and the way they work have no geographical or linguistic boundaries. These children have unrestricted access to the internet, twenty-four hours a day, seven days a week, 365 days a year, receiving an endless stream of information that drives how they think and how they make decisions. The idea that we could spend just a few days with them, sitting down face-to-face, talking about family, is just inconceivable to them.'

But Crane had an idea: 'Xinran, you should try making friends with my daughter in the way that generation is used to making friends. We older generations should strive to keep up with the pace of the times our children live in, because that marks the progress of society and the extension of history. To stay in reasonably frequent contact with my daughter, I forced myself to learn how to use a mobile phone, a computer, even video messaging. As she herself put it, if our generation can learn to keep up with their generation, then the communication and emotional connection between us will be stronger and deeper than any other two generations have experienced at any point in history. If not, then we'll be left stranded in the Stone Age, staring out helplessly at the digital age they inhabit.'

And she's right – ever since I started using WeChat,* I can contact her any time of the day; I can even see her on video. It's not an issue if she's travelling on the other side of the world; we can still chat whenever we feel like it, and it's all free. I think if you learn how to use WeChat, my daughter Lili will agree to an interview with you.'

I'm someone who tends to stick to traditional ways of doing things, my excuse being that I refuse to become a slave to modern technology. I can see and understand the benefits brought to people's lives by modern means of communication, but I feared that joining WeChat would open the floodgates to too much information and messaging, and I'd be left struggling to keep my head above water. If I was travelling, resting, working or for whatever reason unable to reply straight away to my friends and relatives, I was afraid that they'd be left worrying for no reason. Sometimes waiting can be sweet, but most of the time it's not. It's bitter, terrifying, and can even breed resentment.

But I was determined to find out more about how China has changed over the past century, and how one family's story could reflect those changes. I knew that if I couldn't get to hear the stories of the younger generation, I would never be able to follow up on this particular family's present or its future. And this is why, against my better judgement, I decided to set up WeChat on my phone. Learning to speak with this younger generation on their own terms was the first step to understanding their stories.

---

* A multi-purpose messaging and social media app popular in China.

From what I could make out from the image on my computer screen, Lili was very petite. That, coupled with her sweet-sounding voice, meant you would never know she was a young woman in her late twenties – I guessed most people would take her for a sixteen-year-old girl.

Like so many Chinese girls of her age, Lili had perfected the art of finding the exact 'selfie angle' on screen that made her eyes appear bigger, her nose higher, her chin sharper and her mouth smaller – all the hallmarks of 'feminine beauty' as defined by the younger generations of China today.

But the way she spoke and thought made it clear that behind that facade was a mind growing more and more conscious of its roots, and a heart with a growing taste for the sweetness of love.

So you've heard all about my family, I suppose, at least the older generations. Didn't it seem like my great-grandparents lived in a fairy tale? That's how the family legend goes, anyhow. My mum's parents were more like statues, cast in the bronze of the Chinese revolution – I mean that you rarely catch them displaying any kind of human emotion. They say my mum and her siblings lived in a political zoo, with its terrifying tiger, wayward wolf, contemplative crane, mischievous monkey and daring duck! I think our generation is more like a mini United Nations – we all have such different views on the world.

Of grandma Green's children, uncle Tiger had two kids, a boy and a girl. You know, Grandma always reckoned the one-child policy was delayed specially for them. Second uncle Wolf and third uncle Monkey don't have any. I'm the only child of Crane, and my aunt Ducky also has a daughter. If you count the children of all Grandma's brothers and sisters as well, there's just too many of us to keep track of. We've got cousins over in the States and Hong Kong, but they've all married and settled down, and we might as well be living on two different planets – we hardly ever speak. Of those of us left in mainland China, the one we keep in touch with most is Wuhen, Aunt Kangmei's daughter.

First uncle's two children may technically be from the same generation, but they're both much older than us. We always joke that they're like trams, because they've got the country and the Party directing them with cables from above, and the tracks laid down below them by our ancestors. They'll never leave that set path to walk off on their own.

First uncle is the kind of guy who does political background checks on his children's partners. Since we were young, he's always made sure that when the family gets together at Spring Festival, the first thing his kids do is report to our grandparents on how well they've been doing at school or at work. This is always pretty embarrassing for Yoyo, Wuhen and me; but then again, I can tell that for all their achievement, they've had to sacrifice a lot of their own dreams in the process. Don't just look at how successful they've been in their careers; listen to how they constantly complain about their families. I've always felt there is a kind of sadness to their lives.

That's why I think of Yoyo, Wuhen and me as truly being part of one generation. Why just us? My grandmother said you write books about Chinese women and Chinese families, so at some point you must have written about how wide the generational gap is in China? There's no other way of putting it really – it's huge! Let's look at Chinese love lives for example. But first I should apologise in advance that I can only speak for the women of this family. The men were all very silent figures, kind of passive when it came to family affairs, and it was only ever the women who bothered telling their children about family history. Sometimes these accounts differed greatly between two people, but sometimes they were exactly the same. They all loved talking about women's stories though, that's for sure. I guess they didn't know what to say about the men.

My grandma told me that in my great-grandmother's era, it was always the parents who arranged their children's marriages. Back then, it was rare to find newlyweds who actually loved each other, and most of the time it was only a sense of filial duty that kept people together in marriage. Very occasionally people dared to pursue love and physical desire. The lucky ones were punished accordingly to family law, while the unlucky ones ended up riding the wooden donkey.* When I first heard that, I thought my grandma must have been trying to scare me. It wasn't until someone sent me a link to an article titled 'Immoral Criminal Law' that I found out she'd been telling the truth all along.

My grandmother's generation was caught up in all kinds of revolutions, and those new ideas divided up the fates of all her brothers and sisters: her brothers watched things play out from overseas, while my grandma and her sisters threw themselves into the revolutionary cause.

My mum was one of five children. The first three were teenagers during the Cultural Revolution — the most emotionless time of our country's history — when even a kiss could land lovers in jail, and the last two came of age during the Reform and Opening Up period. Uncle Monkey described that period as being full of life, a crazy, enticing, exciting time to be alive. My aunt Ducky called it an international feast.

For us, we find it strange if someone's got siblings, but think it's perfectly normal to have slept with a dozen guys by the time you're sixteen or seventeen. How's that for a generation gap? There are still Chinese parents out there who think family is the absolute root of everything, and children who are still hung up on the whole filial piety thing. It's no wonder they can't jump over the generational gap into the present day. I mean, haven't even our country's leaders exhausted themselves by constantly jumping over the gap and back again, trying to please everyone?

Come to think of it, maybe it's not even that accurate to describe Yoyo, Wuhen and me as one generation. There are just a few years between us, but our views on marriage, society and the future are all very different.

There's something my mum and I argue about all the time: she thinks that falling in love is the basis of all life, that it transcends

---

* As recorded in the *Twenty-Four Histories*, a woman committed of adultery or conspiring with a lover to kill her husband was sometimes punished with a device known as the 'wooden donkey'. This was a contraption made from wood, with a sharpened wooden stake attached that would be repeatedly forced into her vagina until she bled to death.

faith, politics, culture, folklore or anything material. But how is that possible? Don't we Chinese always say that you've got to 'talk reality' first before you can 'talk love'? So basically you've first got to establish whether being together is practical before any kind of love or emotion can grow. Isn't that what finding a partner really is about? In the 1950s you had to be make sure they had the right political background; in the 1960s it was their social status; in the 1970s it was all about the worker-peasant-soldier classes, but peasants were too poor, so it was better to find a worker or a soldier. By the 1980s you had no prospects without an education, so university students became the most attractive option. In the 1990s, the truth was hidden among so many rumours that you just had to trust your own instincts!

'Now? With the arrival of the internet, there's no such thing as universal truth any more. Suddenly everyone's free to create a new identity for themselves online, and people look for partners based on a set of very rigid factors like height, wages, et cetera. So with that in mind, do you really believe that love transcends faith, politics, culture, folklore and anything material? Of course it doesn't! My mum's a bit of a – what's the word? – dreamer. I guess she's just a bit of a dreamer. And by the way, Xinran, please don't go telling her I told you so!'

'Of course, but I can't guarantee she won't read this book!'

Well, that's true enough. But how many people who read books remember specific sentences from them anyway? I'm impressed if they can just remember the outline of the plot. Books are like drops of water dripping into the great library of the sea.

I asked Lili whether her love life had been determined by those factors outlined by her mother – faith, culture and so on. Her response, shouted at the screen, was somewhat telling.

'All right, Xinran, I'll do the interview, then. I know exactly what I want to say anyway.'

While Crane had asked me what I wanted to hear, her daughter was telling me she knew exactly what she wanted to say. As Lili began recounting her story, I wondered to myself if this was yet another sign of the generational gap.

I didn't have much of a relationship with my mum until I graduated from university. Before that, as long as I wasn't failing my exams or dying of some disease then my parents didn't seem too bothered about what I got up to. Most of my classmates' families were the same. We awkwardly fumbled our way through adolescence, learning about the changes to our bodies and our emotions as they happened to us. Thank God we had the internet to turn to for sympathetic and anonymous advice. Sometimes I really feel sorry for you older folks. I've no idea how you managed in life.

My experiences in love were kind of like the backdrop to my life growing up, but I wouldn't say you could call them 'spectacular landscapes'. I've got no particularly moving stories to share. What I do know, though, is that those 'landscapes' were absolutely defined by faith, politics, culture, folklore and material things.

My first love was unrequited. Have you ever heard of unrequited love? It's not narcissism, it's more like being an obsessive fan of somebody. But unrequited love is more ... how can I put it? Anyway, that was my love for a famous Chinese singer — I'm sure you've heard of him. Every single one of his songs makes me burst into tears. I really don't know how it's possible for someone's voice to make your heart ache so badly. I was only around fourteen at the time, being treated like a princess at home and always getting top grades at school.

You've met my mother, and now you're looking at me, so you can probably guess that my father's very handsome as well. I've never known what it was like to be an ugly duckling; I've never been depressed or anything. But for some strange reason, his songs made me feel a kind of sadness I didn't even know lived inside me. One time when I was listening to him sing, my whole body went limp and I nearly fainted. Can you believe it?

The first time I had an orgasm was from listening to his music, and for those few seconds I felt like I was some kind of goddess from another world. When it was over, though, I was terrified – I didn't know what had just happened! I even thought that someone might have slipped some drugs into my lunch at school, because I'd seen people in films acting that way after they took drugs. I hope you're not laughing! Anyway, don't worry, the singer I'm talking about is Leslie Cheung, and he's even older than my dad. Well, he's dead now; he committed suicide. But his voice is still young!

Later, I developed a crush on one of the maths teachers at school. He looked a lot like Leslie Cheung, and his dress sense was way better than any of the other male teachers. He was never actually my class teacher though, so I never had the chance to spend much time with him. In any case, that crush didn't last long. I saw him arguing with one of the female teachers, and he was pushing her about like some kind of barbarian. He had none of the style you'd expect of an educated man.

For a long time after that, I wasn't interested in men. Lots of my high-school classmates started dating, but I was left by myself to simply watch. None of those boys moved me in any way.

But I've always been a real believer in the idea that everything is predestined. I know 'the one' is waiting for me somewhere out there. When I went to the US for university, I thought I'd found him.

I was nineteen when I arrived. The unfamiliar food, language and customs put me in a kind of ivory tower, where my only comfort was in listening to Leslie Cheung's music. I'm sure you can imagine that, alone in a foreign country, that kind of music really resonates with you.

One day, I found myself sitting alone on the campus lawn, listening to a song called 'I Am What I Am'. Tears were streaming down my face, thinking about whatever awful Western meal I would have to eat next.

'Are you all right? Need any help at all?' a Chinese voice called out, and I looked up to see a young man approaching from the other side of the lawn.

'I ... I'm fine. I just got caught up in a song I was listening to; I guess I went too far.' I tried to cover for myself.

'Glad to hear it. Have you just started school here? I don't think we've met, but I've seen you in the cafeteria. You always look so hesitant, kind of cut off from the crowd. A few of us Chinese students guessed that you might need some help.' As he spoke, he turned to face a group of students sat not too far off, chatting on the grass. A few of them waved at me.

His name was Gao Ming; he was a financial management sophomore who was also chairman of the Chinese students' union.

It was as if Gao Ming's sudden appearance brought me back to the mainland from a lonely desert island. The kindness and consideration he showed me made me feel that this was a man straight out of a Leslie Cheung song! I opened myself up to him, and in time I sensed he too began to enjoy the affection between us. But Xinran, there were two sides to that 'affection': my gratitude for his support, and his urge to protect me. We weren't lovers back then. To be honest, I didn't think I was good enough for him.

With Gao Ming's encouragement, I started getting more involved in the students' union. My talent and energy attracted the attention of lots of male students, and it wasn't long before my dorm became a kind of meeting point where people would come to hang out and watch movies online. Most of them were boys, obviously.

Gao Ming and I were always coming up with new ideas for the union. We even invented a slogan for the Chinese students: 'Have Peace in Your Life and Pride in Your Study: Live Peacefully and Work Happily!' We took it for granted that Gao Ming, as chair of the union, would act as our dormitory leader as well, which worked out for me as I loved being with him in my room, seeing how comfortable he seemed in this intimate setting.

Around Easter time the following year, a few friends and I decided to make the most of the holiday and drive out to the Grand Canyon. We were happily chatting away and discussing plans over supper in the cafeteria one evening when Gao Ming came over to join our table.

'What are you guys talking about? You all look so *high*!' His question was clearly directed at me.

'We're gonna take a drive to see the Grand Canyon. Just booked a 4 x 4!' one of our friends butted in.

'Lili, are you going too?' Gao Ming seemed surprised.

'Yeah, all four of us are going,' I said with a mouthful of food.

'Well, why didn't you tell me?' Gao Ming's voice had suddenly become very aggressive.

'You ... Aren't you going back to China for the holiday?' I didn't know what was up with him.

'So you just waited for me not to be around, then made plans with other people?!' His eyes were blazing.

'I ... Why can't I go? I don't understand what's wrong.' Our friends mumbled their excuses and slipped away from the table, leaving us there alone.

'How could you treat me like this? You obviously don't care about *us*!' Gao Ming was pretty much shouting by this point, and everyone around us was staring.

At that moment, I wasn't exactly best pleased with him either. 'Why are you so angry? What's got into you? You're going back to China to see your family, and I'm going on a trip with friends. *The river water hasn't touched the well water* – it's got nothing to do with you!'

'I mean, how ... how could you just take it upon yourself to make plans with the others without even letting me know?' Gao Ming slammed his fork down on the table in anger.

'Why, though? This isn't a union event.' I thought he was being very unreasonable.

'I know it's got nothing to do with that, but it's got a lot to do with *us*!'

Hearing that, I stood up. It had suddenly dawned on me that he saw me as more than just a friend.

Gao Ming saw that I was lost for words. He took me by the hand, sat me down and said something I didn't even register – my brain was too full of muddled thoughts to be fully aware of what was going on around me. Gao Ming was in love with me? This 'Mr Perfect' was really in love with *me*? I mean, he seemed to really care about me; was what I felt for him perhaps love too? I had always been very grateful for what he had done for me, but did those feelings amount to love?

I spent that whole night lost in confusion. Later, Gao Ming would tell me that we went back to the dormitory together, but that he didn't come in with me. Seeing how I was acting, he thought his behaviour had really frightened me – damaged me, even – and he too felt scared.

Did you know the word *jingxi* – 'pleasantly surprised' – can also mean *xijing* – 'surprisingly pleasant'? Well, whatever it was, the two of us really did become lovers. He never did go back to China that Easter holiday, and I never made it to the Grand Canyon. Instead, we took a trip to New York together. Who paid? We both did, split down the middle. In the whole time we dated, we never fell out over money. We both came from one-child families, so all the money from our parents' and grandparents' wallets tended to end up in our hands, but that didn't mean we were those kinds of kids who just lived off their parents.

Why did we break up? Less than six months after we became official, Gao Ming developed a bad case of love OCD. It started with him texting me constantly throughout the day – there wasn't WeChat back then:

'What are you doing right now?'

'What time are you coming back to the dorm?'

'Who are you with?'

It was like a non-stop, 24/7 interrogation. I even had to tell him exactly what time I'd be going to sleep, what exams I was taking – everything. If I didn't reply straight away he'd come and wait for me outside whatever classroom I was in. My classmates would see him through the window in the door and tease me: 'Come to check up on you again?'

When he stopped letting me have any contact with other male students, that's when it began to feel like he was trying to put me in a cage. Sure, he loved our romantic strolls around different parts of the campus, but he wouldn't let me live a free life, and never let me off the leash. He used to go crazy whenever he found out I'd spoken to another man, no matter what excuse I gave him. In the end, what led me to suggest we break up was finding out that he'd been going through my inbox and reading my emails. I told him I couldn't take his possessive behaviour any more; I'd lost all the respect I once had for him.

But Gao Ming was too proud to accept the break-up. It wasn't so much his feelings that got in the way, more that a woman breaking up with him would have been a blow to his self-esteem. 'Ever since I was a little kid,' he explained, barely concealing his rage, 'I've been in charge. That goes for my parents as well – they do what I say. So how *dare* you say we should break up! That's for me to decide.'

That chairman of the student union, that kind young man, that tender loving Gao Ming. That image shattered in front of my very eyes.

I stared at him with a cold gaze: 'Well, then, why don't you hold a meeting at the union to announce that you want to break up with me? Or how about we go to the cafeteria together, and you humiliate me in front of everyone eating their supper? Better still, let's go to the campus lawn, and with the whole school watching, you can tell them all what a bitch I am! Whatever you choose, I'll go along with it. I'll go along with it out of respect for how you once helped me. But just know that I'll never have any feelings for you ever again.'

Gao Ming never did do any of those things. In fact, he dropped out of school and went back to China. I heard his parents got him a job as a civil servant.

How did I feel about that? When I first heard he'd dropped out, I did feel a dull pain and a trace of guilt. He had only been half a year away from graduating; maybe I should have seen our relationship through until he finished school. Maybe if I'd gone along with his demands he would have gone on to become one of the pillars of our country.

But that's not how I see it now. Self-confidence without limits is just arrogance; ambition without empathy is just selfishness. If people don't see eye to eye in a relationship, then it won't work. If you don't miss them every second they're not around, then it won't work.

When you start going out with someone, you enjoy doing whatever they want to do and giving them whatever they need. You're eager to please and desperate for gratitude. But as time goes on, love can breed jealousy in the heart and start wanting to control the other person. A mature love is one which accommodates the needs and individuality of both sides. Only when both sides are equal can love be true, don't you think?

I don't think that sacrifice is necessary for love either. For two people who are joined in love, their sadness is shared, as is their happiness. It's not a sacrifice if you *want* to do something. Besides, if there's no trust and respect between two people, they can have no future together. Am I right, Xinran?

In my second year, I decided to give myself a birthday present from my parents, and I went out and bought a new iPhone. That ridiculously convenient tool of communication immediately opened me up to a world of opportunity when it came to finding new online partners. Since then I've never stopped using it, but although I've met countless people, I've only had two online boyfriends. They acted like mentors and friends to me, sharing their experience and philosophy on life. It's just a shame we never met!

I don't think you could say that we were lovers; I don't know if that's how they'd see it either. Sometimes they'll be quite flirty with me, but when it comes to online lovers there are real ones and then there are fake ones. If you don't ever meet them, who's to say which is which? If we had met up, maybe we wouldn't have felt anything for each other.

I think I might want to meet them one day. Of course, I wouldn't say no to having a few boyfriends on the go at the same time. Nowadays, if a girl only has one lover, she's kind of looked down on.

You can have multiple lovers? How do these people cope? I realised that the China I knew was quite a different place from the China inhabited by this new generation of children. It felt as if my ignorance would never catch up with their times.

As I thought of my China, Lili continued speaking about hers.

I've got a 'proper' boyfriend now, though. When you're in a relationship, everyone around you feels way more relaxed. When you're not, your parents will worry about whether you'll ever get married and your friends will always be busy trying to set you up with somebody. It can even make you even feel worthless yourself: 'Is my life a complete mess?' 'Am I so terrible that no one will ever like me?' That kind of thing.

I met my current boyfriend while studying in the States. An English guy called Ben. He's tall, thin, easy to be around. Very … English-looking, I guess. We met at a student party through mutual friends – he knew a friend of mine and I knew a friend of his. We all had a few drinks together and had a great time just chatting away. The four of us started going on trips, going out, having fun.

I was a third-year undergraduate back then, while the other three were doing master's degrees. When our two friends graduated Ben stayed on to study for his PhD, and I took his advice to do a master's. When I'd finished, my mum and dad wanted me to come back to China, saying I was their only child, *the only blade of grass on the field*.

So I went back, and soon started working at a foreign company. I never expected Ben to follow me back to China so soon after that, but he found a job researching the Chinese internet as part of his doctoral research. I guess at first I saw Ben as a minor detour on the journey of my life, but when I heard the news that he'd got a job in China, I began to think that perhaps our fates were intertwined.

Ben later told me that he liked me from the moment we met. Doing a PhD was also just a way to be with me. Doesn't it sound just like a love story from a movie? He loves joking around, and I never used to take things that seriously either, but we've started calling each other boyfriend and girlfriend.

Although we're in different cities, the bullet train makes it super convenient to see each other – it only takes four hours now from Nanjing to Beijing. And of course WeChat makes everything much easier as well. We're lovers who just happen to do most of our dating online, but in a completely different way from the two other secret online boyfriends I had.

What do I like about him? He's sunny, he's inquisitive, he's witty. I feel very relaxed and safe when I'm around him. For Ben, there's nothing worth complaining about. Even if his bag was stolen, or if he lost his passport or wallet, he would just say something like: oh well, at least the money will go to someone who needs it! Don't you think he's a bit of an Ah Q?* Very carefree. When he speaks about something he's really passionate about, though, he can be quite ruthless.

Our biggest attraction to one another is the way we argue. That doesn't make a lot of sense, does it? We rarely agree with each other's point of view, despite the painstaking lengths we both go to to try and persuade the other we're right. We just enjoy the endless debates.

What do we argue about? Back in the US, we would argue about world politics.

I support the US Democrat Party, the UK Labour Party and the China Association for Promoting Democracy. Ben supports the US Republican Party, the UK Conservative Party and the Chinese Communist Party – I could never understand why he saw the CCP as being right-wing.

I'll say to him that the parties I support are all advocating a democracy that will bring most benefit to the working classes. Unless a society is made up of many different voices, you won't be able to achieve any form of social equality. The right-wing parties all exploit minorities and those living on the fringes of society for their own gain.

Ben, on the other hand, will argue that without a structure in place, the masses will just end up a group of followers, believing that power can protect them no matter where it comes from. He said they don't have the strength or the capital to take responsibility for the

---

* Ah Q is the protagonist of Lu Xun's 1921 novella *The True Story of Ah Q*. Lu Xun used the character of Ah Q to reflect many of the character flaws he saw in the Chinese of the time: ignorance, arrogance and smugness. Today, the name is used to describe two types of character: 1. Those who always consider themselves to be right, and lack the ability to be self-deprecating; and 2. Those who are oblivious to humiliation or hardship.

development of society, and any society that aims for equality has to be built on a material basis. He claims that all the parties he supports build on characteristics unique to their own country, while integrating social resources and strengthening society's stability.

He'll say to me, 'Don't think that just because it's called the Communist Party that its politics simply involve going around preaching equality and communism. What about the positives? Without the paternal control of the government, could China have gone within just thirty or forty years from being a country whose entire population relied on coupons to survive to becoming an economic superpower buying up companies across the world?' It sounded like something my father would say. Then again, my father is a Communist Party official.

I particularly dislike US policies in the Middle East, and the way the US acts as if it is the world police. But Ben argues that you can't say now whether these policies are good or bad; you have to wait and see how they are judged by history. To back this up, he always says that half the US was against Lincoln when he was in power, but now people think he was the greatest president ever!

There are some things we agree on, though. Not many, but still . . . We both think the US should ban the widespread sale of firearms, stop selling weapons to the world, and control the way Hollywood blockbusters profit from showing violence to young people.

Back in China, our arguments tend to be about Chinese society. Ben loves China more than I do, no doubt about that. He thinks all the mistakes of the past can be explained away with simple excuses.

For example, I always say how disgusted I am by the hypocrisy of the Chinese elite. I think the government have bred them into a crowd of running dogs that they can use for their own benefit whenever it suits them to do so. But Ben says that it isn't that simple, and that it isn't so easy for the elite: 'Chaos had reigned in China for many years, followed by a century when the country had shut itself up in a box. The distance between China and the rest of the world was vast – both literally and spiritually. Hardly anyone back then could speak a foreign language, and people had to grow up fast, yet those members of the elite emerged as heroes from a time of chaos.'

At least he admits that those heroes, just like the heroes of the past, couldn't have got where they are today without others having to shed blood, sweat and tears. The only difference is that the heroes of today don't carry knives.

Another thing I can't stand today is how Chinese education, health-care and law have become businesses, and I'm worried that if China continues down this route, our people's faith and quality of character will be weathered away by money. But Ben always says that it's all the West's fault, that they had infected China. He thinks that we've been cheated all along by American banking, telecoms and pharmaceutical industries, and is adamant that even though there are always reports into corruption and other scandals, there's even more going on behind the scenes. He used to ask me: 'Why do you think there's a higher percentage of lawyers in the US than in any other country in the world, but they still can't put a stop to fraudulent behaviour?' According to him, it was because law is the most profitable industry in the States. He thinks lawyers are the worst of the lot!

So basically, we disagree on just about everything. He always takes a different view from me; I mean, even when we're discussing the differences between men and women, he claims to know women better than I do!

He's said things like:

'Women are emotional creatures who always assume the worst in any given situation. They are a hundred times more stubborn than men.'

'Once she's been hurt by the man she loves, a woman will give up on everything, sometimes even take her own life.'

'Women are two-faced – they'll laugh on the outside while crying on the inside.'

'Women like to listen to sad songs more than men do, because they're more easily hurt.'

I couldn't let that last one go, so I shot back at him: 'I've always liked listening to sad songs, and I've never been hurt by anyone. I cry because I feel empathy for others.'

'External wounds are easy to see,' Ben replied, 'but emotional pain is very different. People gather up information from the world around them all the time, without even noticing they're doing it. These small pieces of information become subconscious feelings that cause you to react emotionally or physically to something without even knowing why. For example, if a woman sees a man she doesn't know, she may blush. Why? Because the man has something about him that the woman's subconscious is attracted to.'

To prove his point, Ben told me about a Harvard study on the phenomenon of emotional telepathy. After a couple deeply in love had stared at each other for three minutes, their hearts would begin to beat in sync, as if they were being conducted by a doctor. He also loved repeating that thing people say about couples starting to look more and more like each other during the relationship.

Hearing that really made me laugh: 'I could never look like you, with your pointy chin and big nose!'

Ben laughed as well: 'I don't know about that. Lots of Chinese girls get plastic surgery to give them pointier chins and bigger noses. But, you know, if we stay together, you won't need to go through all that pain – you'll just end up looking like that naturally!'

We usually speak in English, but sometimes I help Ben with his Chinese. The four tones, various regional dialects, modern slang and endless vocabulary really confuse the hell out of him, but helping Ben study isn't such an easy task for me either. Having lived in the world of my own language for so long, I'd never stopped before to appreciate just how magical Chinese really was.

Our vocabulary has evolved over five thousand years. Every character that makes up every word is rich with its own unique meaning. For example, the two characters of *Fu Gui* (富贵), can have three different meanings: *fu* (富) means wealthy, *gui* (贵) means expensive, and *Fu Gui* together means 'wealthy and in possession of a high social status'. But Ben can never tell the difference between *fu* and *gui*. He writes things in Chinese like: 'After Reform and Opening Up, Chinese peasants were increasingly expensive.'

Then there's the phrase *Gu Niang* (姑娘), meaning 'young woman'. The character *Niang* alone has the same meaning as *Ma* (妈), meaning 'mother', but that doesn't mean they are interchangeable, right? Ben told me about a French classmate of his who had taken a fancy to a Chinese girl. When he wrote her a love letter, he forgot how to write the character *Niang*, so he thought he was being smart when he just replaced it with *Ma*. So instead of addressing her as 'Dear young lady', he ended up writing 'Dear paternal auntie'...

The topic of the twelve signs of the Chinese Zodiac is something else Westerners find fascinating. They all love talking to Chinese people about their sign and what it means. The unfortunate thing is, many of them don't know that *Shu Yu* (属于, 'to belong to a category of something') and *Shu* (属, 'to be born in the year of') have completely different meanings. Some end up learning the hard way, like Ben's Canadian classmate who excitedly told us: 'I belong to a pig!'

Ben always says that the four tones are the 'natural enemy' of any Westerner learning Chinese.

I've always done my best to comfort Ben. I've told him that there are so many customs in China that even the most experienced Sinologists can't avoid certain mistakes. For example, there was the German businessman who'd studied Chinese half his lifetime but couldn't understand why his Beijing business partner was so put off by the idea of selling German sausages for 250 *yuan*. He didn't find out until a local told him later that the phrases *Er Bai Wu* – '250' in Beijing and *Shi San Dian* – '13 o'clock' in Shanghai – both mean 'idiot'!

Because of their lack of understanding of Chinese folklore, Ben and the other foreigners in his group were the butt of many jokes when they first arrived in China. There was the time when some of his female colleagues unwittingly walked into a shop that sold burial clothes and found themselves so attracted to the 'fashions' on display that they each bought dresses and wore them to a banquet that night. They ended up scaring the wits out of the Chinese guests, who saw these pale 'immortal souls' walking around in traditional Chinese burial clothes.

I've also heard of Westerners mistaking the yellow paper Chinese burn to worship dead souls for festive greeting cards. They write

'Merry Christmas and Happy New Year' on top and send them to Chinese friends, making them think they're receiving a message from another world.

I think opening up to the world must have had a big effect on Chinese people, as it's becoming more and more mixed up with other languages. And the people who really understand the essence of Chinese, who know what's behind these changes, are few and far between. Sometimes I think even we Chinese don't realise this is happening. Ben's always asking me about certain words, and although they're very simple, the kind you use without even thinking, I always struggle to explain clearly how they're used. Sometimes I'll type his questions into an online search engine, fishing for an answer, but all I end up catching is a load more jokes!

'Xinran, didn't you used to teach Chinese at SOAS? Well, you must understand where I'm coming from. Don't you think all those mistakes and mistranslations are *hilarious*?

'Chinese people are extremely hospitable. Even if they've prepared a feast, they'll tell their guests it's just a *bian fan*, a simple home-cooked meal. At a dinner party where one such *bian fan* had been prepared, a foreign guest, feeling confident in his command of the language, turned to his host, stuck his thumbs up in the air and said "*Hen hao de da bian fan*", "What a great pile of shit!" Unfortunately for him, adding *da* to the *bian fan* gave it a quite different meaning...'

My final question for Lili was to ask whether she intended to be Ben's bride someday.

Lili told me that she still hadn't thought of a way to introduce Ben to her parents – she was worried they would object. When they had sent her away to study in the States, they had told her endlessly that she shouldn't trust Westerners, let alone marry one. For her part, Lili understood that her parents' military status meant that a foreign son-in-law would lead to more political background checks and make family reunions difficult affairs.

She truly admired her parents and respected their views, but she confided in me that she just didn't like Chinese men in that way. This was partly because of how the men in her family had acted in the past, for example the way her paternal grandfather had forced her father to grow up as if he was an orphan, or the way her maternal grandfather treated his wife like one of his many subordinates at work, sitting around reading all day, waiting for his three meals while she rushed about doing the housework. There's no question her father was devoted to his work, but what effect had this had on his wife and daughter? After supper, her mother would often keep guard over the TV by herself watching the news or the latest Korean drama. Even her great-grandfather, a legendary figure in her family, had been a slave to the patriarchal, male-dominated culture of his time.

Lili told me something her father had once said: 'A great man is bold and uncompromising in his work. Day after week after year, these qualities are hammered into him, until finally he has enough metal to grind an iron rod into a needle. Only then can he call himself a man of steel!' But, she said, if he's bent on becoming a 'man of steel', he obviously has no time for a family. So what does he need a family for?

In 2016, when I was back in Beijing to take part in the Bookworm Literary Festival, I made sure to meet up with Ben. He was indeed, as Lili had said, a very 'English-looking' young man, tall and thin with an untidy mess of brown hair. He wore a pale blue coat, jeans with holes in the knees and a pair of worn-out leather shoes. He was very polite, and spoke with an attractive voice. In a rush, I asked him how he felt about his relationship with Lili.

Ben's immediate response was: 'I really like her.'

'Why?' I was a little surprised at his frankness.

'Because she made me love China! We come from very different backgrounds, but there's also a lot we have in common: we're the same age, we share an interest in each other's language and culture, we're both well-educated. As for the differences between us, the internet helps us overcome those boundaries of faith, politics, culture, folklore and so on. I like the fact we argue all the time – I think arguing helps us better understand the way other people think. It's like the Chinese say: *The eyes keep watch on the six roads, while the ears listen in all directions.*

'I think that when it comes to defining right and wrong, Chinese people are much more extreme than Europeans and Americans. I'm currently researching Chinese social media trends, and they all point to the idea that nearly all Chinese netizens follow popular opinion. Even the younger generations, the most dynamic, lively, opinionated children of the 1980s and 1990s, are really just taking one of two prevalent standpoints when they think they're expressing their own "personal opinions". Very rarely do they have an entirely unique opinion on something. It's almost impossible to find people with independent or forward-thinking views.

'Compared with her contemporaries, Lili is a very smart young woman, and the topics we argue about stick in my mind for a long time afterwards. For me, she's the perfect partner. When she sets her mind on loving something, she'll do anything to nurture and protect that love. But in her eyes, I'm not sure I even count as her full-time partner yet, or what percentage I'm at now!'

'So have you thought about marriage, then?' I teased him.

A distant look came into Ben's eyes: 'I really care about Lili, but like I said, I don't know what I mean to her. Sometimes I wonder whether she's another one of those young women with several social-media "lovers". I'm not saying I'm worried about her having other lovers right now; even if she does, I'm confident that she'd choose me over them. For Chinese people today, there are virtually no guidelines for dating.

'There's a popular dating show on TV here called *If You're the One*, where you see so many young Chinese women who think the only way to prove your love is with a house, a car and high wages. You must have heard the infamous quote from a contestant a few years ago: "I'd rather be crying in the back of a BMW than be laughing on the back of a bike."

'I'm just a poor student; my mind is my only real asset. I've got several brothers and sisters, and my parents can't give me much in terms of material support. In today's China, I'm what you'd call a "naked-marriage man". Would Lili dare go against social customs and marry me? I can't say for sure, but I'll do my best to make it happen. Or, as you say, I'll "give my guts a shake"!'

Ben's Chinese wasn't bad at all.

'Well, then,' I asked, 'when do you plan on proposing?'

'I'll propose the moment the new US president takes office. During the election campaign, Lili will just say no.'

'Why?'

'Because we always have to be on different sides!'

In 2016, the States were going through an election that was slowly sliding into the realms of fantasy. Outspoken businessman Donald Trump and member of the US political elite Hillary Clinton were fighting for control of the White House. I hoped at the time that whoever was eventually elected would have the chance to hear about how young people like Ben and Lili view the world. After all, theirs is a love which spans the two biggest global languages and cultures.

Yoyo, 2016: a backpacking lover

Next I interviewed Yoyo, Green's other granddaughter; Crane's niece; Ducky's daughter.

The first time I met her was on Skype. She introduced herself to me straight away as a 'backpacker of love', while drawing her face closer to the camera lens so that I would be able to 'download the information of her language more accurately'.

Yoyo had eyes that could speak a thousand words, and a nose somewhat larger than most Chinese. Her mouth was slightly upturned in a way that somehow reminded me of the actress Catherine Zeta-Jones, and when she smiled you couldn't help but feel that everything in life was worth smiling about.

Every time I spoke with her on-screen, all of her facial features seemed to come together to emphasise the words she spoke, and the memory of her face in my mind is that of hundreds of different opera masks. But Yoyo was indeed a master of her feelings, and before I had the chance to say anything she was already off, telling the colourful story of her experience in love.

I've had my fair share of different love experiences. If my mum knew the full extent of them she'd be bouncing off the walls! Don't get me wrong, I actually really admire my mother. That's not just because my grandma is always going on about how she's a really great person, but mainly because of what she's done with her life. She's travelled up and down the country, achieving anything and everything she's put her mind to. She's not like those other *dama* her age, who fill their days with idle gossip, pyramid schemes, public square dancing and Korean dramas. My mum, she's an unstoppable force, diving head first into all kinds of new and exciting adventures, dragging my dad along for the ride.

I don't listen to the people who say my mum's just a brainless, big-mouthed duck. She's more than capable of passing on a few words of wisdom when she feels like it.

Among my mum's contemporaries, there can't be that many people who can keep up with their children's generation the way she can. Anyway, we're talking about me! I'm not a daughter of the elite or some genius who knows exactly what they want to do in life, but neither am I a spoiled, fragile little girl who hides behind her parents. If we still had the kinds of personal files they did back in my parents' day, the identity column of mine would say: backpacker, *sheng nu*.*

But my kind of backpacking is different from the usual kind. I'm not exploring new places, I'm exploring all that love has to offer in search of what true happiness is and where my future home might lie. I've tried nearly all the popular dating trends – flash love, flash

---

* *Sheng nu* is a derogatory term for unmarried women in their late twenties and beyond. It is often translated as 'leftover women'.

marriage, rented marriage, internet dating — I'm just missing being someone's *xiao san*.* I've never been on the TV dating show *If You're the One* and never been to the marriage market in the park with my mum, either. At the moment I'm still just a poor little *sheng nu*, waiting for the next trend to appear so I can try that too. It's not a joke; I'm being deadly serious! I see love as a playground set among a hundred blooming flowers — why shouldn't I pick them to see how they smell? If you're sure of who you are, you'll be fine. Who cares what other people say, anyway?

I started with a 'coffee shop lover'. You know, I'm already over thirty and hurtling fast towards forty. When I first entered adolescence, it was around the time China was opening up to the world and Western cultural influences were starting to rush in. When any kind of special occasion or festival came around, we'd be clamouring to go and eat at McDonald's. Back then, we all thought eating there was the height of sophistication! Drinking coffee was also a luxury, and the price of one cup would be about the same as half my parents' wages for the month. My friends and I would save on things like textbooks and school supplies just to be able to drink coffee, and when we did, of course we had to bring a camera with us.

Chinese aren't so used to the bitter taste of coffee, but the kind of uplifting feeling you get when sitting in a coffee shop more than makes up for that. If you posted pictures of it on your dorm wall, that would attract more envy than any student prize ever could. I had several of those kinds of photos up, which didn't go unnoticed by the other girls in the dorm. They all looked up to me — not for any academic achievement, of course, but for the sexy poses I pulled in those photos. It's just a pity there was no internet back then, or I'd definitely have been an online sensation!

My coffee-shop lover brought his mum along to meet me. To this day I still don't quite get why. We were classmates, two young people who had arranged to go for a coffee, so why the hell did he bring his

---

* *Xiao san*, meaning 'little three', is used figuratively in China to refer to a mistress, the so-called 'other woman'.

mum? I mean, she paid the bill the first time, so maybe that's why? Maybe it was her decision – I don't know. Maybe she was afraid I'd lead him astray?

The second time it was just us, though. Seeing the other couples there kissing and cuddling, we tried our best to imitate them. That was the first time I'd really touched a man, feeling his body all over. It felt like an electric shock. Thinking about it now, perhaps that was my first lesson in sex education? But we soon realised that the coffee shop was well out of our price range. We were just two poor students, at a time when even the children of high-ranking officials hardly had any cash to burn.

But there wasn't really anywhere else we could go. If we went to the park, we'd have to wait for the cover of darkness to find that 'electricity' again – during the day there were just too many people. In the end, we decided to cool things off for a while. Each of us would keep an eye out for places to go and we'd meet up again once we'd found some-where. We didn't have mobiles at that time, but some of the richer students had pagers, and they helped us send messages to each other. After several rounds of messaging, we gradually began to lose interest. The last time we met, we broke up.

I was later introduced to a friendship club. I guess it was a little bit like today's singles parties in the way young people would use them as an opportunity to meet and get to know each other better. This particular club was different from the rest, though. It was decorated in a very simple but chic way, with row after row of small cabin rooms along a corridor leading away from the entrance hall. The cabins had no lights inside, just a small table and two chairs. People entered the hall – which wasn't very big – and chatted awhile with everyone else there. If someone came up and suggested you go somewhere for a private chat, you'd make your way down the corridor to choose a cabin. Once inside, you'd light a small candle that had been carefully placed there beforehand. As the flickering candlelight flashed across your face, you felt that strong, basic desire to touch each other. But people were still very self-conscious back then. We were shy, I guess you could say.

That's why you would never hear any great sounds from the room next door. At most, there might be a low murmuring or a faint moan. Once, actually, a girl burst out of one of the rooms crying her eyes out, shouting 'Hooligan!' I went on several different occasions, and was 'picked out' by a different man each time. We were all very Chinese about the whole thing, and it was always the boys who would pick the girls. But thanks to my coffee 'experience', and the fact I enjoyed the close company of a man, I never even came close to calling anyone a hooligan. I never let any of those one-off lovers touch me anywhere too intimate, mind you.

The club later got closed down as part of an 'anti-pornography' campaign. I think what we call 'flash love' today is an extension of what went on in that club, or perhaps a rebirth of it. Either way, I really think that for those of us who have grown up in a household or even a society that lacks any kind of sex education, this so-called 'flash love' can actually prove to be a very educational experience. That could be very beneficial for people who want to have their own families in the future, don't you think?

I didn't answer Yoyo's question, because I didn't know how to. Not only had I heard of that kind of club, but I had actually researched them before. In *The Good Women of China*, I had written about them as places where people would meet for sex. Before I left China in 1997, urban regulators cracked down on them as part of their campaign against the sex industry, not really understanding their place in Chinese culture. China has always lacked a completely independent judicial system to define new phenomena that are marginalised by society.

Dating websites in China now offer so-called 'couples contests' and 'eight-minute dates', tugging at people's emotions and drawing them in with a series of little games. Some people say these are harmless fun that can even help introverted youths become more socially active, but others think those who take part in such games do so because their hearts are empty, or that they are simply allowing people to take advantage of them. No one really knows how to define such things.

My 'flash marriage' came about because I wanted to experience love at first sight. I used to see love at first sight as such a magical thing. I mean, humans aren't animals in heat, are we? Our feelings are controlled by the brain's sense of right and wrong. That's why I thought that if you really did feel love at first sight, then that force must be quite something.

My grandmother brought me up. The man in my life back then wasn't my father, but my grandfather. And my God did he act like a grandfather – strict, serious, solemn. On the very rare occasion that he'd crack a joke with us, we'd celebrate as if we'd won the lottery!

Grandma said that when they were young, Grandpa was always teasing her, being silly and messing around. But that all stopped when he got caught in the rain of the political movements. He was terrified of saying something wrong or being misunderstood, something that might bring ruin on the whole family. Anyway, I used to feel so terribly jealous when I saw the other grandfathers out on the street, carrying their granddaughters around on their backs. My grandpa never did any such thing!

Not long after I had graduated from university, I met a man. An older man, I should say. He was a professor, younger than my grandpa but older than my dad. He'd had a wife before, but she had died a few years back, and their two children now lived in the States. We met in the Xinhua bookshop in Wangfujing. At that time, I really wanted to go to grad school, choose a subject that would take me abroad so I could go and see the world.

And so there I was, standing in the World History section of the bookshop, staring pretty aimlessly at a bunch of books I could barely understand. I noticed a very refined-looking older man who'd been standing there next to me for quite some time. We caught each other's eye and smiled, asking at the same time, 'What book are you looking for?' That's when we realised we were both there without any particular book in mind – we were both just browsing.

Later, I got tired of it all and went to rest on a bench by the side of the bookshelf. The man was already sitting there, and when he saw me he shuffled to one side and motioned for me to come and sit beside him. That's how we started chatting. When he found out I was there looking for a book on world history, he said he might be able to help as he taught history at university.

A few days later, I found myself visiting his home to borrow some books. Walking into his house was like walking into a library, with bookshelves lining every wall. In a very gentlemanly fashion, he invited me to sit down and have some tea, showing me a photo of his late wife and telling me stories of their younger days. On his desk there were photos of his son and daughter. Another showed him holding his newborn granddaughter, with such a warm and kindly expression on his face.

That day, I started crying as soon as I left his house. Why didn't I have family like that? I couldn't sleep for days afterwards; my mind was filled with thoughts about the professor and his family. Once I'd pulled myself together, I started reading the book he'd lent me like crazy, just so I could go back to his home and borrow another. It wasn't long before I realised what had been torturing me, what thought just wouldn't let me go – I wanted to live there.

That's when I started to seduce him. Genuinely, that's what I did. I began wearing see-through clothes, doing anything to be as provocative as possible. It worked, of course. He couldn't keep his hands off me, and I couldn't hold myself back either.

When he found out I was a virgin, he panicked. 'If you give me your virginity, what will you do in the future?'

I laughed. 'I'll give you the rest of my life.'

He wasn't happy at all about that, but it didn't bother me. As long as I could live in that house with him, I'd be happy. That's what I thought back then anyhow, because I had decided that what the two of us had experienced was love at first sight.

We agreed to register our marriage but wait until his children came back from the States before announcing the wedding. I didn't go and live with him straight away; one, because he feared his neighbours would think he was a creepy old man – in fact, he was only fifty-six – and two, because I feared my grandparents would drop dead with anger if they found out. I didn't really factor in my parents to any of this; after all, they never gave a damn about me.

It all sounds ridiculous now, doesn't it? But I was thrilled with our relationship – that house was now my house, and the tender care he showed me was something I'd never got from my grandfather or my father.

Less than a month into our marriage, my new husband sat me down for a chat. We spoke for nearly four hours – well, most of the time it was him speaking and me listening. To cut a long story short, he said that he was more than twice my age and fast losing the faint strands of youth he had left, while I was little over twenty, with the rest of my life to look forward to. Being together wasn't fair on my future. He'd come to realise that my feelings for him were just emotions misplaced from an absent grandfather and father. He said he could give me that kind of love without us being married, and that I'd be welcome in his house whenever I pleased – I could even bring my future family there. He ended by saying that our relationship was harmful to both families, and that it should end immediately. I'd never cried so badly, but I knew what he said was right. Luckily, he knew someone to help us with the divorce. In those days, it wasn't such an easy thing.

Some people say men and women who fall in love at first sight are crazy. All intelligence and rationality go out of the window, and you believe that you'll be together for the rest of your lives. Even if it's a 'naked marriage' you still won't care. Then when the passion of being a newlywed has died down, you realise you've made a huge mistake.

But that's not how I see it. People are part of the natural order of the world, and like all living things our actions have a cause and an effect. What I'm trying to say is that, in the end, everything happens for a reason. People must be made up of more than just IQ and rationality – what about desire?

Did we meet again? Of course, but with two conditions. Firstly, he was to treat me as he would treat one of his students, and secondly, we wouldn't meet at his house any more. I didn't want to disturb that family any more than I had already.

Sharing a bed with the professor was a sexual awakening. But after that, I couldn't bear being with someone just for the sex – I needed more. Then online dating started getting popular and I found myself moved by a few warm words read from a screen. But whenever I met those men in person, it was always a let-down. None of them had the same quality of character or elegance my professor had.

I know lots of women aged around thirty to fifty who have been hurt so badly that they've just given up on the idea of trying to find another man. Another real man, at least. On the internet they don't have to reveal anything, and instead create an ideal version of themselves to find their ideal online man. Some of those women even end up in a 'perfect' marriage, enjoying life as someone's virtual wife. This kind of thing can only happen in China, don't you think? And me? I'm from China's 3D generation; of course I can't fall behind the times. I had four online lovers at one point!

Back when I used to use those dating sites regularly, there'd always be a whole group of men waiting for me. I developed a set of 'screening questions' to stem the tide, and after one round usually about 85 per cent of them would have disappeared. Those who remained went through another round of questioning, and even fewer would be left. In the end, I always chose those who gave the most intelligent replies.

We just chatted really, mostly about love and relationships, but sometimes other things too. One of my four online lovers was an excellent wordsmith who loved to argue – he could really drive me mad. One was so warm-hearted and patient with me I often felt like crying when speaking to him. One understood family problems in a way that reminded me of the professor. That leaves my favourite – he was even-tempered, ambitious, and always had something meaningful to say.

Why have so many at the same time? In my experience, you go online to become someone you're not – the protagonist of some made-up story. Then, when you've had enough, you just shut down your computer. The lights come on and you're just you again, without the baggage that comes from real-life relationships. There wasn't any system in place to verify users' real names back then, so one person could open up several different accounts. That's how I opened four – a middle-aged man; a middle-aged woman; a teenage girl; and a teenage boy.

In the end, my act wasn't good enough. The first account to be seen through was the 'middle-aged man', closely followed by the exposure of the 'middle-aged woman'. I should have seen it coming, really – what did I know about being middle-aged? I thought that I understood people of my parents' generation, well enough to hold a conversation at least. But I just couldn't get my head around the way they spoke, using all these metaphors and words people of my generation would never have used.

These days, lots of people argue about whether internet dating is safe. But is that really an issue? I mean, as long as it's just dating, and no one expects to get married or anything, then of course it's safe. Distance creates the safety; anonymity backs it up. I've heard experts say that most 'couples' on the internet know hardly anything about each other, and in most cases the relationship is reliant on software that uses questions like 'What are your interests?' and 'What's your favourite food?' to match people. I suppose one potential danger is that login details or phone numbers can be lost in an instant, and if you lose contact with someone you know online you probably won't ever hear from them again. If you do lose touch – intentionally or otherwise – it could lead to really bad emotional damage.

I came across lots of people playing the 'game' of online dating, for a variety of reasons. Some had no time to go out and make friends on their own, others felt lonely in their marriages, and some just wanted to play with other people's emotions for the fun of it. But I believe the joyful or sad outcome of online dating is not down to the individual alone – it has a lot to do with society, because that's where an individual's ability to understand morality comes from. It's also where we learn to decide what's real and what's fake. Maybe that's wrong, but all I'm saying is that modern technology isn't always to blame.

I've never met up with any of my online lovers. But who's to say I won't meet my future husband online? I just have to use my time carefully and filter through the garbage. I've met up with a few men I met online, but none of them were ever my lovers; we were just playing an extended version of our online game. I always arranged to meet them in a coffee shop – a public place with lots of people. This shows them the kind of lifestyle I like, and warns them not to think that I'm a fish ready to be caught so easily.

Ninety-nine per cent of men try and get me to meet them in a hotel, but every time I get one of those requests I say 'bye-bye'. You know, there are now special 'love hotels' set up specifically for online lovers to meet. Apparently they originated in Japan, but they've become seriously popular in China. They usually have cringey names like 'Love at First Sight' or 'I Love Hotel'. I've never been to one, though; I'd be scared of catching AIDS.

Yoyo's story made me think of a report I'd read in the *Guardian* which asserted that since Mao Zedong's death in 1976, China had not only gone through an economic revolution, but also a sexual one. The first 'love hotel' in China popped up in the south-western city of Nanning in 2008, and since then thousands upon thousands of these types of venues have appeared all over the country, like bamboo shoots rising up after a spring rain.

Over the past few years, online abuse of *xiao san* has been pretty savage. But the weird thing is, the more abuse they get, the more there are. Not only that, but the quality of these *xiao san* keeps getting higher, and their age keeps getting lower. Like a lot of other people, I think I saw all the commotion online and it made me really want to go and try it to see what all the fuss was about. The only thing that worried me was that the wife would bring her whole family along and beat me to a pulp!

A few years back, I got a job working as a PR at an ad agency. The manager of the company was really handsome – like film-star handsome. He wasn't just a pretty face, either, he was quite honestly the nicest man I've ever come across. When I later heard that he was married – to an absolute stunner, of course – my sense of adventure and excitement went into overdrive, and I decided to test the depths of his love.

First I used the excuse that I needed to talk about a project to invite him to a high-end coffee shop, which I'd hope would show him how classy I was. Next, I organised a small get-together in a French bar near the office, just with some friends from the company. I even ended up spending a fair amount of my own savings, but it was worth it. After a few more little parties like that, I got transferred to his office to work as his secretary, which is the first step to becoming a *xiao san*. Our conversations shifted from work to our hobbies, and then seamlessly to outright flirting.

But then, just when I was on the brink of becoming his *xiao san*, I got promoted. I was transferred to work in the office of the general manager – who just so happened to be his wife! She was no fool, and had obviously worked out what I was up to. In response, she took me under her wing. She was very friendly, very considerate, and always took great care of me. This, of course, made me feel terribly ashamed, enough at least to make me abandon my plans of becoming a mistress.

The single life started taking its toll on me, and I gradually began to think of dating as a form of travelling. The journey is always exhausting, then when you finally arrive you have your moment in the sun, a brief time to admire the scenery and take a photo before you have to leave. Then you're just left to think about where to go next, to do it all again.

I later tried out a 'rented marriage' just to help out a guy in need. His family back in Changchun were always putting pressure on him to find a wife as soon as possible. He said that for the past four years, his trip home for Spring Festival had been like crossing a mountain of daggers and a sea of flames. Not one day passed without him being interrogated, harassed or criticised by his family, seemingly backed up by all the neighbours along his street.

That's why he went online to find a girl willing to take a wedding photo with him, preferably someone who'd also be willing to spend three days with his family during Spring Festival. He'd be willing to pay 3,000 *yuan* in marriage rental fees, plus travel expenses and other costs incurred on the visit. Lots of people online asked what was wrong with just getting someone to stand in as his girlfriend. But he said that his grandparents were still clinging to the hope that they might one day hold their great-grandson in their arms, or at the very least have their grandson's wedding photo to place on their mantelpiece. Only then would they be at peace. His online friends said it would be impossible — who would agree to do such a thing as take a wedding photo with a stranger? What if they themselves wanted to get married one day? How would they explain things if they were found out?

But I agreed to it. After all, I was a backpacker of love, and I saw this as being just another stop on my journey. I wasn't planning on spending one day of my life dependent on a man, nor was I interested in being just another submissive daughter-in-law. As they say, *if you're helping Buddha on his journey to the West, you may as well take him the whole way* — if you're going to try and explore all that love has to offer, you may as well do it properly! But actually, when we got the wedding photo done, I definitely felt something I wasn't expecting. That bride staring back at me was really beautiful.

Anyway, because of that whole rented wife episode, the producers from *If You're the One* got in touch with me, asking if I'd like to take part in the show to talk about my experience, but I refused. People already secretly thought of me as being kind of perverted: if it all came out in the open, how would my highly traditional grandparents cope? As for my mum, I knew she liked catching the tides of her time, but she didn't know her daughter liked doing the same. The main difference between us was that we were in very much different seas — she was sailing in business and I in love.

What did my family think? Well, that depends on who you're talking about! What my grandma worried about most was that if I kept 'jumping from one man to another', as she put it, I would never have a baby. I used to tease her, saying: 'I've been flicking through the Chinese law books recently, both the women's and marriage sections, but I can't find anything that states women have to have a child!' My grandma Green is a cultured individual, and very articulate, but she can be very frank when she wants to be.

'That may well be true,' she said, 'but the basic law of humankind states clearly that women should give birth. Unless you're burdened with some kind of physical defect, you're clearly defying the established social order by not having a child. And if you don't, mark my words, people will be shouting at you so much that you'll be drenched in spit!' Her words might have sounded a bit excessive, but she wasn't wrong. This kind of sentiment is rooted in almost every person's heart – or in every Chinese heart, at least.

I think it's hilarious the way that, just because you're a woman, just because you have a womb, you have to have a child. Even though it could lead to pain and suffering, even death in some cases, you still have no choice but to go ahead and face the risks. I read an article once that said the maternal death rate in China is very low, achieving the target set by the UN a year early. But the way I see it, what do those figures matter to the women who are already dead?

I think my mum and dad like the fact I've always stood on my own two feet. My 'look after yourself and the family will take care of themselves' outlook on life hasn't interfered with their desire to travel around the world, nor have they had to worry about the burden of looking after me. Sometimes I think my existence was just a way for them to prove their sex organs worked OK. They probably don't have the faintest idea how I grew up!

I suppose most people would say I'm already an experienced *sheng nu*, but given what some others get up to in China today, I think I'm more like the other *sheng nu*, a 'saintly woman'. Firstly, when it comes to dating men, I have standards; I have a bottom line. Secondly, I gave my virginity to a Chinese history professor, not just any old fool.

Thirdly, I have a compassionate heart. Fourthly, I know when to stop before things turn ugly. Fifth and finally, I've never brought harm to any family through my backpacking of love.

Wuhen, 2016: a wounded lover

Of that generation of Red's sisters' grandchildren, I also interviewed Orange's granddaughter, Wuhen.

The first time I spoke with Wuhen was over the phone. Her painfully serious tone of voice made it clear she was only speaking to me out of a sense of duty to her family elders, and for my part, trying to get her to speak was like trying to squeeze the very last remnants of toothpaste from the tube. Only after I practically begged her did she finally agree to a video interview, on the condition that we would not use cameras. But how would that differ from a phone call? After a few rounds of failed negotiations, I turned to Red and Green for help.

With Red's help in persuading her great-niece, I met Wuhen when I was next back in China, in the spring of 2016, speaking for three hours in the teahouse of a Nanjing hotel. The first thing I noticed about her was her slumped shoulders, suggesting that she had borne a heavy burden in life. Also, despite her name, her face was prematurely lined, with creases around her eyes and cheeks that belied her young age. Most prominent of all the creases on her face were the three lines between her eyebrows that resembled the character *chuan* (川). Those furrows, wrinkles that spoke of her heart's suffering, opened and closed with the narrative.

Wuhen didn't have the youthful and mischievous grin of her cousin Lili, nor did she have Yoyo's bold and unrestrained manner of speech. But I felt very strongly that her heart was like a clear spring formed from the drops of her tears, whose calm surface didn't tell of the hardships she had suffered in her young life in the same way her face did.

She had obviously come prepared, knowing exactly what she wanted to say. Each sentence was like a brick which she piled on top of the others one by one to build the story of her life. All my pre-prepared questions for the interview went out the window, and I just wrote down what she said.

Lili, Yoyo and I come from the same root. We have the same great-grandparents, and are part of the same generation. But political fate split the six surviving children of those great-grandparents into two main camps in the 1940s. The two sons took the family business along with Western capitalism, and the three eldest daughters married revolutionaries.

In the late 1960s, the daughters were split up again, this time by the Cultural Revolution. Red and Green – Lili's and Yoyo's grandmothers – seemed to benefit from the events that took place, becoming part of the ruling proletariat class, unlike my nana Orange. Because Grandpa got caught up in the political problems with the former Soviet Union, the family were cast into limbo, and eventually left broken.

For almost half a century, Nana's brothers and sisters had lived and raised their children on opposite sides of the earth, but during the Reform and Opening Up period of the 1980s the mistakes of the past were finally rectified, putting an end to the years of complete chaos. Nana's political status was restored, and our big family was finally reunited. However, the political and social climate in which we had grown up had given us completely different outlooks on life, just as in *Tales of Yanzi*, the famous book written sometime between 475 and 221 BC:

> Plant an orange tree south of the Huai River and you'll get the sweet and tasty Ju. But plant an orange tree north of the Huai River and you'll get the bitter and distasteful Zhi. They are the same fruit, but the environment has changed them.

And so we granddaughters, despite being from the same generation, have a very different understanding of society and have adapted to its changes at very different speeds.

In many ways, I think Nana Orange has actually been very lucky. In most people's eyes her life was destroyed the day of her husband's tragic death, but I think the mental illness she has suffered since has in fact saved her. Without it, she'd have died from the pain long ago. Some people say she'll 'wake up' the day she finds her husband's remains, but if she did, would she be able to cope? Would she understand today's society? Would she be able to endure hearing how her daughter Kangmei has suffered in silence for nearly forty years because of her? Would she even recognise her granddaughter?

My mother Kangmei and my father Wu Ping are children of the 1950s — both were born into so-called 'black category' families, and both grew up receiving re-education from the worker and peasant classes. They not only suffered political oppression and revolutionary humiliation, but also endured extreme poverty and hunger. They lived just the same way as those workers and peasants who existed on the lowest levels of Chinese society, who by the hard work of their own backs supported China in the midst of a political storm. I am a witness to this — I saw what happened and I heard what was said, leaving mark after indelible mark on my heart. My parents gave me the name Wuhen, meaning 'no scars', in the hope that my life would be free from the pain they suffered. But perhaps they didn't realise I was born into a scarred family.

Wuhen's words reverberated around my head for a long time. My name is Xinran, which means 'to always be happy in work and deed'. But in nearly sixty years of life, have I always been happy? Sadly, it wasn't until I moved to the UK when I was forty that I finally understood what it meant to be truly happy with your life. Her words reopened a wound of my own that had closed fifty years ago, a scar I imagine

Wuhen's mother would also have. What pained me now was that I had never imagined our future generations, the children we struggled to look after and worked our hearts out for, would also carry such pain in their hearts.

I felt as if my whole existence had the sole purpose of making up for and remedying the pain of my ancestors. Not long after I was born, my father reluctantly parted with three generations of women – Nana, my mother and me – and set out to do business in the south. He's a man, and he wanted to make sure that his family, who had lived in the shadows for so long, would walk into a better future in the sun. He wanted to seize back the thirty years the political movements had snatched away from him. He fought for us like a man possessed by some indomitable spirit.

Even in my earliest memories, I don't think I've ever seen my mother Kangmei have a moment's rest. Her hands were busy the moment she opened her eyes. Aside from her exhausting job working a lathe in a factory, she had to look after her chronically ill mother and the infant me, all the while researching ways she might find her father's remains. When I was small, I had this theory that my mum was actually a fairy from another world, because she never seemed to sleep. Before my father went south for work, the two of them would help each other study for a university correspondence course every night. One studied physics, the other English.

The poorer the family, the earlier you have to start doing chores around the house, and I began helping Mum look after Nana when I was eight. At ten, I started cooking. By the age of twelve, I was looking after Nana by myself. I had very little time to study, but my grades were consistently very good. By the time I started high school, I could instantly memorise the works my parents studied through the night to make sense of them. When it came to registering for university entrance exams, I really wanted to apply to Tsinghua, but in the end

I couldn't bring myself to let my mother look after Nana by herself. She had worked tirelessly half her life, and it wasn't as if Nana was going to get better any time soon.

That's why I ended up applying to read Media Studies at Fudan University. I thought being a journalist would be a great way to connect with all kinds of different people and all kinds of different issues, which at the same time would help me better understand a society I had never truly been involved in. By the time I graduated, my father's business had achieved some degree of success, and he came back to Shanghai to set up a boutique media agency specially for my mother and me to work at, renting out a shop front in the community where we lived. He just wanted us to be able to do something we enjoyed doing.

Our company was very small, but things started very well. It wasn't long before several media companies got in touch, looking for animators and graphic designers. Very soon, Mum and I were being run off our feet, so we hired a young guy who had studied IT to work as our assistant. His name was Wang Peng. He had a sharp mind and was also capable of putting up with great hardship.

Wang Peng came from a very poor peasant family in Jiangxi Province. Not many children in his village had finished middle school, so when he later came to Shanghai to attend professional training college, his family all saw him as a phoenix who had risen up and flown the coop. In fact, he didn't just work hard in his job; he also helped us with a lot of housework.

Back then I had a lot of classmates in Shanghai, and knew a lot of people I'd met on the internet. But those people didn't mean much to me; I was just waiting for the opportunity to go and study abroad. I wanted to see the world.

One day, Nana had a bad fall. She ended up lying motionless on the ground, Mother and I trying in vain to lift her. We were thrown into a sudden panic – the two of us had no idea what to do. That's when Wang Peng showed up. He quickly but calmly called an ambulance, telling us not to move the old lady until the doctor arrived.

After the doctor had left that day, Wang Peng stayed behind to help us settle Nana. Without even stopping for something to eat, he stayed with us past nine in the evening, fixing things around the house, replacing light bulbs which hadn't worked for as long as I could remember.

After he left, Mother and I fell exhausted onto the sofa in the living room, staring out at a house which was now so much brighter than before. She turned to me and said, 'This Wang Peng, he's just like your father at his age, always willing to help out.'

That night, I lay awake deep in thought. Was there something more to my mother's words? Father's hard work was just a way to make our days a little happier and more comfortable. If I was to go abroad, how would they manage?

From that day on, I began to see Wang Peng from a different perspective; a woman's perspective. He was a very typical southern man, small and wiry, very calm and serious in how he went about his business, and very kind in how he treated others. No matter whether it was a delivery man or a potential client, he would treat them both with equal respect. He was also very good at saving money, which he did to bring his parents over to see Shanghai – the big city.

I soon began asking myself if I could ever fall in love with this man. First, I decided to turn to my online friends for advice; after all, they didn't know who I really was. I submitted my question anonymously online, and within a few minutes I'd received a long list of comments:

'It's not love, it's sympathy playing tricks on you. Watch out, sympathy is the trap of love.'

'I can understand your feelings, but if you marry him, you might regret it for the rest of your life.'

'What age are we living in? What do you think this is, a Qiong Yao movie or something?'*

'Read romantic novels much?'

'Are you sure you're not just looking for a male nanny for your mum?'

'Follow your heart!'

---

* Highly successful Taiwanese writer whose work often focuses on the feelings of young women.

'Don't treat this peasant guy as your doll. The feelings of two people can't be decided by one!'

Feeling even more confused after reading all those comments, I decided to consult 'North Star', a university teacher I had met online when I was in my first year at Fudan. That had been a difficult period for me; I had found it hard to adjust to my new university life, and there was always something I needed help with. That's how I ended up talking to him. No matter what questions I had, he would always guide me with the utmost care and patience, which is why I nicknamed him North Star. When we'd first started chatting, I'd been worried he'd take me for an ignorant fool if he realised I was already a university student, so I'd told him I was still in junior high. I thought this would allow me to be more unrestrained in the questions I asked. After all, at that age you're supposed to be more inquisitive, aren't you? Later, in order not to reveal my true self, every time before we chatted I'd have to remind myself over and over again – 'I'm in junior high, I'm in junior high' – to get in the right mindset. Trying to keep up with your own lies is perhaps the worst form of torture.

When I logged on that day, I casually mentioned that I'd seen a thread recently about a young woman fretting over a potential partner – had he seen it too? I was, of course, referring to myself, but I wanted to know what he thought without asking him directly.

North Star said that in China, love is often lost to reality: 'Dating is more often than not about the need for survival. Politics, family property, status, even Chinese nationality, become bargaining tools in relationships. In today's China, marriages are often the culmination of these trades. From the recent fad of 'speed dating' to the old-style 'marriage markets', all these things point to the loss of our Chinese civilisation. And not only this, there is also a 'poison' instilled into Chinese culture from ancient times – the poison of sympathy and gratitude.

'Sympathy and gratitude put lovers in unequal positions, whereby love becomes a source of blame on one side or tolerance on the other. Blame and tolerance are the mortal enemy of love. We are the product of a deformed love that has arisen from our deformed history.

This is why online dating is on so big a scale in China. You don't have to speak face-to-face, so both sides are free to instil the idea of a fantasy partner in their online partner. Once you've done this, it's almost impossible to escape from this artificial reality, even if you want to. Online love is mysterious and illusory.

'On the internet, people can speak out to their heart's content without worrying about being impolite or offending others. In this space, people can find a release from their depressive lives. That's why online love in China is just like playing games at a carnival – very occasionally you get lucky, but mostly you just get fooled.

'In any case, the woman who posed that question is very fortunate. She's contemplating a man who appears very trustworthy and respectful, and most importantly without any concept of the idea of love as trade. The only thing to worry about is her mother's warped understanding of gratitude influencing her own true feelings. In that way, the woman is unfortunate. I can deduce quite clearly that the woman's parents are not a loving couple.'

I had never openly disagreed with North Star before, but that day I could barely hold back my anger. Who was he to judge whether my parents were happy or not based on one fleeting comment? But of course I couldn't say anything. I couldn't let him find out that woman was actually me.

To cut a long story short – I don't want to simply echo everyone else's take on the subject – I decided to take a leap of faith with Wang Peng. We could at least give things a try, and this way we might offer my mother, who had eaten enough bitterness for one lifetime, some comfort and support.

It wasn't long before Wang Peng moved in with us. With him living there, the housework never seemed as exhausting as it had done before. It's certainly true that men and women working together makes for light work. The furrow between my mother's eyebrows smoothed, and her shoulders became much less tense.

All these factors influenced my feelings towards Wang Peng, and I sank into a complex mix of emotions. It was only when I went to visit his home town for the first time that I made the decision to marry him.

Wang Peng's family live in rural Jiangxi Province, a long way from Nanchang, the closest city. From the main railway station, you have to take a bus for four or five hours until you reach a small town, and then to take a van from the market square. When you reach the start of a mountain pass, you change again into a pedicab, which takes you up a long, winding, bumpy road which is extremely narrow and cut into the edge of a steep cliff. On that final leg, my legs didn't stop shaking until we arrived at his village.

Wang Peng's family only spoke their local dialect, which I didn't understand a word of. When they were talking to one another, I would just sit there in a daze. There was no network out there in the mountains, and his village didn't even have a phone signal. Several times I thought to myself that with the language barrier and my lack of knowledge of the roads, I wouldn't be able to escape such a deep mountainous area even if I wanted to.

This wasn't even the biggest headache – that was using the toilets and the baths. The toilets out in the mountains were something else, basically just a huge pit of human and animal excrement which would also be used for fertiliser, and they had no roof or door. The smell was almost impossible to bear. Every time I went to the toilet, I was scared out of my wits.

Having a bath was treated like celebrating a festival. Until two years before I went, they didn't have a water-heating system. Almost all the villagers would bathe just two or three times in winter, based on the key dates of the lunar calendar, and every few days in summer. Each time, you had to heat water in a pot and pour it into a big barrel, then you'd sit and wash inside it. The toilets and the showers were enough to put me off my food, and every time I went back to Shanghai my mother would ask: 'How have you lost weight again?'

Visiting Wang Peng's rural home town wasn't just a physical shock, but also a spiritual one. The women in those impoverished villages weren't allowed to eat at the same table as the men and family elders, and in some places they even had to wait until the men had finished until they themselves could eat.

The son's standing in the family was paramount. Whether it was cooking, cleaning dishes or mucking out the pigs, the household chores always fell upon the women. As a woman, I had to make Wang Peng his tea or otherwise find myself guilty of offending family rules. Wang Peng argued with his parents several times over this, to no avail.

Shanghainese families are notoriously fussy when it comes to how we use our chopsticks and our bowls. The style of cooking takes precedence over the size of the portions, and we prefer to have a variety of dishes. We care about flavour and nutrition, unlike those northerners who pile up their plates, eating until their bellies nearly burst.

Visiting Wang Peng's home town really opened up my 'eating eyes'. There was no particular style to the way they ate. They'd have vegetables according to the season, but always with the same staples of sweet potato, rice noodles and chillies, all mixed together in a huge pot, which people would sit around, extending out their chopsticks to share its contents as everyone laughed and joked away.

If a family had something to celebrate, they would kill a pig for the occasion, and the whole family, young and old, would take their time in eating it. After the guests and friends had finished eating the meat, the family would eat the offal. When the offal was finished, they'd eat the hooves. When the hooves were gone, they'd eat stewed pigskin. Last but not least, the various parts of the pig's head would be stewed together and eaten over the next few days.

That was probably the first time it dawned on me the lengths to which these villagers would go to save things. The food we couldn't finish was eaten on the second day, the leftovers of the second day would be a meal on the third day, and it went on like that until the last mouthful in the pot had been finished. This was especially true of the elderly in the village. Whether it was a pot of vegetables or a bowl of rice, whether it was boiled or fried yellow, they wouldn't be happy until it had all gone.

The old people there used to say: 'Good food takes a good amount of time to eat!' That first time I went to Wang Peng's house, I don't think a single day went by without there being leftovers. I thought to myself that perhaps the only day they didn't eat leftovers was New Year's Day. Wang Peng said that for the first meal of the year they don't eat meat, they eat taro, tofu, celery and other vegetables – some kind of symbol that the coming year will be a rich and auspicious one.

Perhaps it was because I was the first city girl to visit that village, or perhaps it was because Wang Peng was popular with everyone there; either way, the villagers were all extremely hospitable, always picking out nice little things to give to me, like bacon they had cured specially for New Year. Once a family even killed the prize cockerel they had been going to take to relatives in a neighbouring village. They said that it would help a woman like me replenish her qi and give birth to a son. I hadn't even married Wang Peng at that point!

To be honest, the vegetables there were much fresher than they were in Shanghai; when you ate them there would be a sweet taste left in your mouth. As for the better quality of air in the village, it was extraordinary. I even felt somewhat reluctant to bid farewell to the people of his village. But all things considered, life is tough out in the mountains, which is why on the way back to Shanghai I told Wang Peng that even if I had to make sacrifices, I still wanted to help his parents move out of the village and experience the comfort of the city. They'd worked hard all their lifetime; they had a right to enjoy the rest of their lives.

I married Wang Peng on an autumn day in 2005, just after I had turned twenty-five. We had the wedding in Shanghai. According to his family customs we should have got married in Jiangxi, but there was really no way I could have taken Nana and my parents all the way there to take part in the wedding. So instead we brought his parents and two younger sisters over to the city.

On Christmas Day 2006, our daughter Dong Dong was born. When she was just over a month old, Wang Peng went back to spend New Year in his home town. I remember feeling so relieved when he suggested we shouldn't all go back together, thinking how our tiny daughter would have suffered along the bumps and bends of those roads.

But then, after a call from him on New Year's Day to wish us a Happy New Year, Wang Peng disappeared. We thought he must have had some sort of accident, and we hired someone to go to his village to find out more. The news he brought back was that two weeks after New Year, Wang Peng had returned to Shanghai. But we were both his work unit and his family, so if he wasn't here, where had he gone? I filed a missing persons form with the Public Security Bureau and waited for months without any news. It was as if he had evaporated.

On Christmas Day 2007, the day of Dong Dong's first birthday, I received a text message:

> I wish Dong Dong a happy birthday. I'm sorry, I have another family now. In my home town, a man without a son is the most unfilial. Without a son, I can't see my parents into old age. Tell Dong Dong her father is dead. Thank you all.

In a state of complete shock, I rang back, but the phone was turned off. I haven't heard another word from him since, and Dong Dong has grown up without a father. I don't think I've even heard her utter the word *baba*.

It was around then that internet dating started growing very popular, although it's not as crazy as it is today, mind. Yes, in those days, people still had at least a sliver of honour and respect for family values. Now, it's just out of control. Going online is like taking drugs – as soon as you get on, it's almost impossible to get off. And yes, I'm also talking about myself here.

Have you heard of a game called *Uncharted Waters*? I've been addicted to the internet ever since I first played that game. I was invited to join by a friend, and when I logged on I found myself in the most spectacular church setting, surrounded by more than a hundred people wearing beautiful dresses and morning suits. The entire screen was filled with messages of congratulations, and people asking each other how much money they had spent to attend this 'wedding'.

The groom was the 'Venetian Merchant', the bride the 'Spanish Princess'. No expense was spared, and the costs for the entire wedding totalled around four billion 'Navigator Dollars'. This included hiring the beautiful church, paying for several banquets, not to mention all the red *hongbao* envelopes full of money given by each guest. The groom also spent a 'fortune' on a wedding dress made from the finest Indian silk, and on inviting the best craftsmen in the land to build an extravagant wedding boat. Five impeccably dressed musicians serenaded guests with a faultless performance of the 'Wedding March', and of course a priest was on hand for the occasion. I don't believe there's a single woman in China who wouldn't have been touched by that online wedding.

I later found out more about that 'Venetian Merchant'. In real life he's a civil servant from Changchun, and the father of a three-year-old child. He'd become obsessed with online games a few years back, and he would spend at least ten hours every day gaming online. Through his obsession with these games he's gained a stellar reputation and great wealth in this virtual world, becoming a so-called 'Chamber President'.

In March 2006, a user called 'Spanish Princess' came into his gaming world. He found himself so deeply attached to this virtual love that he would lie awake at night thinking about his alter ego. His real wife even suspected him of having an affair. A real wife, by the way, that this 'Venetian Merchant' would never give flowers to, let alone the beautiful homes and luxury yachts he didn't even have to think twice about giving his new online partner, the 'Spanish Princess'. As he spent more and more of his time gaming, he began to realise that what he was doing was tantamount to having an affair.

But he was hooked, and to avoid his real wife finding out about his dubious relationship with the 'Spanish Princess' he would go online in internet cafés, and before he came home he would delete those 'kisses' sent to his phone from the 'Princess'. She actually ran into the same kind of trouble when messages regarding the wedding 'budget' were discovered by her real-life boyfriend. This gave her no choice but to tell him the truth; it was the only way for her to be forgiven. The 'Spanish Princess' sent a warning message to the 'Venetian Merchant': 'a game is just a game; we can't keep confusing what we have online with our real lives. If my boyfriend objects, I will have to give you up.' But later, to everyone's surprise, her boyfriend ended up joining the game, and was even the best man at her wedding.

After I heard this story, I asked myself: why do I need a man? Why not just create a 'perfect family' for my daughter Dong Dong online? Why should I let the scars of my life bleed? Why should I ache for my family history? So I started joining in these types of online love games. Very soon I came across an online 'river of love', where I met several online 'lovers'. We took care of each other there, enjoying our love in peace.

On 28 October 2015, China ended the one-child policy after thirty-six years. Women my age were now able to have a second child, but I still hadn't found another husband in the real world who would have a baby with me. I really enjoy internet love, and am getting better at it all the time. I've had a trial marriage, dabbled in being a lesbian, all kinds of things. Nowadays, my love is like a ship that follows whatever direction the latest internet wind is blowing. I've long forgotten the home shore from where I set sail.

By the end of 2007, the number of Chinese orphans adopted world-wide had reached 150,000. These children had gone to twenty-seven countries – and almost all were girls. Most Chinese find the adoption figures almost incredible, just as they find it hard to believe that Chinese children have found mothers and homes in so many countries.

Why does China have so many orphaned girls? Personally, I feel there are three main reasons. Firstly, female babies have been abandoned in farming cultures of the East since ancient times; secondly, a combination of the economic boom and sexual ignorance in the 1980s created warped and confused attitudes to sexuality; and finally, there is the one-child policy. Most Chinese would say that it is because there is something inherently wrong with traditional culture; in other words, old customs are rooted in ignorance. Westerners, on the other hand, believe that the one-child policy is to blame.

I first began researching this kind of 'abandoned girl' in 1989, when I started hosting *Words on the Night Breeze* on Nanjing Radio, a Chinese version of the BBC radio show *Woman's Hour*. As this job took me all over China doing interviews, I came across many women who had been forced to abandon their babies.

Favouring boys over girls is now generally acknowledged as a sign of backwardness in developing countries. I think that the preference for male children in these developing countries is connected with the fact that they still have communities which rely on primitive methods of farming, or on hunting, gathering and fishing. Hard manual labour is necessary for survival, making a preference for boys inevitable in primitive agricultural societies all over the world. Males have an indisputable physical advantage over females when it comes to labouring, carrying goods, hunting, defence and so on. This is perhaps the basic reason why matriarchy evolved into patriarchy; it might even explain a similar universal shift to the 'masculine' across human cultures and different languages.

But another factor which cannot be ignored in China is an ancient system of land distribution which still persists today. It began with the Xia dynasty (*c.*2070–1600 BC) and found its most complete form in the well-field system of the Zhou dynasty (*c.*1045–256 BC) and the equal-field system set up around AD 485 by the Northern Wei dynasty rulers. What these had in common with the present system is the principle of allocating fields based on the number of household members. Discrimination in favour of men became, therefore, an immutable law. In the AD 485 edict on the implementation of the equal-field system, a list was drawn up of households and then land was allocated based on the number of permanent family household members. Land was divided into two kinds: arable fields, for growing grain, and mulberry tree land, for feeding the silkworms. Every male of fifteen or over received 40 *mu* of arable land, while females only received 20 *mu*, and slaves and servants could also be allocated land. This land reverted to the government on death. As for mulberry tree land, males received 20 *mu*, and this became their property – they could buy and sell it and it did not need to be handed back to the government.

During the Tang dynasty from AD 618 to 907, it was clearly stipulated that females were not normally to be given their own land. Dynasties have come and gone through Chinese history, but the ways in which land is apportioned has never really changed, and the basic inequality between men and women has become a deeply entrenched tradition. In the villages, boy children not only carried on the family line and inherited the clan name, but they were also the source of the family's property and the creator of its wealth.

Article 22 of the 29 December 2001 Population and Family Planning Law of the PRC states: 'Discrimination against and mistreatment of women who give birth to female children or who suffer from infertility is prohibited. Discrimination against, or mistreatment and abandonment of female infants is prohibited.' However, a 'good woman' must give birth to a boy – every married village woman knows this. It is both her God-given duty and her parents-in-law's most fervent hope. So in some poorer villages, if the first child is a girl, the unfortunate child is abandoned, or even smothered at birth. In poor villages where birth control is unavailable or not understood, abandoning infants is a fact of life, just another law of nature which has operated since time immemorial. If the extra infant the family cannot raise is a boy, he will often be adopted by another family or sold. For a girl, death is sometimes almost inevitable.

Lili, Yoyo and Wuhen first found out about my interest in writing a book of their family history while I was back in China in autumn 2015. The night before I returned to London, one of the three young women printed out nearly a thousand pages of exchanges between her and an online lover, and secretly sent them over to the hotel where I was staying in Beijing.

I read deep into the night, unable to take my eyes away from the thick pile of papers. The final page told the story of how after a year and a half of passionate but ultimately blind love, she and her lover decided to meet in a neutral city, to take their love to the next level and to give it some form of recognition.

The next few lines, handwritten, left me in utter shock:

Xinran, can you imagine how my heart ached? For as I stood waiting in the hotel room where we had arranged to meet, the man who opened the door was my father.

When I was next back in Beijing in April 2016, I asked Red and Green if they could help me arrange a meeting with the three granddaughters while they were together at home for the Tomb-Sweeping Festival. I wanted to find out which one among them was the protagonist in this story of a father and daughter's inadvertent online love. I failed, but they are all daughters of the 3D generation – it could have been any of them!

That day, looking at the three granddaughters, I remember thinking how the difference between their love lives was like the difference between heaven and earth, and it made me feel the hand of God hanging over their fate.

I pray that whatever the future holds for them, their bones will pass on the essence of Red's parents' love, their blood will carry Green and Orange's sense of national responsibility, and their breath will continue to nourish the five-thousand-year-old Chinese culture of 'talking love'.

Afterword

In and Out the Door of Life

Two of the women you have just read about have since passed away. I also lost my beloved husband Toby Eady during the writing of this book.

In the early hours of 12 July 2016, I received a text message from Green telling me that her big sister Red had died the previous day. Five hours later, still reeling from the pain and regret this news had brought me, another message arrived: my father had passed away in Nanjing.

I don't know why, but the news of these deaths sent me into an overwhelming sense of panic, and it was a struggle just to get through the rest of the day. Later, having helped my cancer-stricken husband get to sleep, I had an irresistible desire to pick up this book's manuscript and read about the lives of Red and her family again, as if something written inside would help me come to terms with my loss. I was searching for answers to the questions I still had, fearing they might be lost forever.

Death had closed the door on their lives, but in doing so had reinvigorated my pursuit of their memories. That night I awoke from a dream and realised that my planned fifth section, a collection of ancient Chinese love stories, no longer belonged in this book. That door on the past had closed, while that of the memory of my parents and of the Han family had opened wider and wider during the writing process.

This book has taken over three years to finish, from spring 2013 to autumn 2016. It has been an emotional process throughout, right from carrying out the first interviews and researching, fact-checking and writing, and eventually to translating. As the women's stories unfolded around me, I was pulled into their world. Layer by layer, drip by drip, the experiences of four generations of this one family cast a light on my own family – my grandparents, my parents, myself and my son. Never before had I felt that my family bore the 'Chinese characteristics' that I had so often come across in others.

Like many Chinese people, I thought I knew all there was to know about the different types of marriage – the sweet, the sour, the bitter, the spicy – but never had I experienced for myself the brutality of those political marriages, the suffering those great social changes brought to Chinese people's love lives and their cultural heritage, or the changes to the cultural linguistics between the generations who grew up during this time.

This Chinese linguistic culture is a tree rooted in more than five thousand years. It is a tree that not only has been eroded by all the different political environments it has known over time, with their unique weather systems, but also by the suffering and wounds from all kinds of political storms. What's worth celebrating is that as of 2018, about 18,000 Chinese characters have survived the storm of history. Compared with the twenty-six-letter structure of most European and American languages, the Chinese linguistic landscape is still capable of offering a much wider view of the world.

Just because I share a native language with the leading characters in this book – and indeed a sixth of the world's population who call Chinese their mother tongue – you'd be wrong in assuming that we'd be able to communicate without any difficulties. When most people say 'Chinese', they are referring to both the written language and the spoken language – two sides of the same coin.

Classical written Chinese is known as *wenyanwen*, whereas modern written Chinese – the version of the language which adheres to modern standards of grammar and word usage – is known as *baihuawen*. The *baihuawen* form of Chinese came out of the 1917 New Culture Movement that Red's parents lived through, and was quickly adopted as the standard writing style for Chinese speakers. It wasn't until the late 1950s, however, when the likes of Green were leading China into a new age, that *baihuawen* was officially recognised. The simplified characters of the mainland differ greatly from the traditional characters of the past – some would even call them 'deformed' – but their pronunciation has stayed the same. Within this Chinese family of languages there are thousands of different dialects, some completely unintelligible from the next, based on seven different subgroups: Mandarin, Cantonese, Wu, Xiang, Gan, Hakka and Hokkien.

Along with the process of internationalisation, the Chinese language, which has grown over thousands of years by constantly evolving and accumulating new words, has also gone through many other changes. Even though I was born in China and grew up with the Chinese language, I often need the help of internet translators to understand the true meaning of many conversations I hear today. Every time I go back there, I always struggle to work out what certain 'new words' mean and where they come from.

This is why Red and her siblings had no way of expressing their true feelings to each other when they were reunited after nearly forty years apart. Those brothers who had settled down abroad not only brought with them a world view influenced by democracy and an instinctive fear of Chinese politics, but also a language mixed with English or Cantonese. As for the three sisters on the mainland who had survived the political movements, they had become cut off from the rest of the world, accustomed to the current political system and its control on communication over many years. They found it nearly impossible to understand and identify with their brothers' views on family and the world.

At the same time, Red and her siblings also had to try and overcome the ever-growing language barrier between them and the younger generation, whose means of communication by touch-screen seemed like magic to a group of people accustomed to only ever reading and writing on paper. Then there are those cherished legends of love passed down from the generations above, now being neglected, forgotten, even ridiculed by their own children.

The word *liàn ài*, for example, was traditionally used to describe feelings of love between a man and woman, whereas now it is used to refer to both the emotional and physical strands of love. From Red, who always followed the natural cycles of the earth, to her younger sisters Green and Orange, who embraced the Revolution, the older generations were heavily influenced by traditional classical love stories. Those were the models on which they based their idea of love, models which instilled in them a promise that they too would find love.

Those love stories were originally passed down generations through thousands of years of oral tradition, drama and *shuochang* storytelling; that is, until the Cultural Revolution put a stop to the spreading of such 'poisonous weeds'. When these forms of art returned to the artistic stage after Reform and Opening Up, Red and her sisters revived the memory of their mother's teachings in those familiar stories and music, and found themselves longing for their own childhood. But just as they thought they were getting their history back, the younger generations were on a train speeding away from them, bound for the future. They had no chance to share this oral history with them.

In the 1980s, Deng Xiaoping opened a door that China had left closed for hundreds of years. For so long a grey and impoverished nation starved of enough food to eat and enough colour in its everyday life, China began to greedily embrace the cut-price American way of life – McDonald's and Starbucks became symbols of fine dining to the Chinese, while the most basic of American daily products became known as the extravagant indulgences of the country's social elite.

But then, with the accumulated wisdom of five thousand years of civilisation, coupled with the pent-up energy of a hundred years of chaos and turmoil, China erupted with unimaginable force and speed. In just over thirty years, one hundred million people were lifted out of poverty, and the faces of China's 660 cities were transformed beyond recognition. Chinese started buying global products, and even began purchasing property in neighbourhoods all over Europe and America.

Thanks to the inevitable increase in exchanges with the outside world, parents and grandparents found themselves forced into awkward conversations about sex. Meanwhile, Western arts and music began to infiltrate traditional Chinese culture more and more with each passing day.

The fourth generation of Red's family – Lili, Yoyo and Wuhen – not only grew up during China's period of Reform and Opening Up, but also in the lonely households of the one-child policy. Many of their generation looked upon their great-grandmothers' arranged marriages as mere fairy tales, and turned their grandmothers' sense of revolutionary duty into the butt of jokes. As for their mothers' stubborn devotion to love, it seemed somewhat childish to them.

With the passing of each of the past three generations, family values had time and again been turned on their head. But school history textbooks still stuck strictly to a unified vision of history, and all the while news swirled around them of the soaring pace at which their country was developing. That's how their generation missed the chance to learn traditional Chinese values and to take in a genuine account of history – the true DNA of Chinese culture.

This generation possessed freedom and material wealth their elders could only dream of, and they looked for the miracle of love in the void between Chinese and Western culture. They created idealised versions of themselves on the internet, and pushed the boundaries of what they thought love could be. But as this generation grew accustomed to the loneliness of living without brothers and sisters, the family could no longer be considered the backbone of Chinese culture.

Wuhen appears in many ways to embody those traditional values. She sacrificed her own dreams for the sake of her grandmother Orange and her mother Kangmei – history even seemed to have repeated itself when she, like her mother, married out of kindness. However, fate did not repay her in kind, but rather left more emotional scars that would never fully heal. Her parents' dream that her life would be free from the pain they had endured remained just that – a dream.

But why? Why do so many Chinese people of today ache when they devote their love to someone else, feel so lonely in their pursuit of feeling and so disappointed in their pursuit of faith?

I believe it is apathy and greed eating away at the respect and understanding we once had for our families. This was an all-encompassing respect. For Chinese people, family was the very substance of our being. Our culture, ideology, spirit and social structures were all intrinsically bound to the family. Take the Chinese language, for example: this ancient tongue with five thousand years of history is scattered with references to the family. Whereas Westerners cry out 'My God!' to express their shock at something, Chinese people are much more likely to yell 'My mother!' When insulting one another, Chinese people will target their rival's mother and grandmother rather than the person themselves.

When an official gets promoted, they may well be greeted with the words 'Congratulations on becoming my "parental guardian"!' This title of respect is granted even if the person is an eighty-year-old grandfather speaking to a young man no older than his grandson.

In terms of both education and family values, the position of family elders is insurmountable. The principles and rules they pass down, and the standards they set for all types of family occasion – be it wedding or funeral – are undisputable. Any challenge or alteration to these rules constitutes a betrayal, like a plant breaking away from its roots.

However, over the past thirty years of listening and learning, I have come to understand how traditional Chinese family values are being slowly eroded by the tide of modernity. Political fears, material desires, changes in social status and the ever-growing presence of Western culture and modern technology all pose critical challenges to this ancient civilisation.

For new generations of Chinese, the family is no longer a part of the Chinese identity that they feel the need to consider and protect. Some are so busy with other things that they don't return home and visit family elders and have no time to tell their children about their family heritage. Their relationships are no longer focused on building a family; instead, they are driven much more by physical attraction.

Taking Red's family as an example, will their records of their family lineage live on after that fourth generation? How many of their children will know about Red's parents' love of poetry? How many will hear the stories of Green and Orange's passionate love of their country? How many will understand the unconditional love between Tang Hai and Crane? Will anyone ever know about Wuhen's sacrifices for her family?

After my father died, I became even more aware that this also applied to my own family history, that my son and I were very much part of this question. If this was the case, how would we find the answers? Had we run out of time to find them?

On the afternoon of 12 September, two months after Red's death, I received a message from Green: 'Orange passed away today … Her daughter said that she had long since lost any feeling; her passing was just a confirmation of a death we knew about long ago.'

Orange 'had long since lost any feeling'. These words swirled around my mind for a long time. We may be healthy in body, but do we have any real feelings? Feelings for family, for people around us, for the natural world?

For a long time, I didn't know how to end this book. Then one day a letter came to me in a dream.

Dearest Red,

I hope that in the spirit world you will be able to read this letter sent to you from the human world. The day you left us, you opened a door that had long been left closed in my heart.

Thank you for your trust in me, and for sharing the stories of your life under the ceiling with Baogang. As you wished, the tales of your life alongside those of your parents, sisters and later generations have been made into a book that will be read by friends around the world in many different languages. They will read how your life is the epic story of one woman whose secrets were once only held by a Chinese ceiling but are now carrying her family forwards, breaking historical taboos and walking out onto the world stage.

Aunt Red, have you met your sister Orange in heaven? Please pass on my thanks to her as well, for sharing her pain with the rest of humanity so that we children of China might better understand the chaos of war and the serenity of peace.

In heaven we do not suffer for our emotions or our desires; we do not have to wait for grace and love, because we are living in it. The sixty-one years you waited in the human world have transcended into your long-cherished wish – you are now finally flying free as an angel of love.

My dear Red, as you may already know, my husband Toby peacefully passed away at our home in the early hours of Christmas Eve 2017, finally succumbing to the sickness that he had been fighting for over two years. But I know that his spirit and soul have not left me, my writing, my day and night, nor my love for him. Not one bit.

He once told me he believed that the love stories from four generations of your family will create reflection and sympathy throughout the world, just as *The Good Women of China* did, because mankind has always been seeking the hope of peace in war, the understanding of human nature in the passing of time and the commonalities between family love and the love between men and women despite cultural differences.

He was looking forward to holding this book, and to talking for hours on end with friends and family about his love of Chinese culture, his shock at Chinese history, his feelings for the Chinese people and his love for his Chinese wife. Now his expectations have become a reality. If you meet him in heaven, please give him a message from me:

My darling Toby, you have made a lovely family for us as a husband and father. We had nearly a twenty-year 'honeymoon', as you kept telling everyone, by sharing love, talking love, writing love and making love, together as lovers and soulmates . . .

I still talk with you, read for you and water our love with my tears every day. I can't say goodbye to you because you never left me in my heart and life. As Thornton Wilder says in The Bridge of San Luis Rey*:*

We ourselves shall be loved for awhile and forgotten. But the love will have been enough; all those impulses of love return to the love that made them. Even memory is not necessary for love. There is a land of the living and a land of the dead and the bridge is love, the only survival, the only meaning.

My darling Toby, I miss you, I miss you talking love with me, and your love for me and my Chinese people!

XINRAN

11 February 2018 (the anniversary of the day I married Toby)

Author's Heartfelt Thanks

Whenever I sit down to record how grateful I am towards the family, friends and everyone else who has walked with me hand in hand through each word of a book, I end up writing another book! Brevity is as difficult as it is beautiful, which is why I always try and express to those close to me a spirit of endless thanks.

Allow me to start by expressing my gratitude to Chinese culture, which values age over beauty.

I want to thank my mother. Time and again you have answered the doubts and questions that have come out of my research, drawing from your rich experience and silent observations of life. This is especially true of the stories in this book, for which you acted as a kind of historical aggregator, showing me the China you lived through and the changing of the times.

Thank you to my husband, Toby Eady. You were the love of my life, the mentor of my writing career, and the partner of my soul. No literary agent did as much as you did for Chinese writers, nurturing the seeds of so many Chinese stories, including this one, to grow and flourish in the world.

Thank you to my son Pan and your fiancée Coco, who is Japanese but speaks Chinese much better than a lot of Chinese people. Not only did you give me time, space and support, but your youthful vitality and grasp of modern technology helped me to understand three vital elements of a new generation of young people in this book – their outlook on life, their values and their world view – and to understand the recent youth trends in China that have baffled me for years.

Thank you to the three sisters in this book, and every woman in their family I interviewed. Through their big sister Yaohong (Red), we became not just friends, but family. We may not share the same blood, but you have become part of my life, helping me to learn about modern Chinese history, breathe in the very essence of my culture and understand the roots of Chinese feelings. Without the trust you invested in me, your open-minded approach to history and your acceptance of the future, my research and writing on Chinese women would be profoundly lacking.

Thank you to William Spence, the English translator of this book. We met as volunteers for the Mothers' Bridge of Love, became close friends in the study of literary translation, and became fellow travellers in the translation of this book. Your love of Chinese culture, proficiency in Chinese and dedication to translation have brought this book out into the world.

Thank you to my dear friend Wu Fan, the author of *February Flowers* and *Beautiful as Yesterday*. Your passion for building literary exchanges between China and the West, not to mention your talent for writing in both Chinese and English, has given me great encouragement in my writing.

Thank you to Veronique Baxter and the team at David Higham Associates for being with me throughout the journey of writing this book. I feel fortunate and proud to have such a talented group of agents. Thank you to my English editor Tomasz Hoskins, whose broad vision of multiculturalism and insightful opinions made me feel fortunate to be his student. Thank you also to your team at I.B. Tauris and to Sarah Terry, my copy-editor, for their wisdom and hard work in getting this book out to its readership.

Thank you to every foreign-language translator and publisher of my books. Without your hard work, the stories of Chinese women I have written would never have been read by readers in over fifty countries in more than forty different languages.

Last but not least, thank you to all those who have ever helped me gather historical material and acted as go-betweens with my sources, and to the MBL volunteers who have guided me in our work to help disabled and displaced children around the world. I thank you from the bottom of my heart for your selfless dedication, for sharing the burden, and for walking the road with me between China and the West.

The Mothers' Bridge of Love

www.mothersbridge.org
Culture for Children, Books for Kids

The Mothers' Bridge of Love (MBL) is a UK-registered charity (registration number 1105543), set up by Xinran and a group of volunteers in 2004. MBL's aim is to support children of Chinese origin from all corners of the world by creating a bridge of understanding between China and the West, strengthening the ties of birth and adoptive cultures and helping bring education to rural China. As of 2018, MBL has built twenty-three village school libraries in rural China.

Xinran would like to invite you, her readers, friends and family from all over the world to support MBL.

For online donations, please use the link http://www.everyclick.com/mothersbridge.

Cheques made out to The Mothers' Bridge of Love can be posted to MBL, 19 Queens Court, London W2 4QN, UK

Money can be wired to The Mothers' Bridge of Love (MBL) using the following details:

Sort Code: 400607
Account Number: 11453130
SWIFT Code: MIDL GB2142E
IBAN No.: GB08MIDL40060711453130
HSBC Bank, 1 Woburn Place, Russell Square, London WC1H 0LQ, UK

Your support will help educate children in the poorest parts of China.

Thank you.

2019

12/12/19   3x   LAD 9/15/19